C000181876

Au Revoir Now Darlint

AU REVOIR NOW DARLINT

The Letters of Edith Thompson

LAURA THOMPSON

unbound

First published in 2023

Unbound
Level 1, Devonshire House, One Mayfair Place, London W1J 8AJ
www.unbound.com

Text design by PDQ Digital Media Solutions Ltd

A CIP record for this book is available from the British Library

ISBN 978-1-80018-246-2 (hardback)
ISBN 978-1-80018-247-9 (ebook)

Printed in Great Britain by Clays Ltd, Elcograf S.p.A.

1 3 5 7 9 8 6 4 2

To Milo, the darlingest boy

Letter to the *Daily Telegraph*, published June 1951:

On the direction of the judge about 120 typed foolscap sheets of the whole of Mrs Thompson's correspondence were handed to the jury to be studied by them, and it was my duty to read them to the members of the jury, which included two women. 'Nauseous' is hardly strong enough to describe their contents...

The jury performed a painful duty, but Mrs Thompson's letters were her own condemnation.
ONE OF THE JURY, London EC1.

From the closing speech for Edith Thompson's defence, December 1922:

You have read her letters. Have you ever read... more beautiful language of love?

CONTENTS

INTRODUCTION

A hundred years ago, on the night of 3 October 1922, a thirty-two-year-old man named Percy Thompson was stabbed to death as he walked home to his suburban villa in Ilford. With him was his wife, twenty-eight-year-old Edith. His killer was Edith's lover: Frederick (Freddy) Bywaters, a merchant seaman aged twenty.

Freddy Bywaters was soon arrested, charged and tried. He was hanged at Pentonville on 9 January 1923. So too, a couple of miles away at Holloway, was Edith Thompson.

There was no proof whatever that she had anything to do with the killing of her husband, no material evidence of foreknowledge or complicity. What condemned her, essentially, were her own words: the letters that she had written to her lover, which were used by the legal system to 'prove' that she had conspired with Freddy and incited the crime.

The moral condemnation of Edith Thompson was not merely about murder, however. It was the fact that the letters were a prolonged celebration of an adulterous affair, with a man almost eight years her junior; a luxury add-on to a perfectly good husband, at a time when the First World War had left 'decent' women with no men at all. Moreover the letters portrayed pride, rather than shame, in love rather than marriage. And although they were, in fact, very little about sex, they were quite astonishingly sexy. Had they not been, people would not have been so ready to believe that they were also an exhortation to murder. It was a simplification to say, as Edith's defence counsel would later do, that she was 'hanged for adultery'; but at a time of great societal unease, not unfamiliar to us a century on, she became – in the totality of her transgression – a symbol of something that the nation wanted to purge. The idea of doing so was cleansing, restorative. 'Even those who objected in principle to her execution can hardly regret her absence from this sphere,' as a commentator put it in *The Times*. But plenty, as it happened, did not object to the execution.

A century ago, the content of the letters was what signified, although a handful of people saw them as remarkable in themselves. Now it is possible to see them as a record, perhaps unparalleled, of a woman seeking to vault the walls around her life and scale the twin towers of class and gender: an Everywoman who was also a supreme individualist, and who suffered an outlandish fate that might – in mitigated form – befall anybody who takes the wrong risks.

The letters were her great autonomous act, an attempt to release the self that had no other means of expression. But it is the *way* in which she does it, clear and direct and almost appallingly alive, that speaks across the years. Edith was a natural born writer. She left school at fifteen and had a taste for literature of the superior-popular kind, whose style would not have been a beneficent influence; but that was irrelevant because her style was entirely her own, and in fact not a style but a voice. Her sentences are shapeless and repetitive, in no way 'correct', yet some of them stick in the mind as correctness rarely can.

Darlint, I've surrendered to him unconditionally now – do you understand me?

We ourselves die & live in the books we read while we are reading them...

I just tried to make you live in my life...

He has the right by law to all that you have the right to by nature and love...

Darlint – do something tomorrow night will you? something to make you forget...

'It is gush, it is not?' said the judge at her trial, a voice from the pre-war era that she offended so profoundly. Even Edith's supporter F. Tennyson Jesse, who in 1934 wrote a sympathetic novel based upon the case, *A Pin to See the Peepshow*, said that she had found the letters grating to her nerves – that she couldn't take all those 'darlints': a contraction of 'darlingest'. Edith's signature word is, as much as anything, a punctuation to her sentences, which otherwise unfurl in stream-of-consciousness ribbons: the untutored kin of *Ulysses* with a pagan Lawrentian sensuality. Hers is a modernist voice, boneless and fluid, disdaining the formalities of grammar and snapping the shackles of morality. Freddy Bywaters had it right when he explained her thus: 'When writing letters to me she did not study sentences & phrases before transferring them to paper, but, as different thoughts, no matter what, momentarily flashed through her mind, so they were committed to paper.'

Edith, who wrote *to* Freddy, was really writing *for* herself. Part of the appeal of this young man – her only extra-marital lover; she flirted indiscriminately but took love intensely seriously – was that he was hardly ever there. Fifteen months spanned the start of the affair in late June 1921 and its ending in early October 1922, and of that time the couple spent more than three-quarters apart. So the affair was epistolary, perforce; but the letters acquired their own importance, over and above her feelings for their recipient. And she believed, of course, that he was the only reader that she would ever have. She had no thought of being judged on what she wrote – not in a literary sense, and certainly not the literal sense applied by the No. 1 court of the Old Bailey, where her letters were read to suit a particular end, the one that would kill her.

A century before the advent of cancel culture, this woman was cancelled – obliterated – for word crimes, thought crimes, the crime of being herself.

For this reason, above all, her letters demand to be published for a new generation.

Edith Jessie Graydon was born on Christmas Day 1893. Her family was loving, warm, lower middle class – William Graydon was a clerk and part-time dance teacher, his wife Ethel a policeman's daughter. Edith grew up in a tiny terraced house in Manor Park (now in the London borough of Newham) that she always thought of as home, and married at twenty-two because that is what young women did. So far, so ordinary. She read novels and became intensely involved in the lives of the characters, rather as today one might in a TV soap opera; she took immense pride in her home and her appearance; she relished London life, its bars and theatres; she suffered the terrors of ageing and of illicit pregnancy. Again, nothing extraordinary in any of this. She was typical, average, a figure one might recognise today, although in the early 1920s it was unusual that she worked throughout her eight-year marriage – as a highly efficient buyer and manageress in a City of London wholesale milliner's, Carlton and Prior, where she was always known as 'Miss Graydon' – and earned more than her husband. The marital home at 41 Kensington Gardens, an attractive double-fronted property (slightly marred by the presence of the Lesters, a family of three sitting tenants), was registered in Percy Thompson's name, as was then the norm. But Edith was its part-owner, her high achievements had helped to buy it, and hers was the taste that decorated it: a cabinet filled with Limoges in the drawing room, a mahogany suite with silk upholstery, ebony elephants, Japanese prints. She continued to work after her marriage, because that was what she wanted to do, and – most unusually – she had no children.

She enjoyed freedoms that her mother's generation could not have imagined: no corset, no skirts trailing in the dirt, electric light in the home, rudimentary contraception, the prospect of the vote (although, as she died before the age of thirty, she never exercised that right). Much of this came about because of the First World War, when women worked, and thus had greater control over their bodies, their minds, their biological destinies. And these freedoms were not illusory; they were the beginnings of change; nevertheless they were revealed, when Edith's life went wrong, to be fragile. Like so many women (this remains true today) she believed herself to have more power than she had. The years after the war, when jobs were handed back to men, were marked by a craving to return to the old certainties; Edith represented a future – and the kind of woman –

that Britain feared. She became a scapegoat, hurled into the darkness. Not by blocking her on Twitter or forcing her resignation. Literally.

Even now, Edith would be at risk of the rage of the mob. She did not 'fit'; never the best idea for a woman, and especially not if she arouses perturbation rather than pity.

She was aspirational, she was flighty, she was discontented, she was competitive, she was self-centred. Above all she was overwhelmingly attractive to men, a *femme de l'homme,* and this would still arouse the mixture of misogyny, envy and sanctimony that helped to bring about her downfall. She also possessed a capable business brain, which would get a better press today than a century ago; although the way in which she played up to her boss, Mr Carlton – rumoured to have paid for her expensive defence counsel – would assuredly be condemned by the Roundhead tendency.

Ours can be a prudish, prurient race, which struggles to treat sex in a grown-up manner. Faced with genuine erotic power, it can become censorious. All the more so in an age when marriage was for life and vamps were Theda Bara on the silent screen, not bob-headed girls walking the streets of Ilford.

Edith was sometimes beautiful, sometimes not; like her personality, her looks were protean; but her appeal was about more than that. Gender has become a construct, a choice. Yet nobody who reads her letters could honestly doubt that Edith was possessed of a lush and intrinsic femininity; that femaleness rippled through her genes, her flesh, her nature. She had, moreover, an irresistible quality of *absorption*, in life and her feelings about it, which she discovered and uncovered as her words tumbled on to the page.

In her letters she described her existence both as it was and how she wished it to be, and the two threaded in and out of each other, plaiting a pattern of truth and fantasy. The dream world that she conjured was one in which Percy Thompson did not exist. Her relationship with her husband was complicated, like everything to do with Edith. It is hard now to understand why she married him, and perhaps the surest sign that she knew she was not really free: that class decreed she should settle for a boy next door, who stood with her on the platform at East Ham Underground every morning on his dutiful journey to the City.

He was in some ways her counterpart, a hard-working shipping clerk who had risen in life – in his case, from a deeply deprived childhood near the east London docks – and who had, at first, appreciated the specialness in his partner. In other ways he was hopelessly inadequate. Edith sometimes portrayed her marriage as dreary, sometimes as downright abusive. It may well have been both. Yet she did not leave Percy – admittedly a seismic step a century ago – and the couple socialised regularly together, including on the night of the murder, among people who considered them to be happily married.

In the letters, however, the yearning refrain was for a Percy-free future. Sometimes this theme played a darker variation, and became an avowed desire to eliminate her husband. Sometimes this variation was luridly coloured, with references to substances that she might add – or have added – to his food: poisons, pieces of lightbulb.

In fact it was Freddy Bywaters who killed Percy Thompson, solus and with a knife. The Thompsons were walking home from the train station after an evening spent watching a Ben Travers farce at the Criterion Theatre. They had almost reached their house when Freddy appeared as from nowhere. He stabbed Percy several times, three of the blows being deep and lethal, then ran off into the night.

It was never openly suggested that Edith played any physical part in the murder, although there were whispers – perhaps inevitably – that she had carried a small weapon and caused some of the minor cuts to her husband. The evidence for this is absolutely non-existent. The speculation arose only because of what she had written in the letters. They were the whole and the heart of it. Because of them she was tried, as was Freddy, for murder and conspiracy to murder; additionally she was charged with incitement, and with administering poison and glass with intent to murder.

In flat contradiction of this last indictment – and, indeed, of what Edith had written – her husband's exhumed body was found to contain no trace of any injurious substance. After the post-mortem, a detective remarked that 'the case against Mrs Thompson has failed.'

Yet it was pursued with quite extraordinary vigour, and its chief ally was the letters; although when their writer was asked to explain her own words, which was impossible because they had so little meaning outside her own head, the prosecution found that Edith Thompson herself was quite helpful too.

Murder writes human nature large; that is perhaps the essence of its fascination. In essence the Thompson–Bywaters case fits a familiar template, that of the eternal triangle (although there was, as will be seen, a shadowy fourth person in the mix). It also conformed to the Orwellian criterion of 'classic' English murder, wherein godless passions churn behind respectable facades. When Percy Thompson was stabbed, net curtains metaphorically twitched.

The case centres upon a love affair, and it says a great deal about the nature of romantic love. It deals in the whole question of illusion, without which romance cannot subsist, and in the solipsism that prevails within those who believe themselves to be inseparable from another person. Edith's letters, which are like a continuous free-form poem, show her to have been semi-lost in a dreamscape, whose great delight was that she herself was conjuring it. It was as Flaubert wrote of Emma Bovary: 'She was becoming a part of her own imaginings'.

From the outside one can see that she was also, more prosaically, an unsatisfied woman with an unsatisfactory husband, who started flirting deliciously with Freddy – another boy next door, a school friend of her younger brother Bill* – when he returned to Manor Park at the start of 1920, a few months before his eighteenth birthday in June. He had been on a tour with the SS *Plassy*, taking in China and Japan, having joined the merchant navy in February 1918, at the age of fifteen. Although extremely young he was, decidedly, a man.

In May 1920 he moved into the Graydon family home, at 231 Shakespeare Crescent, as a paying guest. The *Plassy* was in dock at Tilbury, and Freddy's widowed mother, Lilian,† had moved to Norwood in south London, so it was far easier to live eastwards. The

---

* Edith had four younger siblings: Avis (b. 1895); Newenham (a family name, from her father's Irish forebears, b. 1899); William (b. 1901); Harold (b. 1902). Like Freddy, Bill was in the merchant navy; as will be seen, the two friends sometimes met up abroad.

† Freddy's father, who served in the Royal Field Artillery during the First World War, died in 1919. Lilian was obliged to sell the family home in Manor Park and start her own small business.

Graydon house held other diversions, of course. During the eight weeks of Freddy's first stay, he aroused the interest of the unmarried younger sister Avis – pleasant-looking, what would have been called a 'nice girl' – who became the object of his official attentions. Unofficially his real inclination lay elsewhere, upon the star of the family: Edith. She, in her turn, was attracted. She was also unable to resist the occasional meeting with the young man whom her sister clearly adored.

Thus things stood, in the relatively uncomplicated sphere of physical desire, not acted upon, with no danger in sight. Then, in June 1921, the two couples – the Thompsons, Freddy and Avis – holidayed in a boarding house on the Isle of Wight (the furthest afield that Edith ever travelled). A photograph taken during the journey, on the beach at Southsea, shows Percy reclining on a bed of pebbles, grinning into the camera with a pipe clenched between his teeth. Edith, beside him, openly cradles the head of Freddy Bywaters on her voluptuously raised hip. The photo, with its great erotic charge still pulsing through the dead chiaroscuro, prefigures all that would happen on this holiday. The person behind the camera – Avis – must have seen it; although she did not know for sure until the Thompsons left for London after a week and Freddy, who was supposed to stay on with her, trailed after them. She remained alone in the boarding house. When she returned to London, Freddy met her train and told her that he wanted to be friends, or some other time-honoured evasion. Yet she did not quite give up on him.

Percy, meanwhile, had seen nothing. Indeed his blissful ignorance was such that on 18 June he extended an invitation to Freddy to move into the Thompsons' spare room, at the very reasonable cost of £5 a month. Nine days later, on Freddy's nineteenth birthday, the lodger and the lady of the house became lovers.

Through late June and early July there ensued a sunlit honeymoon period, to which Edith's letters would make frequent reference a year later.

> Darlint this month and next are full of remembrances – arnt they?

Her second week of holiday was between 3–10 July, when the

sitting tenants were away. During the days the lovers did as they wished: the illusion that the house belonged to them was only shattered when Percy turned his key in the front door. The Lesters returned, and Edith went back to work, but the affair continued to bloom in secret; until the afternoon of Monday 1 August, towards the end of the bank holiday, when a showdown between the parties created another prefiguring: of murder.

It began with an incident of ridiculous triviality. Percy, Edith and Freddy were in the back garden at the Ilford house; Edith was sewing and found that she needed a pin. Freddy offered to go into the house and get it for her. Something in the manner of Edith's demand and Freddy's response seems to have told Percy a part, at least, of what was going on. A quarrel began between husband and wife. It calmed down – started up again – then moved into that stage where all care and control is lost (the sitting tenants were out for the evening – had they not been, things might not have gone so far). Edith would later tell the Old Bailey that Percy hit her several times. According to corroborated evidence – Mrs Lester saw the black bruise down her arm – she was thrown across the room, overturning a chair and falling against a table. Freddy, who had sensibly remained outside, heard the crash and ran into the house as Edith fled upstairs. The two men squared up to each other, but Percy had no fear at all of his future killer. He demanded that Freddy leave, which he did immediately; clearing out for good on Friday 5 August.

Freddy's reaction to Percy's behaviour towards Edith, as described in a statement to the police, was characteristic. 'I thought it a very unmanly thing to do and I interfered.' He would make a similar remark with regard to the second confrontation, fourteen months later, a few yards from the house where he had spent that dangerously seductive idyll.

'The reason I fought with Thompson was because he never acted like a man to his wife. He always seemed several degrees lower than a snake. I loved her and couldn't go on seeing her leading that life.'

As an analysis of his own motivation, it was deceptively simple. It certainly lifted any shadow of guilt from Edith Thompson. Yet it was she who created a killer out of a tangled string of words, even though the question of intent is what truly signifies. As does this: in the end, did the pair of them still believe that it had all happened because of love, or did they think that they had sacrificed themselves for not very much?

Edith Thompson, Everywoman, was defined by the desire to realise her extraordinariness. According to many commentators this was a self-delusion, which made her all the more ordinary: a *Love Island* contestant who dreams of walking the red carpet at the Oscars. Margery Fry, sister of the Bloomsbury Group's Roger, and a notable penal reformer, visited Edith in Holloway and thought her 'a rather foolish girl'. T. S. Eliot wrote to the *Daily Mail* to praise its cool reporting of the trial, 'in striking contrast with the flaccid sentimentality of other papers I have seen' (this was probably aimed at the *Daily Express,* whose editor, the future MP Beverley Baxter, was anti-death penalty and sympathetic to Edith).

Yet why did these high-end people bother to be dismissive, if the case – the personality of Edith – had not in some reluctant measure compelled them; as it did the ageing Thomas Hardy, who wrote a wretched poem about the 'plain, yet becoming' prisoner and her 'Clytemnestra spirit'. Not for a moment was her guilt in question, but neither was the dense spell that she wove.

She was a cause célèbre, in fact, although it was Freddy who aroused most of the sympathy. Edith attracted fascination, but also blame. She was deemed, almost universally, to be the agent behind the murder, the cougar who had compelled a besotted youth to do her killing for her. Again, the lack of evidence was overwhelming; but so too was the narrative. People subscribed to it in their millions, devouring pages of newsprint that knew exactly what to give them: the story of a wicked woman whose sins must be expiated for all our sakes. No man could possibly have aroused such powerful emotions as Edith Thompson did, this slim pale figure in her musquash coat, arriving at the Old Bailey like a doomed film star. Even now, a story that centres upon a female tends to be more compelling, more visceral in the response that it generates; even now, women touch nerves that a man cannot. Think Meghan. Think Amber Heard. Think of the careful path that female celebrity treads in order to keep the world onside, in order not to alienate: feminism and #metoo and all the rest notwithstanding.

Back in 1922, when Edith was condemned to be the first woman to hang for fifteen years, the equality argument was turned very smartly against her, in a way that is also familiar. Listen up, women, was the subtext of those advocating her execution. You campaigned to live like men, to vote and work and desert the home; you need to take the consequences and be judged like men. 'If there was some plausibility before 1920 in the proposition that a woman's sex disqualified her from suffering capital punishment,' ran a letter in *The Times*, 'there is none now.'

That was a male voice, discreetly revelling in a kind of puritan glee. And this – unlovelier still – was a woman's voice, to the Home Secretary, after he refused to commute Edith's sentence: 'Thank you for defending the honour of my sex.' There was more where that came from. 'I do not think,' wrote a Home Office civil servant, 'we have a single application from any one of the women's societies in favour of the reprieve of Mrs Thompson, and I believe that so far as those women's societies are concerned any differentiation between these prisoners, purely on the ground of sex, or the respite of both prisoners on the ground that one of them is a woman and therefore if she is not executed the other ought not to be, would be bitterly resented.'

And the conclusion, to the vexed debate about executing a woman, was invariably this: given that young Bywaters had to hang, how was it fair that Edith Thompson should not? This was the outward, rational mood. Yet the secret, excited mood of the country held the reverse view: it wanted to hang Edith, and this meant that it also had to hang Freddy Bywaters.

Then, quite suddenly, it was all over. And a kind of unease began, almost instantly, to permeate a nation that had been so fervidly desirous of this particular cancellation.

I have been compelled by this story since my teenage years, drawn initially by the coincidence of the surname (there is no family relationship). As well as in factual accounts, it recurs as a cultural reference in several works of fiction. I first became aware of it in Agatha Christie's *Crooked House*, a 1949 work through which the case runs like a motif. It is mentioned in Nancy Mitford's *Love in a*

Cold Climate, published the same year as Christie's novel, in an ice-cool droplet that shows the perverse fame Edith had attained post-mortem. 'I'm in a terrible do about my bracelet of lucky charms,' says a woman who has suffered a jewel theft. 'Just when I had managed to get a bit of hangman's rope, Mrs Thompson too, did I tell you?' But my fascination really flowered when I first read *A Pin to See the Peepshow*; a wonderful book to which I never return without longing for the story to play out differently, as it so easily could have done.

> Forget the ends lose yourself in the characters and the story and, in your own mind make your own end. Its lovely to do that darlint...

With Edith Thompson, who sought to create her own story and – because of that – had it taken from her, the ending seems so random as to be unfathomable. A woman who could be so many of us, who could be me, who made mistakes and found that others were setting the price for them.

So much still resonates, beyond the ongoing dilemma of how to negotiate life as a woman. The instantaneous efficiency with which the 'system' enmeshes an individual and blocks every exit route. The incipient hysteria that turns upon certain categories of person and seeks their immolation. The prudery and judgmentalism within the national psyche. The terrifying manipulation of the concept of 'truth'. The anger against words, and the wilful refusal to see nuance and ambivalence within them. Although the hanging of a twenty-year-old is a grotesque barbarism, Freddy Bywaters had at least committed a recognizable offence; but what happened to Edith is the stuff of Kafka, of show trials, of *The Handmaid's Tale*... and, albeit in a different sphere, of the viciousness of internet culture, its howls against the very process of argument, its pathological hounding of those who have written the 'wrong' things. Prejudice changes with the times, yet it is always essentially the same; that is to say, resistant to reason.

Today the stakes are lower. But for those of us who are ambitious and foolish and – worst of all – unlucky, they remain in essence the same.

THE LETTERS

First things first: this book would not exist, and the name of Edith Thompson would be a mere footnote in an unmemorable murder case, if her lover Frederick Bywaters had done as she asked him, and destroyed her letters.

She burned his, all except three, and the contents of what was lost are the great lacuna at the centre of this story. 'You don't know what sort of letters he was writing to me,' was her riposte to her mother from her cell at Holloway, when asked how she could have written such things.

There are two other mysteries relating to the letters. First: what happened to the physical objects, the pages on which Edith wrote, after they ceased to be private documents and became exhibits? Nobody knows, and their disappearance does have the air of a further 'cancellation' – and indeed of an irony: because Freddy did not destroy them, the authorities did.

Second: how many letters did Edith write of which we know nothing? Quite a few, it is safe to say, although not from the period that this book covers – one cannot be sure, but in text form these all appear to have survived.

The first known communication is a telegram, sent to Freddy's then ship, the SS *Malwa*, on 22 September 1920: 'Chief away today cannot come' – the chief presumably being her boss, Herbert Carlton. This may have referred to a romantic assignation, although as yet nothing of consequence. Then, in April 1921, Edith signed another telegram 'PEIDI', the nickname given to her by Freddy, which both use throughout these letters and which implies a heating-up of the collusive flirtatiousness.

The love affair proper began on 27 June 1921, after which Freddy lodged at the Thompsons' house, meaning that he and Edith spent a lot of time together before his departure on 5 August; but physical proximity never stopped her writing to him, and the first document in this collection – a note, dated 11 August – relates directly to the existence of other letters. Freddy departed with the RMS *Morea* on 9 September, returning on 29 October 1921, and told the Old Bailey that he and Edith wrote to each other during those seven weeks. None of that correspondence survives.

So the question, perhaps, is not so much why did he keep Edith's letters, but why did he start keeping them after the subsequent leave, which ended 11 November 1921?

In a letter to the Home Secretary in January 1923, Freddy argued plausibly that he would have kept none 'if I had, for one moment, thought or imagined, that there was anything contained in Mrs Thompson's letters to me, that could at any time, harm her'. Nevertheless Edith had believed him to be destroying them. The fact that she was disposing of *his* letters surely suggested that he should do the same, even though he had no spouse to find them. He felt safe, keeping them; but still it is odd, and one can only imagine Edith's feelings after the murder when she discovered that he had done so.

Were the letters so precious to Freddy, of such emotional and/ or erotic value, that he wanted to preserve them, to read them over and over as he lay in his cabin on the *Morea*? Possibly. Therefore he may have started to keep them when it became obvious that the sunlit love affair, so alive with hope for the future, was settling in to a rhythm of prolonged separations: Edith's letters were yearningly entwined with the fact of her absence.

Alongside this, it had become equally obvious that her husband was not going anywhere. In her soft, highly charged way Edith had told Freddy of her unhappiness in the marriage – there had been the big showdown during the August Bank Holiday, which seemed to have brought matters to a head: yet it had not. The Thompsons were together, an entity, in the sight of God and Ilford.

At his trial, Freddy said that when he returned home on leave in October, 'Mrs Thompson and I spoke about the desirability of her getting a separation from her husband. I said to her, "Can you not come to any amicable understanding or agreement with your husband to get a separation," and she replied, "I keep on asking, but it seems no good at all.'"

Then, on 5 November, Freddy went to the Thompsons' house:

> I made a request to him [Percy] that he should have a separation. I had taken Mrs Thompson out previously; apparently he had been waiting at the station for her and he had seen the two of us together. He made a statement to Mrs Thompson, 'He is not a man or else he would ask my permission to take you out,' and she repeated that statement to me the following day. In consequence of that I went and saw Mr Thompson...
>
> I said, 'Why do you not come to an amicable agreement; either have a separation or you can get a divorce,' and he hummed and hawed about it. He was undecided and said, 'Yes – No – I don't see it concerns you.' I said, 'You are making Edie's life a hell. You know she is not happy with you.' He replied, 'Well, I have got her and I will keep her.'

Assuming that the account is essentially true, is there a connection between this meeting and the fact that, thereafter, Freddy kept Edith's letters?

One analyst of the case, Filson Young, who unlike most observers thought Freddy the dominant partner in the Thompson–Bywaters relationship, believed him capable of blackmail; in other words, that his reasons for preserving the letters were basically suspect. Blackmail is a strong term, but certainly the correspondence constituted a hold over the Thompsons. In some indefinable way, Freddy may have thought that it might be of use in the future: if Percy tried to threaten him, if Edith turned against him, if things got complicated...

Speculation only, although the question of whether Freddy's motives were venal or sentimental goes to the heart of his character, which was at least as complicated as that of his flagrantly mercurial lover.

Alternatively it could have been nothing more than happenstance that led him to keep the letters after November 1921; and perhaps that is the most likely explanation of all.

Twenty-seven of Edith's letters, plus a number of telegrams and cuttings, became exhibits at the trial, together with the three letters from Freddy that had been kept. Twenty-nine others by Edith – plus two postcards and a couple of telegrams – survive, but were not submitted as evidence. A facsimile reproduction shows that they were written in a surprisingly neat, legible, almost schoolgirl hand.

They have been in the public domain for a century; they were read aloud at a magistrates' hearing and – by a succession of determinedly unembarrassed barristers – at the Old Bailey, where a prurient crowd revelled in a thrill way better than any theatrical spectacle. Yet magically, touchingly, they hold their sense of privacy. In a way that is almost lost to us today, such is the impulse to play to an inescapable digital gallery, these letters were aware of nothing except themselves. Therein lies their innocence, even when their subject matter is anything but. Freddy Bywaters was by his own admission a killer; and yet to read what he wrote to his lover in his tiny bedroom, beneath the grubby glow of the gas... it is hard not to feel the shift, between the intimacy of his intention and its monstrous exposure to the light.

As for Edith: it is possible that the greatest suffering of all was caused by the reading aloud of her words.

Therefore this is not an easy admission to make. One is glad that the letters still exist.

PART I: BEFORE

Editor's note: Edith's punctuation and spelling have been slightly regularised for ease of reading.

1

This letter would become Exhibit 49 at the Old Bailey trial. No envelope exists.

Immediately there is a mystery: what 'letters' does she mean? It must be the ones that she had written to Freddy... although it is unclear why she had been keeping them.

Presumably these earlier letters were destroyed, in accordance with her wishes.

The cash box to which Edith refers was, indeed, a key element in her undoing; as will be seen.

※

August 11th, 1921

Darlingest, Will you please take those letters back now? I have nowhere to keep them, except a small cash box I have just bought and I want that for my own letters only and I feel scared to death in case anybody else should read them. All the wishes I can possibly send for the very best of luck to-day,

From PEIDI.

Later Exhibit 12, this was sent to the house of Freddy's widowed mother, Lilian, from which she ran what she called her 'costumier business'.

'He', of course, is Percy, who had rid the house of the lodger but not solved the problem that he presented. Edith had returned home late on the 19th, the Friday night before this line was sent, after a tryst with Freddy in the City.

Percy's suspiciousness – understandable, yet so unappealing – merely intensified thereafter, reactivated every time Freddy came home on leave. Although Edith resented and chafed against this, and although her letters are a reiteration of the unhappiness that she felt within the marriage, she never took any decisive step towards changing her situation. Separation was constantly mentioned. Nothing ever happened. Of course it would have been an immense and difficult thing to do, especially within the 'respectable' class to which the Thompsons belonged; but there were no children, Edith was capable of earning money, she had a supportive wider family, she regarded herself as a modern woman... It could have been done.

Yet it is a complexity of this case that Edith, although in her deepest soul dissatisfied with Percy, on another level rubbed along with him. After his death, during the brief time that she spent in the marital home before being taken to the police station in Ilford, she said to her mother: 'Oh Mum, I did love him, and he loved me.' A composite of rue, grief and half-truth? Almost certainly; although not according to the authorities. The remark was reported by the detective inspector who overheard it, and a Home Office memorandum – untroubled by doubt – labelled it firmly as 'playacting'.

Mr F. Bywaters, 11 Westow Street, Upper Norwood
Postmark: Ilford, 20 August 1921, 8.15 p.m.

Come and see me Monday lunch time, please darlint
He suspects

PEIDI

Later Exhibit 62. On the envelope, addressed to Freddy's ship RMS *Morea* in Marseilles, Edith had written the words: 'Pour Vous'.

This letter was written in November 1921 – Freddy had sailed for Bombay (as it was then called) on the 11th. Although undated, the mention of a racing bet enabled the police to establish when it was sent. The first extant to show Edith in full flow, it is a perfect example of her epistolary style; it also touches upon most of the themes that pervade this story.

As, for instance, in her reference to 'that compact we made' – a proposed suicide pact, in which the couple would kill themselves at an appointed future date if nothing in their situation had changed. At the Old Bailey trial, Freddy told the court: 'I suggested it as a way of calming her, but I never intended to carry it out.' No more of course did Edith; although their attachment did, effectively, lead to the involuntary fulfilment of the pact.

Meanwhile Edith, even as she was conceiving melodramatic notions such as this 'pact', was deeply engaged with her everyday life – writing for instance about 'Mel', a local man who (as he himself was all too aware) held a lowly rank among her band of admirers, and 'Molly', who had been a casual girlfriend of Freddy's. This capacity for banality – which so forcibly struck her prison visitor Margery Fry – is key to her Everywoman fascination. She was aspirational, and she was supremely imaginative, and at the same time she was trying to arouse Freddy's jealousy with a man in whom she had zero interest and making bitchy little remarks about his ex. Mel's spiteful ribbing of Avis shows that he was well aware of Edith's romantic friendship with Freddy, which – despite her careful destruction of his letters – she made no real attempt to hide.

Certainly Lilian Bywaters knew all about it, and was far from happy – no wonder Freddy didn't want Edith ringing her. He had already tried to bring the two women together, but his mother was having none of it. Later Lilian would say to the police: 'My son Fred told me she was in the millinery line, and suggested I should do some business with her. I ordered a hat which she sent on from her place at

Aldersgate Street [Carlton and Prior]... She then suggested I should meet her and we met by appointment at the Strand Palace Hotel... I have seen her since on several occasions but have merely said Good morning or words to that effect.'

As Lilian told the Old Bailey, it was around that time – in the autumn of 1921 – that Freddy 'asked me if I could tell him how she could get a separation from her husband... I said that there was no law to compel her to live with a man if she was unhappy with him.' In other words, Lilian saw that this was not merely a question of unhappiness; that for Edith to leave Percy required a bold desire to do so that she did not really possess. Unsurprisingly, Edith was wary of Lilian's fierce, indomitable shrewdness. She knew that the mother's eye pierced the necessary fantasies of the love affair, and feared that Lilian would persuade her son to view it in this same realistic light: as something that would never come to anything.

It is arguable, in fact, that Lilian is the person most deserving of sympathy in this story. From the first she saw danger, and she was wholly unable to prevent it.

There are two specific passages in the letter that led to it being put in evidence at the Old Bailey. One comes early: 'Yesterday I met a woman who had lost 3 husbands in eleven years and not thro the war, 2 were drowned and one committed suicide and some people I know can't lose one.' The idea that this implies intent to murder is laughable – who hasn't said something similar at some point? – but that, of course, is part of the terror of the story: something of the kind, some sudden unintended descent, could happen to almost any of us.

Then, after more than 2,000 words of flitting butterfly-like from subject to subject, there is this: 'Thank you for giving me something at some future date, when both you and I are ready.'

Was this 'something' a substance designed to harm Percy? It certainly read that way, if one were sufficiently determined to link it with the woman who had enviably lost three husbands. In truth, however, and as subsequent letters make clear, it was almost certainly designed for use on Edith herself: a drug, or herb, picked up by Freddy on his travels, deemed to have abortifacient properties.

For all the frankness of these letters, many of the passages were obscure, and in contrast to her later reputation Edith is strikingly innocent about sexual matters. It is clear that both she and Freddy were aware of the possibility that she had very recently fallen pregnant, something that seems to have worried him more than her. She fainted at work on 7 November (a doctor was called out, costing her 10 shillings and sixpence) and no doubt this increased her suspicions – about which she remained oddly unperturbed, as if the matter could be dealt with quite easily at a time of her choosing.

But her reference to 'something' would, a year later, force her defence to make a seriously invidious choice. Was it better – in the already prejudiced opinion of the courtroom – for Edith to be using a drug to effect a miscarriage, or in order to poison her husband? Incredible though it may now seem, it was regarded as more dangerous to admit that she had self-aborted. And this lie helped to make everything that Edith said in evidence sound like obfuscation; a century ago, however, admitting openly to what thousands of women did in secret was simply not an option. If one is honest, that might still be the case today. When a woman's 'right to choose' is not universally accepted as a right, aborting a baby is not something to which a defendant would admit without qualms. Especially if she were – as Edith so damagingly was – vulnerable to accusations that she had put her career, her freedom, her pleasure, her very self first.

꙳

Darlint, – Its Friday today – that loose end sort of day (without you) preceding the inevitable week end
I don't know what to do – to just stop thinking, thinking very very sad thoughts darlint, they will come, I try to stifle them, but it's no use

Last night I lay awake all night – thinking of you and of everything connected with you and me

Darlint I think you got into Marseilles last night did you? anyway I felt you did – perhaps you got my first letter, the other one you will get today

All I could think about last night was that compact we made. Shall we have to carry it thro'? don't let us darlint I'd like to live and be happy – not for a little while, but for all the while you still love me   Death seemed horrible last night – when you think about it darlint, it does seem a horrible thing to die, when you have never been happy really happy for one little minute

I'll be feeling awfully miserable tonight darlint, I know you will be too, because you've only been gone one week out of 8 and even after 7 more have gone – I can't look forward can you? Will you ever be able to teach me to swim and play tennis and everything else we thought of, on the sands in Cornwall?*   you remember that wonderful holiday we were going to have in [19]22, and that little flat in Chelsea that you were coming home to every time and that 'Tumble down nook'† you were going to buy for me, one day. They all seem myths now.

Last night I booked seats for the [Ilford] Hippodrome – the show was good – not a variety, but a sort of pierrot entertainment and 2 men opened the show with singing "Feather your nest". I wished we could just you and I – but we will yes, somehow we must   I enjoyed the show immensely – you understand me don't you darlint. I was dancing the hours, I was forgetting, but by myself in bed I was remembering

* Neither of them ever visited Cornwall – this was simply part of the fantasy.
† A recurring phrase in the letters, taken from a popular song.

Altho its Friday I'm not going anywhere, I havn't been asked Darlint

Yesterday I met a woman who had lost 3 husbands in eleven years and not thro the war, 2 were drowned and one committed suicide and some people I know can't lose one.   How unfair everything is. Bess and Reg' are coming to dinner Sunday.

Today is the Derby Cup and I have some money on 'Front Line'. I don't suppose it will win, I'm never lucky not in anything darlint, except in knowing you.

I don't think I'll be able to buy that watch for you by Xmas, darlint, I'd like to ever so much, but as things are, I'm afraid I can't afford to, but the will and the wish to give is there and I know you'll like that just as well

A man on the stage said this last night "Marriage is the inclination of a crazy man to board a lazy woman, for the rest of his natural life."   Rather cutting I think, but there it came from a man.

Au revoir darlint, until Monday, I'll write some more then and hope I'll be able to talk with you as well.

*****

Altho' I said Au revoir until Monday Darlint it's only Saturday now. We are opening Sats always now. I don't like it a bit because I'm thinking of that Sat about the 14th [January – in fact the 18th] when you will be home but perhaps I'll manage to get that one off   He's grumbling

---

* Bessie Akam, with whom Edith had gone to school, was one of her few female friends.

fearfully about it – 'No home comfort whatever, you'll have to stop at home, no other man's wife wants to gad the town every day. They all find enough interest in their home'. It's his Saty off today.

When I looked at you* to say "good morning" an irresistible [sic] feeling overcame me, to put my fingers thro your hair and I couldn't   I love doing that darlint, it feels so lovely – you don't mind do you? most men don't like it, in fact they hate it, usually, but I know you're different from most men. When I got to 231 [Shakespeare Crescent] last night only Avis was in. Mother and Dad had gone to Highbury to see Grandma,† I believe she is sinking fast.   Avis said at the class‡ Mel mentioned he had seen me "with a friend of yours" he said to Avis, but when Avis was telling me this she said "I asked him who it was and he wouldn't tell me." She didn't actually ask me to tell her, so of course I didn't mention you, but she knows I am sure.

On the Friday you left, Mel rang me twice and both times I was out, he hasnt rung again

Yesterday I lunched opposite a Major and his typist   I'd love you to have been there   The conversation consisted of "How extraordinary," "really" and giggles   She did manage to say – rather loudly too "I do wish I'd come into my money soon, I'm tired of being poor." I'm sure they would have amused you, it reminded me of what you said Molly's stock of conversation consisted of.

---

* Edith kept a photograph of Freddy in her office desk.
† Her maternal grandmother, Deborah Liles, widow of a police constable.
‡ The Graydon sisters and their father both taught at a friend's East Ham dancing school. One of the young men who learned to dance there was Alfred Hitchcock, who some years later met the ageing Avis Graydon – by then, like him, a Roman Catholic – at a church event; out of consideration for her, he asked his biographer, John Russell Taylor, not to include an account of his connection with Edith Thompson.

People tell me I have got fatter in the face this last fortnight, darlint do you put on flesh when your heart is aching, I suppose you must if I am fatter because my heart aches such a lot. When I lay awake at nights and think, the small ray of hope seems so frail, so futile, that I can hardly make myself keep it alive   It's 12 noon now and I am going to get ready to go – no not home, but to 41 [Kensington Gardens] to get dinner ready, first, and then do shopping and clean the bedroom and dust the other room and do God knows how many more jobs, but I suppose they will all help to pass the time away   If I could only go to sleep tonight and wake up tomorrow and find it was the 7 1 22   But I can't – I know nothing ever comes right in this world, not right as we want it to be. It's an awful sort of state to get into, this morbid feeling and I hope I shan't give it to you, darlint when you're reading this   Perhaps I ought not to write at all when I feel like this, perhaps I'll feel better on Monday, anyway I'll put this away until then.

*****

I've had a funny sort of week end darlint I want to tell you all about it and I don't know how. I am staying in this lunch time, especially to write to you   First of all on Sat. at tea, we had words over getting a maid*   He wants one, but wont have Ethel 'because my people wont like it' he said   I was fearfully strung up and feeling very morbid so you may guess this didn't improve things. However at night in bed the subject – or the object the usual one came up and I resisted, because I didn't want him to touch me for a month from Nov 3rd do you understand

---

*   Ethel finally arrived to take up her new job on 4 October 1922, the day after the murder. She had previously worked for Percy's sister Lily and her husband.

me darlint? He asked me why I wasn't happy now – what caused the unhappiness and I said I didn't feel unhappy – just indifferent, and he said I used to feel happy once. Well, I suppose I did, I suppose even I would have called it happiness, because I was content to let things just jog along, and not think, but that was before I knew what real happiness could be like, before I loved you darlint Of course I did not tell him that but I did tell him I didn't love him and he seemed astounded   He wants me to forgive and forget anything he has said or done in the past and start fresh and try and be happy again and want just him   He wants me to try as well and so that when another year has passed meaning the year that ends on January 15/1922, we shall be just as happy and contented as we were on that day 7 years ago*   These are his words I am quoting   I told him I didn't love him but that I would do my share to try and make him happy and contented. It was an easy way out of a lot of things to promise this darlint I hope you can understand   I was feeling awful – I could have so easily died and I still feel awful today, how I wish you were here – I think only you can make me hope on a little longer [...]

I think I did tell you darlint I had 1 letter from Tilbury on Friday night and 1 long envelope from Tilbury Sat morning and 1 letter from Dover Monday morning.

Darlint I don't like you to say and think those hard things about yourself and I certainly don't like that sentence of yours 'I've run away and left you'   Don't please think them or about them   Truly darlint, I don't,

---

*   The Thompsons married on 15 January 1916, so Edith's reference is to the end of the anniversary year that *started* in 1922. Of course none of the protagonists lived to see this.

I know whatever you say – that it's Fate – it's no more your fault than it is mine that things are still as they are, in fact perhaps I really know, deep down in my heart, that it is more mine, but I try to stifle those thoughts, I only keep them locked up in my heart and I say to myself 'He won't even let it be my Fault this next time'. Am I right darlint? It's the only thought that makes me want to live on Darlint, you say do I remember? that Monday Oct 31*
I'll never never forget it, I felt – oh I don't know how, just that I didn't really know what I was doing, it seemed so grand to see you again, so grand to just feel you hold my shoulders, while you kissed me, so grand to hear you say just 3 ordinary commonplace words "How are you" Yes I did feel happy then

[...]

I'm sorry you asked me about a photograph, really sorry, because I never make a good one, darlint, not even a natural one, when I pose, and I don't know that I will have one taken, even to please you [...] However I'll think about it   You know I'm really a coward   I'm afraid you wont like it – or perhaps see things in it you wont like You remember what you told me you thought of and felt about a photograph you had sent you on the 'Orvieto'†
That's why I'm afraid

I will do as you say about when I want you, I'll even bruise myself, as you used and then take myself to Court for cruelty to myself, eh darlint?

---

*   This particular leave had begun on the 29th.
†   Freddy worked on the *Orvieto* between February and June 1921. Presumably an unknown girl sent him a photograph that he subsequently disparaged.

I've thought about the hair torture* and Im feeling quite prepared to undergo it now   I don't vouch for how I shall feel when the time comes, so be prepared for a stand up fight – it'll be rather fun.

[...]

About books I have already sent out and obtained the 'Trail of 98' [by Robert W. Service] and am going to start it perhaps tonight – no not tonight I think because Avis just phoned me and asked to go and see Grandma as I'm the only one she has not seen and she keeps asking for me I suppose I shall have to go – altho I don't like it much, I'd far rather remember her as I saw her in the Summer They say she looks terrible now

I think the Guarded Flame is difficult to read and I dont know whether you will like it – W. B. Maxwell writes very strange books – some are very sensual – but in a learned kind of way   I can't explain any better than that.

Why don't you want your mother to ring me darlint?

[...] Yes, I think I do feel a bit no not cross – but what shall I call it – disappointed about the lady and the mail bag   For a start I don't like the expression about the coffee and milk coming from you to me – from you to anyone else – perhaps yes and after all is she any worse for being a native [...] I thought you were beginning to think just a little more of us than you used.

Thank you for giving me something at some future date, when both you and I are ready.

---

* The reference is to having her hair bobbed, which she did the following spring.

I'm glad you told me you wouldn't worry about me darlint. Yes of course I will tell you everything, when the time comes, but you wont worry about it, will you darlint, whatever it is, because I don't and won't.

In that last note of yours you said 'you had been pushed to blazes for the last 3 hours'   Do you know Darlint I can just hear you saying that, yes hear you really – it's so like you.

Yes, darlint, I shall say it and I mean it – you're not to feel like it, I won't have it, (I've stamped my foot here) so just forget and obey

PEIDI

4

Later Exhibit 27, undated. Again the mention of a horse race established that the letter was sent in November.

Edith's love of a gamble – she was fascinated by luck, as well as by fate – was the norm in an era when racing was hugely popular, although ten shillings each way was a big bet, one-sixth of her weekly wage. Her habit was later used to bolster the image of a hopeless wanton. In January 1923 her brother-in-law, Richard Thompson, gave a series of vengeful interviews to *Lloyd's Weekly Newspaper*, which characterised Edith as not merely a murderess, but a woman of almost fathomless depravity, an amateur prostitute and a spendthrift of Percy's money (of course Edith's money was her own, and when bonuses were included her income exceeded her husband's).

This 'suburban Messalina', as she was called, had an incongruously childlike habit: she would earnestly cut out articles from newspapers and enclose them with her letters. The police later found some fifty clippings, of which about forty were of a frivolous, coquettish bent: 'Battle of Calves and Ankles', 'Do Women Fail as Friends' and, as here, 'Husbands and Dance Partners'. The only cuttings actually put in evidence were the remaining ten, which were concerned with matters of poisoning.

And poisoning was deemed to be at the heart of this letter, which contains the infamous sentence: 'I had the wrong Porridge today...' – a throwaway line, as it seems, amid the chatter about the Waldorf and the 'Guarded Flame', and the agonised (but perhaps deliberately provocative) confession that she had slept with Percy again. This is the great thing about reading Edith's letter in context. One realises, as could never be the case at the Old Bailey (not that they wanted it to be), just how incidental were most of the remarks that went on to hang her.

The prosecution would interpret that casual inclusion of the 'porridge' phrase in a different way. In his opening speech to the jury, the solicitor general, Sir Thomas Inskip, said: 'The unexpectedness of the passage, the inappropriateness of the passage as it stands, is startling. It will be for you to say whether the line of thought that was in Mrs Thompson's mind was that the existence of her husband was a bar to the happiness she thought she could attain.'

Does it strike a reader quite like that? – a reader, that is to say, who is not already looking for a particular narrative, the one that leads to a guilty verdict? Not really.

Yet even when Edith was questioned by her own side, junior defence counsel Walter Frampton, her replies came across extremely badly; revealing the impossibility of parsing, in a literal manner, what was in effect a literary text. Asked to what the 'porridge' passage referred, she said: 'I really cannot explain.' Frampton continued: 'The suggestion here is that you had from time to time put things into your husband's porridge, glass for instance,' to which Edith replied firmly: 'I had not done so.'

All well and good, if the questioner had only left it there. Instead Frampton pressed Edith for an 'explanation of what you had in your mind when you said you had the wrong porridge', to which she answered, near-incomprehensibly:

> Except we [she and Freddy] had suggested or talked about that sort of thing and I had previously said, 'Oh yes, I will give him something one of these days.'

Even now, reading this, one gets a desperate queasy sense of doom, of the churning fear that must have taken possession of the woman in the witness box. The exchange continued:

'We had talked about making my husband ill.'

'How had you come to talk about making your husband ill?'

'We were discussing my unhappiness.'

'Did that include your husband's treatment of you?'

'Yes.'

'Now you say you probably said that you would give him something?'

'I did.'

'Did you ever give him anything?'

'Nothing whatever.'

Again that steadfast denial – together with a suggestion of abuse within the marriage, which today would be taken seriously, but then was not. In this trial, any allusion to Edith being ill-treated by Percy went unremarked. One can be pretty sure of the general feeling, that she had deserved whatever she got (and of course the defence had to be careful not to intensify her motive for murder). The passage in the letter, regarding the 'heated argument' with her husband, could scarcely be more damning in this regard.

Worse yet, however, the same scepticism greeted Edith's twice-stated assertion that there was nothing injurious in her husband's breakfast meal. Because she could not admit to the nature of the mysterious 'something' mentioned in her previous letter, inevitably it seemed as though this same something had found its way into the 'wrong porridge'. The defence established what would seem to be a conclusive fact: that the concoction was prepared each morning by the sitting tenant, Mrs Lester. 'I never knew Mrs Thompson make it,' she explicitly told the court. It was therefore near-impossible that any extraneous substance – whether that be a poison, some slivers of glass or an abortifacient drug – had been introduced into a bowl by Edith. Like every other piece of evidence in her favour, however, this was swept aside as if it had never been said.

Her leading counsel, Sir Henry Curtis-Bennett, took the view that Edith had entirely invented the porridge scenario for the benefit of Frederick Bywaters: to keep this handsome, virile, much younger man interested, to convince him of her love and, in this instance, to make him think that she was so unhappy with Percy as not to care if she had accidentally taken poison herself. She appears to reference it again, in Letter 6, in the passage that begins: 'I believe I felt about the worst I have ever felt when that happened...'; but that, too, may have been a renewed burst of invention to lend credence to the story.

And indeed the simplest explanation of all Edith's talk of murder, all that insistence and iteration, the urging and goading, the laying of words like soft hands upon her susceptible lover, is to say – very simply – that she did not actually mean it: that she was fantasising, imagining, creating gorgeous word-pictures of a world in which Percy did not exist, without ever really wanting him to be dead. Which is true enough, as far as it goes. Whether it goes quite far enough is another story; as will be seen.

※

Have told you before I put 10/- eh way on 'Welsh Woman' for the M'chester Cup, just because you liked it   I expect you know the result. The favourite won and it (the favourite) was the only horse I really fancied, but as it was only 5 to 2 starting price, I didn't think it was worth the risk and then the dashed thing won.

Darlint, its a good job you are winning some money at cards, for I can't win any at horses.

I have won 14/9 on one race since you have been gone, I've forgotten which one it was.

I've enclosed you several cuttings, please read them darlint, and tell me what you think of them   The one I've marked with a cross I think very true indeed, but I'd like to know what you think about it.

The part about 'a man to lean on' is especially true Darlint, it was that about you that first made me think of you, in the way I do now. I feel always that were I in any difficulty, I could rely and lean on you   I like to feel that I have you to lean on, of course I don't want to really but it's nice to know I can, if I want to   Do you understand? Note the part, 'always think of her first, always be patient and kind, always help her in every way he can, he will have gone a long way to making her love him'.

Such things as wiping up, getting pins for me etc, all counted, darlint. Do you remember the pin incident,* on Aug 1, darlint and the subsequent remark from him 'You like to have someone always tacked on to you to run all your little errands and obey all your little requests'   That was it, darlint, that counted, obeying little requests – such as getting a pin, it was a novelty – he'd never done that.

'It is the man who has no right, who generally comforts the woman who has wrongs'.   This is also right darlint isnt it? as things are, but darlint, its not always going to be is it? You will have the right soon won't you? Say Yes.

The 'husband and dance partners' article also amused me, especially as things are. I think I told you about him wanting to learn

Last Tuesday when Avis came across he asked her to teach him and she is coming across next Tuesday to give him his first lesson   He wanted me to teach him, but I said I hadn't the patience, my days of dragging round beginners were over. Of course this conversation led to us discussing dancing rather a lot and we talked about the nonstop†   We were talking of going as a set with our own partners and Avis detailed them all until she came to me and hesitated so I filled in the gap by saying 'Bill' [their brother]. I felt like telling him who it really was and perhaps had Avis not been there I should have done, but I didn't want to endure any more scenes especially in

---

* This refers to the argument on August Bank Holiday that led to Freddy leaving the Thompsons' house; the fact that it began with Edith asking for a pin connects, one assumes, with the title of F. Tennyson Jesse's *A Pin to See the Peepshow*, although the pin incident in that book is quite different.
† Presumably a benign form of the 'dance marathons' that were a craze during the US Depression.

front of her.   You will find the photos with this letter, I havent looked at them and I hope they are so rotten you'll send them all back   Is it horrid of me to feel like this? I suppose it is, but darlint I want bucking up today I've made a bruise on each side of my left wrist, with my right thumb and finger, but it doesnt do any good, it doesnt feel like you.

We went to Stamford Hill˙ to dinner on Sunday and had a very good time, and were given an invitation to dinner on January 7th to Highbury   We accepted but all the time I was wishing and hoping (probably against hope) that circumstances would not allow me to go, do you understand? but I suppose I shall go

The last 2 Fridays I have been to the Waldorf and on the first occasion it was very foggy – all the trains were late, so had a taxi right to the avenue and got to Mother's at 10 20. He [Percy] wasn't coming for me so it didn't matter much – but I expect they wonder what I do.   I have promised to go to the 'Cafe Marguerite' to dinner tonight   Can you guess with whom?† God knows why I said I'd go, I don't want to a bit especially with him, but it will help to pass some time away, it goes slowly enough in all conscience – I don't seem to care who spends the money, as long as it helps me to dance through the hours I had the wrong Porridge today, but I dont suppose it

---

* Edith had three aunts living in north London: Ada Garnett in Tottenham; Lily Laxton in Stamford Hill; and Edith Walkinshaw in Highbury. She was close to these last two, and it was after an evening at the theatre with Lily and her husband John that Percy was murdered.
    There was another aunt, the never-mentioned Rhoda, a mysterious figure within this family: the 1891 census records her, aged twenty-one, as a patient at the all-female London Lock Hospital in Harrow Road – an institution for the treatment of venereal disease.

† She went with Mel, as later becomes clear.

will matter, I don't seem to care much either way   You'll probably say I'm careless and I admit I am, but I dont care – do you? I gave way this week (to him I mean,) it's the first time since you have been gone. Why do I tell you this? I don't really know myself, I didn't when you were away before, but it seems different this time, then I was looking forward – but now well I can only go from day to day and week to week until Jan 7th – then thoughts and all things stop   How have you got on with 'The Guarded Flame' I expect by now you have [found] it interesting – I have persevered with 'Felix" and have nearly finished it   Its weird – horrible and filthy – yet I am very interested   You'll have to read it after I have finished   I believe if I read this letter through before I sealed it you'd not receive it darlint, I feel that I'd tear it up, it doesn't seem to me that I've been talking to you at all – just writing to you, but I feel like that today, and I know it's rotten because you get this letter for Xmas and it wont be a very nice present will it darlint, but its the best I can do. Perhaps I'll leave this letter open and see how I feel by Wednesday, the last day for posting it

*****

Darlint, Monday – I recd greetings from you and a note 'I cant write to you' and I've been expecting to talk to you for a long time I wanted to   I wanted you to cheer me up – I feel awful – but I know darlint if you can't well you can't – that's all to be said about it, but I always feel I can't talk to you when I start, but I just say to myself he's here with me, looking at me and listening to what I am saying and it seems to help darlint, couldn't you try and do this, I feel awfully sad and lonely and think how much

---

*   A novel by Robert Hichens, whose central theme was morphine addiction.

you would be cheering me up but perhaps you'll think I'm selfish about it all and I suppose I am, but remember when you are thinking badly or hardly of me your letters are the only thing I have in the world and darlint, I havnt even all those

We had was it a row anyway a very heated argument again last night (Sunday). It started through the usual source, I resisted and he wanted to know why since you went in August I was different – 'had I transferred my affections from him to you'. Darlint its a great temptation to say 'Yes' but I did not   He said we were cunning, the pair of us and lots of other things that I forgot, also that I told lies about not knowing you were coming on that Sat. He said 'Has he written to you since he has been away,' and when I said 'No' he said 'That's another lie'   Of course he can't know for certain, but he surmises you do and I'm afraid he'll ring up and ask them to stop anything that comes for me so I must get Jim* on my side   You know darlint I am beginning to think I have gone wrong in the way I manage this affair.   I think perhaps it would have been better had I acquiesced in everything he said and did or wanted to do   At least it would have disarmed any suspicion he might have and that would have been better if we have to use drastic measures darlint – understand? Anyway so much for him   I'll talk about someone else. Have you guessed with whom I went to the Cafe Marguerite? If not you will by the following 'Isn't your sister jealous of you.'

Me – My sister – why should she be?

---

* James Yuill was the driver at Carlton and Prior, who placed Edith's bets for her (in the days before betting shops, many establishments had a 'bookies' runner).

He – It seems to me you see more of her fiancé[*] than she does herself.

Me – Hows that and what do you know about it anyway

He – Well I saw you going down Ilford Hill the other evening and he was holding your arm – did you go to a dance together.

Me – Oh shut up and talk about something else

But darlint he wouldn't he kept on coming back to you and I'd gone there to forget and instead of forgetting I was remembering all the time.

I went to lunch with Mr Birnage[†] today. At the next table 2 girls were discussing Flemings 'Oh a jolly fine place I think   Good food, a nice band, and plenty to drink' The other one – 'Yes I like the place very much but my boy wouldn't be seen inside it'. It reminded me of you with a glass of bass was it? and Avis with a glass of water

Goodbye for now darlint, I'll try and be more cheerful when I write to Marseilles. You say 'Don't worry' – just dance – If I only could.

PEIDI.

---

[*] Freddy was never Avis's fiancé, but such a remark was very much Mel's style. And Edith would assuredly have taken pleasure in his barbed teasing, which after all proceeded from the starting point of her extreme desirability. Her receptiveness, even to his near-valueless admiration, is one of the vivid flaws that make her so compelling a personality.

[†] Sidney Birnage was a well-to-do insurance broker who lived with his wife near the Thompsons in Ilford. Like Mel, he perceived the near-unconscious quality in Edith that – in a fine phrase from *A Pin to See the Peepshow* – she carried for most men 'like a banner'.

5

This letter was not put in evidence.

It raises questions, however, whose answers the Old Bailey had – in its infinite non-wisdom – already decided upon. One sees, for instance, the insecurities that Edith suffered over Freddy, about which she was unable to play it cool (her allure was not of that kind), and which contributed to her ramping up the rhetoric: 'I could dare anything, and bear everything for you.' This relationship was a layering of power-shifts; something that would have been so much clearer if his letters existed.

As would still be the case today, the age difference was at the heart of it. In the eyes of the world, which generally see only what they anticipate, the Thompson–Bywaters love affair was one in which a dominatrix held a spellbound naif in her thrall and caused him to do her bidding. The more perceptive observers, far fewer in number, saw that this was not quite the truth, that Freddy had all the adamantine confidence of hard-bodied youth and that Edith, who as well as being older was less experienced, was in many ways his supplicant. The writer Filson Young, who in 1923 edited *The Trial of Frederick Bywaters and Edith Thompson* for the Notable British Trials series, put it thus in his introduction:

> A great deal of play was made about their respective ages, and it was suggested that she was an experienced woman corrupting a young lad. That is not the way I see it... In some ways he was the older of the two, as he was certainly the more masterful. He was an almost excessively virile, animal type.

Yet that was not the whole truth either: as the thinker, the *writer*, she was the one who could guide the story... until he, in fact, decided its ending.

Complicated indeed.

So too was the fact that Percy was suggesting a baby at a time when Edith was almost certainly pregnant with Freddy's child. When she writes 'it's still the same', the implication is that her period has not come, although her wording is obscure – almost as though she does not want to spell things out, even to the person who has placed her in this situation. She was a spectacularly sensual writer, but never graphic; which has the odd effect of intensifying the sensuality.

So it is hard to be precise about what was going on. In Letter 3 she says that she does not want Percy to touch her for a month after 3 November, but what does that mean? That she and Freddy had sex that day, presumably, but what has that to do with being touched by Percy? That sex with him would have complicated matters about the paternity of a putative baby? Yet Edith, apparently, wanted rid of the baby.

Moreover, if the 3rd *was* the date on which they believed that conception might have occurred, at the time of writing she had only missed one period – or possibly not even one; it could simply have been late. One does have a sense, therefore, that this possible pregnancy, and Freddy's anxiety about it, were means whereby Edith was tightening their bond.

And the real mystery is why she would have fallen pregnant at all, when she had not done so throughout nearly six years of marriage. This was highly unusual, another characteristic that caused her to be vilified and feared: the Lady Macbeth touch. Such unnaturalness, not to have fulfilled her rightful female destiny! (Some people still think this way about childless women.)

There are strong indications that she suffered from endometriosis, which can make conception difficult, but she would certainly have employed some form of contraception. Diaphragms, condoms, douches – and withdrawal – were all quite widely used, as is obvious by the shrinking of the average family size; although the 'Malthusian uterus' was condemned by the Church and by doctors, and those who advised on the subject were liable to be prosecuted. Nevertheless in 1921 Marie Stopes opened her first clinic (for married women only).

Freddy, too, would have known how not to get a woman pregnant. Not that these methods were exactly fail-safe – but Edith seems so sure, in November, that she is at risk, one must assume that passion had overcome them and they took no precautions whatever.

They had so few opportunities, after all. Indeed the likelihood is that, except for the honeymoon fortnight of June–July 1921, they had full sex on just three or four occasions. A remarkable irony, given that their love affair would become the very emblem of adulterous transgression – although without the letters, of course, it would have been nothing of the kind. The sacred institution of marriage would have remained unthreatened by Edith Thompson had she not poured her longings (ineffable rather than sexual, but almost nobody saw that) on to the undestroyed page.

❦

Mr F. Bywaters, P&O, RMS *Morea*, Aden
Postmark: London EC, 6 December 1921, 2.30 p.m.

Darlingest boy I know,

I saw in the paper yesterday you touched Aden on the 28th, I suppose tomorrow or Sunday you will arrive in Bombay & I believe Bill [her brother] left today, perhaps you will just manage to see him tho'.

I am feeling very blue today darlint, you havn't talked to me for a fortnight, and I am feeling worried, oh I don't know how I'm feeling really, it seems like a very large pain that comes from that ceaseless longing for you, words are expressionless – darlint, the greatness, the bigness of the love I have, makes me fear that it is too good to last. It will never die, darlint don't think, but I fear – how can I explain – that it will never mature, that we, you & I will never reap our reward, in fact, I just feel today darlint, that our love will all be in vain.

He talked to me again last night a lot, darlint I don't remember much about it, except that he asked me if I was any happier   I just said I suppose as happy as I shall ever be, & then he frightened me by saying – oh I don't think I'll tell you

*****

I left off there, darlint – thought – thought for ½ an hour & I will tell you now. He said he began to think that both of us would be happier if we had a baby, I said "No, a thousand times No" & he began to question me, and talk to me & plead with me, oh darlint, its all so hard to bear, come home to me – come home quickly & help me, its so much worse this time   He hasn't worried me any more, except that once I told you about, darlint, do you understand what I mean? but things seem worse for all that. You know I always sleep to the wall, darlint, well I still do but he puts his arm round me & oh its horrid. I suppose I'm silly to take any notice, I never used to – before I knew you – I just used to accept the inevitable, but you know darlint, I either feel things very intensely or I am quite indifferent just cold – frozen.

But to write all this is very selfish of me, it will make you feel very miserable – you can't do anything to help me – at least not yet, so I'll stop.

What else can I talk about? only ordinary things darlint, but to talk about even those perhaps will help to deaden the pain. We went to the theatre in the week to see "Woman to Woman" at the Globe. I had the tickets given me. Darlint, it was a lovely play, I think I liked it as much as "Romance" altho the plot is not the same. I have written you a description of it – I should like you to discuss it with me, but better still I should like to see it again with you, but I can't, so I have talked to you about it, that's the next best thing, isn't it darlint?

Also I finished the book "The Trail of 98" & liked it ever so much, I have also written to you, about it   Darlint you have quite a lot of mail from me at Aden, I think, I do hope you will feel pleased – not too miserable, I don't want you to, darlint, just forget all the miserable things I've said to you.

Its been terribly cold here, & foggy – thick real old fashioned fogs for 4 days. I've had & still got such a bad chilblain on the back of my heel – its been there a fortnight now & I cant get rid of it   I think I've tried 5 different things   The worst of it is any shoes I have – the tops of them cut it – the chilblain, right in half

[...]

Yesterday I was taking a country buyer to Cooks, St Pauls, & passing the "Chapter House" he said to me "Would you care for a glass of wine here, its quite a nice place" Imagine darlint, me being told it's quite a nice place. I said "No thanks, really I'd rather not" & yet if it had been anywhere else I should have said "Yes"   Do you know, darlint, when you were home last time we didnt go there once, I feel sorry when I think about it, I should like to have gone, but we will next time, say "Yes" darlint I do so hope you'll be home longer than a fortnight this next time. Isn't it funny the feelings we have about going into the places with strangers that we have been in together. I feel very strongly about it, I couldn't no I simply couldn't go & sit in either of those corner seats at the Strand without you nor at the Holborn, nor "Chapter House", nor the "Coronation" nor anywhere else, where you & I have been & talked, really talked. [...]

What do you think, he is going to learn dancing – to take me out to some nice ones, won't it be fun – as the song says "Aint we got fun", while you are away   About myself darlint, its still the same & I've not done anything yet – I don't think I shall until next month, unless you tell me otherwise, after you get this letter, or the one I wrote previously.

*****

Darlint I got a letter, or rather 2 in 1 envelope on Saturday morning   You say that you can't write but you will try from Port Said. Is this correct? The envelope of these is stamped Port Said. No, you're quite right darlint, when you say you can't talk to me, you can't, these letters are only writing, they are not talking, not the real talking I was looking forward to.

Why is it? darlint, what is the matter? you do still feel the same, don't you? [...] Am I horrid to expect so much, tell me if I am but darlint I feel that I could give all, everything & I can't read between the lines of your letters this time that you even want to accept that all.

One part that did amuse me was over the argument That expression "I do love 'em, etc" made me think of old times, you remember the Shanklin* times, when neither of us had any cares, or worries, personal ones I mean, altho' we hadn't learned to know ourselves or each other, which were the best times darlint? now or then, just tell me, I shan't mind   That was a funny dream you had, wasn't it? I wonder what it means or if it means anything Why do you tell me not to get excited darlint, do you think I would   I don't think I should darlint, over that,

---

* On the Isle of Wight, a reference to the holiday in June 1921. Her references to remarks in Freddy's own letters are unclear.

you & I have too much at stake to take too many risks. But I don't think there is any risk, darlint, it doesn't seem so at any rate, but I feel that I could dare anything, and bear everything for you, darlint.

That's all now, darlint, I've got such a great lump come in my throat & I'll have to swallow it somehow. Peidi does want you now.

6

Later Exhibit 13.

Again the lacuna within this case is all too apparent, as Edith replies – in her hop, skip and jump way – to a succession of points in Freddy's letters, and nobody will ever know quite what she was answering. Here one infers a lot of trivialities, but that was not always so. As Avis would write, after the trial, to Prime Minister Andrew Bonar Law: 'Why was it so emphatically said "She incited Bywaters"? ... Where are Bywaters' letters to prove his statement that Mrs Thompson is innocent?'

But Freddy's letters were dust and ashes, leaving Edith to be betrayed by her own insidious eloquence.

As, for instance, in her second reference to sleeping with Percy in order to 'disarm suspicion'... again, one feels that she could hardly have written anything more damaging. It spoke directly to the image of her as a sorceress, preying upon male helplessness. No wonder so many women hated her and men, filled with a kind of lascivious fear, neutralised her by turning her into a clubman's joke. Mr Justice Darling, one of the three judges who heard her appeal in December 1922, got a big laugh from the courtroom when he conjured a picture of an Edith and Freddy who had got away with murder and were subsequently married: 'One day they might be sitting by the fire and he might be thinking to himself, "That woman poisoned her husband and now I am in his place. What about me?"' The fact that there was no material evidence whatever of Edith actually poisoning Percy made not a whit of difference: 'truth' had become what people wanted it to be.

All the same, one does have pity for Percy here. This is an unusual murder case in many respects, not least of which is that sympathy does not naturally lie with the victim; instead it is with the glamorous, fateful, sexually appealing pair condemned for his dreadful death. Percy was fitted with a metaphorical halo at the Old Bailey – representing as he did the threatened moral order – but since then he has been most unfavourably perceived: as a stubborn, suspicious, sulky man, part-brute part-sitcom cuckold, concealing his inadequacies within buttoned-up pyjamas and lashing out against them with a frustrated, sometimes violent, faux-masculinity.

Some (not all) of the evidence for this comes from sources other than Edith, and by modern standards he is certainly an unattractive figure (more on this at Letter 8). A hundred years ago, however, in a society where there was no such crime as raping one's wife, he was a fairly average sort of husband – and therein lay the problem, because he had a very non-average wife.

It was not his fault that Edith agreed to marry him, which clearly she should not have done. Nor could he help his own ordinariness: it was as though he had used up all his individuality on wanting this woman in the first place. If he had only had it in him to say: all right Edie, here's your divorce, off you go with your fancy man – calling her bluff, in effect. He would have saved three lives and won the day. She would have been stuck with Freddy, reality would quickly have intervened and Percy would have been, quite genuinely, the good guy.

But he was unable to do this. Like Edith he was a member of the respectable lower classes, but unlike her he came from a family in which respectability meant never parting the lace curtains to let in the light and laughter (this, too, was not his fault). He was trapped in his belief system, shared by the vast majority, which said that marriage was for life and a husband's word was law, and he was angrily bewildered by Edith's complex personality. What was an unimaginative bloke to make of this bright, blithe, sexy, elusive woman, the interludes of 'surrendering' and the bursts of apparently contented wifeliness, the round of bridge parties and theatre visits that the Thompsons performed together throughout this whole story, which a part of Edith did genuinely enjoy, and which must have led Percy to believe that their marriage was salvageable? Hence his suggestion of a baby (Letter 5), the time-honoured 'solution' to fixing a relationship. And the fact that he did this, in hope and in ignorance, cannot help, again, but arouse one's pity.

Mr F. Bywaters, P&O, RMS *Morea*, Plymouth
Postmark: London, 3 January 1922

Darlint, I've felt the beastliest most selfish little wretch
that is alive. Here have I been slating you all this trip for
not talking to me and I get all those letters from Marseilles
darlint, I love them and don't take any notice of me, I
know I am selfish – and you ought to know by now, I told
you haven't I? heaps of times   Now what have I got to
talk to you about, heaps of things I believe – but the most
important thing is, that I love you and am feeling so happy
that you are coming back to England, even tho perhaps I
am not going to see you – you know best about that darlint,
and I am going to leave everything to you – only I would
like to help you, can't I?   Of course he knows you are due
in on the 7th and will be very suspicious of me from then,
so I suppose I won't be able to see you – will I? You know
darlint, don't have the slightest worrying thoughts about
letters as "to be careful I've been cruel" to myself I mean.

Immediately I have received a second letter, I have
destroyed the first and when I got the third I destroyed
the second and so on, now the only one I have is the
"Dear Edie" one written to 41, which I am going to keep*
It may be useful, who knows? By the way I had a New

---

* Dated 1 December 1921, sent from Bombay and later Exhibit 14, the letter read:
'Dear Edie,
   Do you remember last Xmas [1920] you wrote to me wishing me all the best. I never
wrote you so this year I'm going to be sure of it. I want to wish you all that you can
wish yourself   I know all those wishes of yours will run into a deuce of a lot of money
Such things as fur coats, cars and champagne, will be very prominent on the list –
anyhow, good health and I hope you get it. Have a very real good time, the best that is
possible. I shall be about 2 days this side of Suez. Never mind I will have a drink with
you. Once more the very very best at Xmas and yours very sincerely...'

Year's card, addressed to me only from "Osborne House, Shanklin" [the boarding house in which they had stayed on the Isle of Wight].

[...]

Darlint, I've surrendered to him unconditionally now – do you understand me? I think it the best way to disarm any suspicion, in fact he has several times asked me if I am happy now and I've said "Yes quite" but you know that's not the truth, don't you

About the photos darlint, I have not seen them, so I don't understand about "waiting for you". Please destroy all you don't want and when you come to England, show me what I look like, will you yes, I was glad you promised for me, darlint, as I most certainly should have refused myself and I should have hated myself for refusing all the time   Darlint, I never want to refuse you anything, it's lovely for me to feel like that about you, I think by this you can understand how much I love you

The French phrase darlint, if I can remember rightly was "I can't wait so long, I want time to go faster"

You used iron and I used my heel and its such a long time ago, or seems so, since I asked a question, to which your "I did that" is the answer, that I have forgotten what my question was [...] About the fortune teller – you have never mentioned "March" before darlint, you've said "Early in the New Year," are you gradually sliding up the year to keep my spirits up? darlint, I hope not I'd sooner be sad for ever and know the truth, than have that expectant feeling of buoyancy for a myth

[...]

About the Stewardess, I'm glad you went to the cabin with her, what is it I feel and think about you? I have someone to lean on – if I need anyone, and she had too darlint, had'nt she? someone to lean on and help her, even against her own inclinations

[...] Darlint, I didn't think it fair about the fight altho most people are disgusted with boxing (women I mean) I always tried to look upon it as something strong and big and when you told me about that I thought   If amateurs even do that sort of thing, then professionals must and I felt disappointed.

Thanking you for those greetings darlint, but you won't always be "The man with no right" will you – tell me you won't – shout at me – make me hear and believe darlint [...] I believe I felt about the worst I have ever felt when that happened' I think when I noticed what I had done I had a conscience prick and felt "I don't care what happens and I don't suppose he does really" but you would care wouldn't you darlint? tell me yes, if I really thought you wouldn't darlint I shouldn't want to die, I just want to go mad

Why have you never told me what you thought of your own photos darlint, you are a bad bad correspondent really darlint I absolutely refuse to talk to you at all next trip, if you don't mend your ways   Darlint, are you frightened at this – just laugh at me

I think you misunderstand me when you think I thought you were cross with me for going out. No, darlint, I didnt think you were cross for that, but cross because something

---

* See commentary to Letter 4.

happened or might have happened to me, that would happen to any girl who took the risks I take sometimes.

Yes, I enjoyed John Chilcote [*John Chilcote, MP* by Katherine Cecil Thurston] ever so much, I admire the force in the man that made him tackle such a position against such odds

The man Lacosta in the "Trail of 98", I didnt give a thought to, he was so vile I didnt think of him at all, and I'd rather not now darlint

I am reading a book that I think you will like darlint "The Common Law" by R W Chambers. We were at 231 [Shakespeare Crescent] for the coming of the New Year darlint – I wondered if you were wondering the same as I What will the New Year give to two halves – to you and I Last night 231 all came over to me and did not go until gone 1 and then I had the clearing up to do and consequently am feeling a bit tired today

If I only had you here to put my head on your shoulder and just sleep and dream and forget. Darlint come to me soon, I want you so badly more and more.

Your cable has just come in, thank you darlint and I think you might get to Plymouth earlier than expected, so am wishing this off.

Goodbye and good luck darlint from PEIDI

I feel quite big, being a member of the Morea˙ darlint

---

* Presumably Freddy acquired some sort of official status for Edith, to facilitate the delivery of her letters.

7

Not put in evidence. Undated, but clearly written during Freddy's leave in January 1922, probably on the 10th (Freddy's presence in Britain never dammed the stream of letters). He had docked at Gravesend on the 7th and the couple met for the first time on the 9th, the day on which they would both die the following year.

The gist of the letter is concerned with the baby that was now, according to Edith, growing inside her. It is a near-certainty (although with this mistress of invention there is always room for doubt) that she had been pregnant when she celebrated her twenty-eighth birthday, on Christmas Day 1921, and was by this time about nine weeks gone.

The air of inconsequence that hovers over Letter 3 – 'thank you for giving me something, I'll use it as and when' – is now far less apparent, although what Edith actually did (and required Freddy to do) to resolve the situation remains a mystery. More on this with Letter 9.

Darlint, it doesnt seem possible you are home again   I can't realise it, I tried all last night   I did not close my eyes once – just thinking & feeling all over again how I felt when I saw you   By the time you read this I shall have asked you to do something for me   I didn't like doing it myself, darlint, in fact I cried all the time, but after it was done I felt easier, & after you have finished it for me I shall feel easier still. Darlint, dont be cross about it, its better I am sure & I was thinking all the time to myself "the next real one I have perhaps I'll be able to keep for always"   I wasn't very nice last night when you were leaving me darlint, I know, but I'll try and be patient, 2 hours after 7 weeks seems so short. I put the violets in my hand bag last night until I went to bed at 9 p.m & then put them in water   They are quite fresh this morning, I wore them & they are now beside our monkey[*] on my desk   I dont think I thanked you properly for the sweets darlint but I was so pleased to see you, everything flew, you understand, I know

I have not put his ribbon[†] on again yet – it will cause comment if I do so am leaving it for a little while.

Thank you for G.M.M.C[‡] wire this morning   Dont forget I want you always so be careful, & good luck darlint

PEIDI

8

Later Exhibit 64.

Undated, but the reference to the 9th implies January 1922 (this was the only 9th of a month to fall within Freddy's onshore leaves).

The letter was put in evidence because of the refrain about fighting, winning, not failing, which would have been deemed to support the charges of incitement. Indeed that repeated word 'fail' has echoes of the supreme inciter, Lady Macbeth – although she, after all, had only been urging her husband to do something he already wanted to do. And, as with the Macbeths, what this letter really shows is the push–pull in the relationship, the impossibility of establishing where its true seat of power lay. 'You are going to help me first and then I am going to help you...'

Along with Filson Young, one of the few people who perceived this was – interestingly – the detective-inspector who headed the Thompson–Bywaters case: Frederick Porter Wensley, crude but shrewd, who wrote in his 1931 memoirs that Freddy 'cannot be set down as an unsophisticated youth, for he was experienced much beyond his age, and of strong and dominating character.' Of course the former DI did not exonerate Edith from the charges that he himself had helped to establish, although his account of the case contained an equivocation of some significance:

> *Whichever of them first thought of murder* [my italics] there is no question that she had such power over him that he was prepared to do her bidding.

As well as the age difference, what complicated matters – and is referred to here – was money. A successful professional woman, who held down what would now be described as a career with prospects, Edith earned £6 a week plus bonuses and owned half a house worth £250 (the earnings-to-property-price ratio was, as will be noticed, somewhat different a century ago). Freddy, although not without ambition, was a fairly lowly member of a merchant ship crew who earned between £5 7s 6d and £13 15s per month, according to the work he was doing. Sometimes a clerk, sometimes a steward, at the time of his arrest in October 1922 he was described simply as a 'daily servant'.

Inevitably the disparity played a part in the relationship between Freddy and Edith (she is extremely alert to any sensitivity on the subject). On the one hand, he would have been bolstered by his ability to arouse such fierce passion in this smart, impressive woman; on the other, as a young man who already held himself in high regard, he would have disliked a scenario (as below) wherein Edith gave him the means with which to take her out. So when he stood Edith up for the lunch date, was it because of money? Or was it, in fact, because at times he wanted something simpler – somebody with whom he felt comfortable – an Avis rather than an Edith, who did not weave spells and make demands of a kind that he nonetheless could not resist. One notes, in Letter 6, the throwaway line: 'perhaps I am not going to see you – you know best about that darlint', as if Freddy had suggested that it would be better if they did not meet; there are hints of that again in this letter, and there would be far more of it later in the year – a conflicted desire, in him, to pull away from her.

This is not unrelated to the issue of income disparities. Alongside it, one could also posit why Edith – so desirous of vaulting the boundaries of her life – did not use her powerful attractions to find a different kind of lover from the admittedly fanciable boy next door.

Darlingest boy, thank you –

I know what you say is really true, but darlint it does feel sometimes that we are drifting. Don't you ever feel like that – and it hurts so – oh ever so much

Yes, we are both going to fight until we win – darlint, fight hard, in real earnest – you are going to help me first and then I am going to help you and when you have done your share and I have done mine we shall have given to each other what we both "desire most in this world" ourselves, isn't this right, but darlint don't fail in your share of the bargain, because I am helpless without your help – you understand. Darlint, this is the one instance in which I cannot stand alone, I cannot help myself (at first) – the one instance when I want a man to lean on and that one man is and can only – always – be you.

Please, please darlint take me seriously – I want you to – I wanted you to before and you didn't. Tell me when you see me next time that you will darlint, for certain, remember Peidi is relying on you and you understand me and know I mean what I say and tell me you know I wont fail or shirk when the time or opportunity comes.

Darlint you say you are looking forward to Thursday night, is this really true? somehow I feel it isn't, I have done ever since the 9th and when I think about it I feel more so about it. You have not asked me all the time you've been home to go with you – except to a dance – which I refused – because I want to wait for that time – that first dance until it will be a real pleasure, without any pain and it can't be just now darlint can it? and when you said you'd take me to lunch and then didn't come and I'm wondering – I can't help it darlint if Ive done right in asking you to take me out. And apart from this feeling that I have, there is that ever present question of money – darlint you've never told me this time once about money – what you had and what you spent and I felt hurt – horribly darlint, especially about the suit – last time you told me about the coat – but not this time – why the difference darlint?

And as I haven't any money to give you, at least not much and perhaps you havn't any I wish you weren't going to

take me out darlint and even now its not too late – if
you'd only tell me, be quite frank about it darlint, I'll
understand – surely you know I will. I didn't intend to
mention this darlint, but neither you nor I must harbour
thoughts that each other doesn't know, must we, we must
be one in thoughts and wishes and actions always darlint,
so I have. Please understand how I feel and know I love
you.

PEIDI.

9

Not put in evidence.

This is a quite extraordinary letter; even Freddy Bywaters was taken aback by it, as will later be seen.

The *Morea* departed on Friday 20 January 1922 and, on the following day, according to her own account, Edith miscarried. How this came about – was brought about – will never be known. She herself seems hardly to have understood the body with which she was so deeply in tune.

In Letter 7, some ten days previously, Edith wrote: 'By the time you read this I shall have asked you to do something for me I didn't like doing it myself, darlint, in fact I cried all the time, but after it was done I felt easier, & after you have finished it for me I shall feel easier still. Darlint, dont be cross about it, its better I am sure...'

As so often, one is left to ponder the meaning of the word 'something'. Did she mean that she had arranged an abortion, and wanted him to accompany her? F. Tennyson Jesse relates such an episode in *A Pin to See the Peepshow*. Yet it seems well-nigh impossible that this happened in reality. Throughout Freddy's leave Edith was (as above) fretting about the kind of trivialities that would have been surely overwhelmed by the imminence of a life-threatening, illegal procedure; and, although the couple did see each other properly on the 19th, they cannot have been engaged upon such dire business – 'it was real lovely on Thursday', is her description of the meeting.

There were other remedies available to those in such a predicament, although their efficacy was of course dubious. Women swallowed quinine, raspberry leaf, purgatives and gin, or bought medicines such as 'Madame Drunette's Lunar Pills', coyly advertised as 'menstrual regulatives'; they threw themselves down the stairs or tried to dilate their cervix with candles; they boiled and steamed themselves in the bath, if they had one. Edith may have tried any of these things – possibly the bath was where she 'cried all the time'. Yet in her often childlike way, and her desire to 'lean on' her teenage lover, she gives the impression of having placed all her faith in Freddy – and, it would seem, in the abortifacient 'something' that he seems to have procured. If so then she was right, because something clearly worked.

Still more mysterious is her behaviour after the miscarriage. She describes it with all her innate, instinctive vividness; any woman who has ever experienced cramps will feel the ghost of them again, reading that she collapsed in an extremity of pain as the foetus loosened its grip upon her womb. Later (Letter 38) she described losing a great deal of blood. But then, instead of seeing a doctor – or, at the very least, taking to her bed for a day or so – what did she do? According to this letter she cleaned up the bathroom, fastened hooks and eyes around her tender stomach and spent the following evening at the Holborn Empire.

Edith had plenty of everyday female guts, the 'chin up' kind that shrugs off pain and puts on a lipsticked smile, although she would fall apart completely in the face of demands for a different kind of courage. And it was extraordinary, not least in the apparent unawareness that there was anything odd about it. The disconnect between incidents in her letter – one minute she was bleeding out her insides, the next mingling with a 'very cosmopolitan crowd' – shows Edith's butterfly-flitting at its most bizarre.

Yet think about it: given the tightrope that she walked in her double life what else could she have done, except pull herself together as if none of it had ever happened?

There is a final mystery in her last words, when she remarks that she is 'a teeny bit disappointed'; an echo of 'the next real one I have perhaps I'll be able to keep for always' in Letter 7. Was this the truth? Would she have liked to keep Freddy's child? Or – given the slight, hinted fear that he is distancing himself from her – was she saying it to flatter him, to please him, to perturb him, to urge him into a reaction? All those things, surely, and in a different mood she would probably have meant none of them. But the mutable nature of Edith's words – tweet-like in the way in which she wrote her thoughts as they burst into her mind, with no intention that they should acquire enduring significance – was not something that the Old Bailey chose to recognise.

Nor, of course, did it recognise her near-infinite capacity for imagination. And one cannot reject the possibility that the whole saga – pregnancy, miraculously induced miscarriage, still-more-miraculous recovery – was invented, a thread spun by this Ilford Scheherazade (perhaps from the starting point that she *might* have conceived Freddy's child) in order to keep her man from wandering. As a theory it is far-fetched, and almost certainly incorrect. But it does explain how she managed that evening at the Holborn Empire.

❦

Mr F. Bywaters, P&O, RMS *Morea*, Marseilles
Postmark: London EC, 24 January 1922, 1.30 p.m.

Darlingest boy I know,

I got your note and enclosure from Tilbury and a letter – a real nice one from Dover this morning.

Yes, darlint, it was real lovely on Thursday – just to be with you for longer than that one hour just to let time slide for a little longer than usual. I'm ever so glad I had you on Thursday – it would have been so hard – yes, much harder than it is now for you to go away without being with you for just that short time.

Darlint don't we set store by just those few hours – can you imagine what a whole long day will be like? Hours seem like Paradise, days will be like well I don't know, because I've never had days before.

This is a vile nib, but I havn't another.

That feeling I had & still have about you going darlint I can't explain – not even to myself – first of all I feel that I shall want you & shall need you to lean on & you won't be there & then darlint – the "drifting feeling" that

I told you about before – I think is mainly responsible I think – if next time – (I mean in March) – things are just the same – we'll feel further apart still, because darlint, I did feel apart this time – its no use making myself say I didn't. But darlint that was your fault – yes, it was & you're going to say "It was" & take all the blame – because I said so [...] Darlingest boy, I didn't go to 231 on Friday – I did want you so much – just to take care of me & help me to get thro', I'll tell you about it.

About 10.30 or 11 a.m. I felt awfully ill – I had terrible pains come all over me – the sort of pains that I usually have – but have not had just lately – do you understand.

These continued for about an hour & I stuck it somehow – feeling very sorry for myself – until about 12 o'c   I went off then into a faint. They managed to get me to with brandy – then I went off again, & again, making 3 times in all. Everybody here was fearfully frightened & eventually sent for the doctor. He told them to partially undress me & give me a hot water bottle – refilling it every half an hour

At 3.30 p.m. he came in again and as I was no better Jim took me home in the motor   Darlint, I was lying flat on the floor inside, with the water bottle.

When I got home I went straight to bed & about 7 something awful happened, darlint I don't know for certain what it was, but I can guess, can you, write & tell me.

On Saturday, I felt a bit better, but not much   I didn't know what to do or take to get better & I looked awful. In the evening I dressed & went out & really enjoyed myself, meeting heaps of people I know & hadn't seen – some for 2 years. It was a very cosmopolitan crowd

darlint & I do wish I had been with you there   I'm so
certain sure you would have enjoyed it   I've enclosed
you a menu & programme, *not ours*, but an extra one I
got Uncle [possibly John Laxton] to give me. On the
back you will see names of artistes "Evelyn Clifford &
John Humphries." They are husband & wife friends of
Mr. Carlton [her boss] & they sang a song the following
of which I remember.

He: One little word.

She: Cheri.

He: Leads to two little words.

She: Ma chere.

He: Two little words lead to 3 little words.

Both   I love you.

It was nice, darlint, you would have liked it

Yesterday darlint was an opportunity lost, it was a thick, a
very thick fog – the worst London has known for years. He
went to bed about 8.30 with a headache – I stayed up in front
of the fire until 10.30 with you darlint – thinking of you &
thinking of us & thinking of that "Glorious Adventure"*
that you are helping me with. You are aren't you?

---

* This refers to a film, *The Glorious Adventure*, released on 1 January 1922 and starring
the renowned British socialite Lady Diana Cooper. In an interview, given some fifty
years after his attendance at the Old Bailey trial, the writer Beverley Nichols – at the
time a very young member of the press – likened Edith's appearance to that of Lady
Diana, as well as to a 'Rossetti drawing'. She was, he recalled, 'a beautiful woman. With
a sort of innate quality of aristocracy.'

[...]

Darlingest boy, I'll talk to you again by Wednesday. Don't worry about me now, I'm feeling much better, but a teeny bit disappointed.

PEIDI.

10

Not put in evidence.

'One Little Hour' is a recurring allusion in Edith's letters – it was a popular song, what one might call 'their' song, and with the capacity for sincere absorption that was at the heart of her personality she lost herself in its sentimental lyrics. 'One golden hour! For that eternal pain!' encapsulated for her the Thompson–Bywaters love affair, with its brief unions and its attenuated separations, filled with words.

The 'rift with Lily' refers to a falling-out with Percy's sister, who lived very near the Thompsons with her husband, Kenneth Chambers (it was their former maid whom Percy did not want Edith to employ – and possibly she *was* out for trouble, why fixate upon that one girl in a city full of domestic servants?).

Edith did not like any of the Thompson family. And they do not come across as in any way likeable; although they could, of course, have put their own side to the story, which even before the murder would have bemoaned the flighty, self-obsessed minx who made Percy's life intermittent hell. Lily, meanwhile, was one of the few women who pricked at Edith's usually buoyant sense of superiority. The two had known each other when both acted in an amateur dramatics society in Stepney, organised by a local church minister – Lily was the star of the company and married the minister's son. Kenneth was a bank worker, thus a cut above Percy on that pinched social scale where every narrow gradation counted. Then, in 1919, the Thompsons had spent ten months as the Chamberses' paying guests before they found their own house in Ilford. Given Edith's queen bee character, it is easy to see that this might not have ended well.

Yet an interview with Avis Graydon in 1973 suggested that the rift was not the fault of Edith, but Percy: 'he was so bad-tempered and he got on so badly with his family'. She said a lot more. Indeed, from the end of the trial to the end of her own life, Avis took on the role of counsel for Percy's prosecution. She was compelled by grief – and by grievance, that Edith should have been portrayed as the monster in the marriage (later it will be seen that there may have been a further, more complex motivation). 'The man is dead, but why should he die blameless', as she put it to PM Bonar Law.

How accurate was Avis's portrait of Percy, as an obsessively jealous heavy drinker with a violent temper? Not entirely, is one's best guess. He was jealous, yes, but he surely had good cause – Avis suggested that he objected to Edith speaking to any man, not just Freddy, but note in this letter how even Freddy accused Edith of being 'fast': she was the sort of woman whom men found intensely desirable, then criticised for that very quality. There was no evidence that Percy drank to excess, although he may have done so on occasion. As for the violence, it is unclear whether this was an occasional expression of extreme frustration, or something grimly embedded in the Thompson marriage. The incident on August Bank Holiday 1921, when Percy manhandled Edith to the extent of badly bruising her arm, is corroborated by the sitting tenant Mrs Lester. Freddy would testify at the Old Bailey that Edith feared 'being knocked about when she was asking for a separation or divorce', and in a further statement said that he had 'extracted a promise from him [Percy] that he would not knock her about any more and that he would not beat her' – but Freddy was hearing these things from Edith, who was the very definition of an unreliable witness. That does not mean that she was lying. And of course it is outrageous that this testimony was completely ignored at the Old Bailey; but even the objective witness has to admit that it is impossible to interpret accurately. (The sexualised masochism with which Edith wrote to Freddy about holding her own wrist, in order to bruise *herself* – 'but it doesnt do any good, it doesnt feel like you' – was, of course, a very different thing; a complication, however, in this context.)

Avis's claim that Percy did not get on with his family was not quite true – he was, for instance, close to his brother Richard. However: her version of the 'rift with Lily' was backed by Mrs Lester, who told the police that the couple had left the Chambers house in a hurry 'owing to a quarrel they had one night in the bedroom, when Thompson was knocking his wife about and his brother-in-law told them to go.' The question is how Mrs Lester could have known such a thing, and the only feasible answer is that Edith had told her. Which means that it is probably, but not certainly, true.

Kenneth Chambers – who seems to have been a decent man, liked by Avis – mentioned no such occurrence when he spoke to the police. His evidence has an air of discretion, and he would not have wished to badmouth a recently murdered brother-in-law. He did, however, say that there had been no visits between the Chamberses and Thompsons since the latter moved out of his house, which is fairly remarkable given that the couples lived less than a mile apart. Chambers went on to say that 'Mr Thompson was a very reserved man and he never discussed his domestic affairs. As far as I could see, they were a very happy and affectionate couple.' A similar view would be expressed by Edith's admirer Sidney Birnage, who with his wife socialised with the Thompsons (triggering no outward jealousy in Percy). He told the police: 'They have appeared most affectionate towards each other.' Then there was this, from John Laxton, describing the night at the theatre from which Percy would not return to his home: 'They appeared a most affectionate couple. When leaving they appeared in the best of good health and spirits.'

Mr Laxton would have said nothing, of course, to give his niece a motive for wanting rid of her husband. Avis's words can actually be said to have strengthened the case against Edith: a woman might well have incited her lover to kill such a pig as she described. What she also does, however, is affect the case for Freddy's defence.

At the Old Bailey it was stated that Percy's killing was cold-blooded and deliberate: murder, rather than an act of justifiable homicide/manslaughter – as argued by Freddy's counsel. This was easily ripped apart by Justice Shearman, whose motive in doing so was surely mixed with the need to bring down Edith as well: *she* was the one deemed to have acted with malice aforethought, even if the decisive action was Freddy's.

Freddy would claim that he had gone to Ilford on the night of 3 October 1922 with no intent to kill, simply to confront Percy. A fellow prisoner in Brixton, who shared a cell with him when he was awaiting trial, later recounted a conversation about this: 'He told me he didn't mean to stab him, see, he meant to talk to him. I said, well, what was you tooled up for? You must have meant something if you had a tool on you.' The salient point, indeed. Why was Freddy carrying a large knife, whose double-edged blade measured five and a half inches? He claimed that he always did so, that it was a shipboard habit; and that he only used the 'tool' on Percy when the other man claimed to be armed with a gun.

As a defence it was somewhat improbable. Nevertheless Edith's aunt, Lily Laxton, who also sent a pleading letter to the government, wrote: 'Knowing the late Mr Thompson very well, I say the lad's story is true & undoubtedly he acted as he thought in self-defence, Mr Thompson being just the kind of man who would bluff having a weapon.'

Of course the everyday shrewdness of a Lily or an Avis, mixed as it undoubtedly was with the urgent wish to help Edith, was dismissed by the forces of law, whose collective mind worked in different ways. But these sensible women were saying something highly relevant: Freddy had knifed a man who was capable of aggression. If the Old Bailey didn't care to investigate a possible tendency to wife-beating (which it did not), it should still have noted what this implied about Percy's character.

The two men had had a confrontation before, fourteen months previously, on the August Bank Holiday. Their final encounter was a re-enactment: a showdown Percy would not have dodged – after a night at the theatre with his wife, the sudden appearance of lover-boy would have enraged him – and he was not frightened of Freddy. The forensic evidence, moreover, told a tale very different from the one of a man waylaid by instantaneously fatal blows.

The killing took place on Belgrave Road, the main thoroughfare from Ilford station, off which the Thompsons would have turned right to reach their home on Kensington Gardens. The trail of blood along the calm residential street – traversing the pavement, the middle of the road, the high fence against which Percy had slumped and died – measured some forty-four feet, and was overwhelmingly suggestive of a prolonged scuffle. Given the size of Freddy Bywaters' knife, and the element of surprise, he could have jumped his victim and despatched him in a moment. Yet the evidence of the corpse, too, says otherwise. The confrontation had demonstrably begun face to face; some slashes to Percy's three-piece suit (and to his tie, which was severed), four minor cuts to the face and four slight cuts to the torso imply nothing so much as an increasingly nasty fight. It was only after an unknown number of seconds that a firecracker explosion of insanity led him to make the three deep plunges of the knife – to inner arm, neck and throat – that ended three lives.

'I pushed her to one side, pushing him further up the street', ran Freddy's statement to the police, which – lacking as it did the detail about the gun, designed (badly) to actualise the claim that this was not deliberate murder – has an air of truth.

> I said to him, 'You have got to separate from your wife'. He said 'No'. I said 'You will have to'. We struggled. I took my knife from my pocket and we fought and he got the worst of it. Mrs Thompson must have been spellbound for I saw nothing of her during the attack...

Had the decision not been made to infer, from the letters, a long-planned strategy against the life of Percy Thompson – poisoning, shards of glass, finally stabbing – then this statement might have been fundamentally accepted. So too Edith's story, which was that having been shoved against a wall by Freddy she was left dazed for a moment, then realised that he and her husband were skirmishing. A woman's cry of 'Don't – oh don't!' was heard by a man who lived nearby; this was dismissed completely, while witness testimony as to Edith's distress and hysteria was viewed as evidence of her deviousness. Such was the desire to view her as a murderous Machiavel, which shut down with it any possibility of understanding what her lover had done. His action had to be seen as the culmination of a coherent plan; not, as it more truly was, of a story that had acquired its own mysterious momentum and had, at last, reached a conclusion.

Mr F. Bywaters, P&O, RMS *Morea*, Marseilles
Postmark: London EC, 28 January 1922, 2.30 p.m.

Darlingest boy, its Wednesday now, the last for posting to Marseilles.

I'll be thinking & thinking, wishing such a lots [sic] of things tomorrow – late – when I shall know you have arrived   You will help me darlint you won't fail me this time. I'm feeling very very hopeful to-day – that "bucked" feeling darlint, you know it, I know, but I also feel how much I miss you – miss so much even that one little hour.

Do you remember the songs darlint "One little Hour," did you like it – well if you did when you first heard it, you dont now, because darlint you've changed, you're different – not a bit like the boy I remember at Shanklin on the last Friday, do you remember darling "I love you," [*] I do & then it was that "One little Hour" kind of love, oh yes it was, but those kind of things that were pleasures to you then are just sordid incidents now aren't they – I mean with everybody but ourselves.

Darlint, about the other song [in previous letter] you never mentioned if you liked the words. I didn't buy it to send to you especially, it belonged to me – no to both of us, & it still does. Not since you've been gone darlint have you had a nice tidy head,[†] I've done it purposely not once a day but 2 or 3 times, it's nice I like doing it. So

---

[*] Freddy's words when he first declared himself to Edith, at the boarding house in Shanklin.

[†] This refers to Edith's pleasure in ruffling Freddy's hair, which in his absence she was doing, as it were in spirit, to the photograph that she kept in her office.

you'll have to, darlint. Just say I'm not to, & I will. Do you remember our Sat. morning [14 Jan] the snowballs & the sweets & the drinks in that "low common place" for a woman to go.

Darlint you know you called me "fast" & the man in the confectioners thought I was terrible spending all your money & darlint I will be terrible, when you have a lot of money for me to spend. All those motor cars & fur coats & champagne you wished me at Xmas I'm going to have one of these days, eh darlint – because you're the only one that I'll let buy them

I went to E.H.S.[*] on Monday night for the parcel & as I had time to spare (I didn't want to get home before 7) I walked back along the High St. to the Broadway – very narrowly missing Mrs Bristow & bumping into Cossy. I dare say everyone at 231 knows I was in the High St. now.

On Monday night we went into the Birnages for a hand of cards. They were very nice, but the strain of keeping out family matters (owing to the rift with Lily) was rather trying.

Darlint, I got your cable this morning, thank you so much the clock indicates handed in at ½ past 7 p.m. on Tuesday. Is this right? It's later than it always has been.

The weather here is frightfully cold again, the wind blows so hard, & I miss you to hold me in the train.

---

[*] East Ham High Street. The people mentioned were obviously known to Edith from her years at Shakespeare Crescent; this little passage again shows the tight boundaries of the world that she inhabited.

Will you do something for me darlint, yes, I know you will if its possible. I want a slide for the back of my hair to match the comb,* do you think its possible to match.

I can't possibly wear my usual one & the comb together. Try for me please darlint.

[...]

Darlingest boy, please excuse me now – I've just had a ring from Avis & Mother was taken ill last night with "flu" & temperature 105 – the doctor is afraid of pneumonia – so I'm just going down to Manor Park. It's 12.30 now. I love you darlint & am living for Monday when you will be talking to me. I hope it will be a long long time.

PEIDI.

---

* A gift that Freddy had brought back from his travels.

11

Not put in evidence.

Freddy was born on 27 June, and it was on the occasion of his nineteenth birthday that the couple first slept together. Edith marked this double anniversary on the 27th of every month.

❧

Mr F. Bywaters, P&O, RMS *Morea*, Aden
Postmark: London EC, 31 January 1922, 6.15 p.m.

27th January, 1922.

My very best wishes darlint and hopes for many real happy ones later. PEIDI.

12

Later Exhibit 15, accompanied by four cuttings whose contents ensured that these, too, would be exhibited at the trial.

As has been said, once these letters were brought into the legal arena they were interpreted in one way only: literally. This is what killed Edith Thompson. To which it might be said: but why was the law involved at all? Because, in the first instance, Percy Thompson had been killed, and everything proceeded backwards from that terrible fact.

So Edith *was* guilty of something, because the letters – even when obviously fantastical; as here when she mentions poisoned cigarettes – played their part in bringing about Percy's death. To say otherwise is to deny that words matter. She was guilty because she had written things; and however much she had been submerged in herself, consumed with the need for self-expression, her words were written for another person; whose reaction she sought, while taking no responsibility for what that might be. The letters did not make Freddy act as he did, but without them he would not have done so. Which makes her guilty of something, but nothing that was the business of the law.

And yet. So many people believed that she was guilty as charged (indeed some still do). Not all of them were carried along on a wave of prurient puritan hysteria, which viewed Edith as a scapegoat for post-war moral decline and contemplated her execution with a kind of dark excitement, yet they still thought she was guilty. For instance Margery Fry – a fervent abolitionist – was, she wrote, '*terribly* exercised about the Thompson case' and in her role as prison visitor met Edith several times. She later described trying to feel her way towards Edith's 'flimsy personality' (few so cruel as the impersonally kind), but what really baffled her was Edith's refusal to accept the verdict, which to Margery was simply beyond question.

The Times, meanwhile, clearly believed itself to speak for the majority of its readers – and for truth – with this calm assertion after the trial: 'The crime was premeditated and long contemplated.'

In other words: what now reads like a series of scattergun assertions by the prosecution, which had picked out every incriminating phrase from within a vast accumulation of words and traced from them a glinting thread of intent, was viewed as absolute proof that Edith had intended to poison Percy. The fact that he died by stabbing, and that there was therefore no 'nexus' (Sir Henry Curtis-Bennett's word) between the letters and the crime, was deemed wholly irrelevant. So too was the evidence of the Honorary Pathologist to the Home Office, Bernard Spilsbury, who testified that he had found no trace of poison or glass in Percy's body. Perhaps it was because he did so in a way that refused to be wholly unequivocal, blurring what should have been a shining moment of triumph for Edith's defence: there was nothing in the body but, at some unspecified time in the past, there just conceivably might have been.

'Did you find any indication of ground glass in the appendix?' he was asked by the prosecution.

'No.'

'Is the negative result of your examination consistent with glass having been administered?'

'Some time previously, yes.'

'Is it possible that a large piece would have passed through the system without injury to the organs, or without leaving any signs behind?'

'It is possible.'

For the defence, Sir Henry Curtis-Bennett asked about poison; Edith's letters contained references to hyoscine, digitalin, bichloride of mercury and ptomaine: 'There are not many of those poisons... that would leave any permanent effect at all,' said Spilsbury, leaving Sir Henry to change tack thus:

'At any rate, there was no trace, either post mortem or by analysis, of any poison having been given?'

'No.'

That was decisive, at least.

Today, of course, an alternative forensic opinion would have been sought to hammer home the findings of the post-mortem.

No poison; no glass; no case to answer. A century ago, however, Spilsbury was regarded as forensically infallible (his reputation is now less lofty), and his reluctance to land full upon the square would have been noticed. In 1973, an explanation was offered by another eminent pathologist, Professor Donald Teare, whose attention was drawn to the last sentence of Spilsbury's post-mortem report: 'The fatty degeneration of the heart muscle, liver and kidney may have resulted from disease, but no disease was found in the body which would account for these changes.' This wording, according to Teare, was carefully constructed to imply that, with poisoning as with glass, nothing was proved but something was possible.

A multitude of poisons, including chloroform or phosphorus, can cause such symptoms as were identified in Percy's body. Although chemical analysis of the organs was negative, Teare suggested that there were 'certain poisons, particularly I suppose the poisonous hydrocarbons, which certainly fifty years ago might be difficult to identify after a month's interment.'

He also believed that Spilsbury might have made representations to the Home Office to the effect that Edith should not be reprieved. 'I haven't any doubt that he would. He was a very conscientious man, in constant touch with the judiciary – people who really mattered – and his words would have had weight.'

Hydrocarbon poisoning, which today is most likely to result from sniffing glue or ingesting cleaning fluids, does not directly connect with Edith. She might have used some household product, such as turpentine, but nothing of the kind was mentioned in her letters – as it surely would have been. It was also the case, according to Teare, that these poisons would have to be administered in a strong-tasting substance. Not tea or coffee, nor indeed porridge. Which brings one to alcohol; thence to Avis's claim that Percy had been a heavy drinker; and on to the thought that this might well have accounted for the 'fatty degeneration' found by Spilsbury.

Yet F. Tennyson Jesse, an expert student of the case, claimed to have been told by Spilsbury himself that he was convinced Edith had never administered anything injurious to her husband. And, if his findings were genuinely indicative of something suspicious, why was he not questioned directly about it at the trial? Why, moreover, is there no record of any of this in the confidential Home Office files, which are chock-full of justifications for why Edith should hang, yet contain no mention of Spilsbury and his alleged suspicions?

At the same time, one has to accept that a handful of passages are hard to explain away, even to those who believe that what happened to Edith Thompson was a grotesquery; and indeed it is interesting to consider how they would be viewed if the death penalty had not been imposed. To put it at its most simplistic: imagine that they were a series of texts, sent by a older married woman to her boyfriend, who then killed her husband during a set-to and was charged with manslaughter. How, then, might they be read? For sure Edith would be blamed (#cougarbitch), but it would also be easier for the cooler-headed – the contemporary Filson Youngs – to interpret the nature of her guilt.

The reference in this letter, for instance, to 'two witnesses' to the fact that Percy was taken ill, by means demonstrably not administered by his wife. This has a careful, thought-out air, which reads uneasily.

And, of course, everything about these letters is *how* it reads, because the pattern that Edith wove of truth, elaboration and lies still defies disentanglement. Nobody knows what she meant by much of what she wrote. It is possible that she herself did not always know. Her gift – a writer's gift – for creating alternative scenarios means that the letters float in a beautiful occlusion; they hover upon the line between fantasy and reality, which is as easy to traverse as moving from one room to the next ('I go, and it is done'), but also a chasm to be leapt.

In the end Freddy Bywaters crossed that line. Sometimes, just sometimes, one wonders whether Edith – however briefly, however non-lethally – did so too. More on that later.

Mr F. Bywaters, P&O, RMS *Morea*, Aden
Postmark: London, 10 February 1922, 2.30 p.m.

Darlint – You must do something this time – I'm not really impatient – but opportunities come and go by – they have to – because I'm helpless and I think and think and think – perhaps – it will never come again.

I want to tell you about this   On Wednesday we had words – in bed – Oh you know darlint – over that same old subject and he said – it was all through you I'd altered. I told him if he ever again blamed you to me for any difference there might be in me, I'd leave the house that minute and this is not an idle threat.

He said lots of other things and I bit my lip – so that I shouldn't answer – eventually went to sleep. About 2 am. he woke me up and asked for water as he felt ill I got it for him and asked him what the matter was and this is what he told me – whether its the truth I dont know or whether he did it to frighten me, anyway it didn't. He said – someone he knows in town (not the man I previously told you about) had given him a prescription for a draught for insomnia and he'd had it made up and taken it and it made him ill. He certainly looked ill and his eyes were glassy. I've hunted for the said prescription everywhere and can't find it and asked him what he had done with it and he said the chemist kept it

I told Avis about the incident only I told her as if it frightened and worried me as I thought perhaps it might be useful at some future time that I had told somebody

What do you think, darlint   His sister Maggie came in
last night and he told her, so now there are two witnesses,
altho' I wish he hadn't told her – but left me to do it

It would be so easy darlint – if I had things – I do hope
I shall

How about cigarettes?

Have enclosed cuttings of Dr Wallis's case. It might prove
interesting darlint, I want to have you only I love you so
much try and help me PEIDI

12 (i)

Exhibit 15a.

Dr Wallis, whose surgery was at the end of Shakespeare Crescent, was the Graydon family doctor. In a very remarkable coincidence he became part of a story not dissimilar to Edith's own, albeit with a completely different denouement. As was surely generally known in that small community, he was conducting an affair with the practice nurse, Mrs Ada Bolding, who lived with him at his surgery while her curate husband studied at Oxford. In 1921 the Rev. Bolding was offered a position at Lingfield in Surrey; Dr Wallis moved in with the couple, oddly enough at about the same time as Freddy Bywaters began living with the Thompsons. In early 1922 Bolding was found dead.

An open verdict was given at the inquest, but the general view was that Bolding had discovered the affair and killed himself. Mrs Bolding and Dr Wallis were exonerated of suspicion of murder; clearly it did no harm, in these situations, to be a member of a highly respected profession.

Extract from *Daily Sketch*, 9 February 1922, page 2, column 1. With headnote:

'Curate's Household of Three
'Mystery of his Death still unsolved.
'Wife and Doctor
'Woman asked to leave the Court during man's evidence.
'Death from hyoscine poisoning, but how it was administered there is not sufficient evidence to show.'

This was the verdict last night at an inquest at Lingfield after remarkable evidence and searching cross-examination.

The three principal figures in the case are –

The Rev Horace George Bolding (39), curate of Lingfield (Surrey) Parish Church, found dead on his bed in his dressing-gown on January 4. Described by parishioners as "Happy, jovial, one of the best of good fellows, and a regular sport."

Mrs Bolding, about 35, the widow, who was in London with the only child, a boy, at the time of her husband's death.

Dr. Preston Wallis, a ship's surgeon, who, separated from his wife, had stayed some time with the Holdings, and who was called to the bedroom and found the curate dead.

On page 15, column 3, the report is concluded with the following headnote:

'Helping the Doctor.
'Why Curate's wife often went about in his Chair
'Practice that dwindled'

12 (ii)

Exhibit 15b.

Extract from *Daily Sketch*, 8 February 1922, page 2, column 1. With headnote:

'Poisoned Curate
'Resumed Inquest to-day following Analyst's Investigation'

Then follows a short paragraph referring to the inquest on Mr Bolding to be held on the 8th February, and referred to in Exhibit 15a.

12 (iii)

Exhibit 15c.

> Extract from *Sunday Pictorial*, 5 February 1922, page 2, column 1. With headnote:

> 'Poison Chocolates for University Chief
> 'Deadly Powder posted to Oxford Chancellor
> 'Ground Glass in Box
> 'Scotland Yard called in to probe "Serious Outrage"'

Then follows a paragraph dealing with chocolates sent anonymously to Dr. Farnell, the Vice-Chancellor of Oxford University, which were examined by an analyst, resulting in the discovery that some of the sweets had been bored underneath and filled with ground glass and what is believed to be an insidious form of Indian poison.

12 (iv)

Exhibit 15d.

> Extract from the *Daily Mirror*, 6 February 1922, page 3, column 4. With headnote:

> 'University Mystery of Poisoned Sweets
> 'Oxford Vice-Chancellor on Deadly Gift
> 'Postmark Clue
> 'Powder containing Indian Drug in Police hands.'

Here follow some details which refer to the same matter as is reported on Exhibit 15c.

13

Not put in evidence.

This is very much a reply to Freddy's last, and the gist of what he wrote to Edith can clearly be inferred. Having received her letter detailing the miscarriage-plus-Holborn-Empire episode, he reacted – as pretty much anybody would – with expostulations of outraged astonishment.

Yet as Edith says to him: put yourself in my place. What else was she to have done?

It is interesting that she confesses to ignorance about 'such matters' – with her solipsistic nature, and the allure that so many of her own sex found instinctively alarming, she had little chance to imbibe the kind of whispered female folklore that informs most young women. Interesting, too, is the way in which she seeks to defend herself against Freddy's criticisms: she did not want a doctor, she says, because she could not bear Percy to think that the baby had been *his*. Appealing to her lover's masculine pride, in other words; of course the truth was that she did not want Percy to think she had miscarried at all. As things stood, her husband was able to tell himself that the relationship with Freddy was an inappropriate flirtation. A baby, even though it could theoretically have been his own, was liable to harden any latent suspicions of an actual affair.

The first lines here, with their reference to 'schemeing' and failing, are typical of the sort of passage that the prosecution required Edith to explain under cross-examination, yet this letter was not cited at the trial. Indeed none of the letters that deal explicitly with the miscarriage episode were put in as evidence. Was this to preserve the remaining decencies in such a high-profile case, which was already causing middle England such collective palpitations, and was described in the *Sunday Express* as a 'grimy surge of moral anarchy... a glimpse of a modern London without a conscience or an ideal'?

Mr F. Bywaters, P&O, RMS *Morea*, Aden
Postmark: London EC, 15 February 1922, 5.30 p.m.

I was so pleased to get your letter, darlint, it came on Friday midday   Miss Prior* took it in & examined the seal – all the time she was bringing it down the stairs. I was looking at her.   Darlint, you say I can't know how you feel, when you failed can't I darlint? dont I know didn't I fail once? I do know darlint, its heartbreaking to think all the schemeing [sic] – all the efforts are in vain But we'll be patient darlint the time will come we're going to make it just you & I our united efforts darlint, I shall be very very interested in all you will have to tell me   I can understand darlint how difficult it must be – all that underwork   I wonder if I could do any more I believe I could somehow women usually can in these things but I'm counting on you putting all my faith in those persuasive powers that I know you possess, because you've used them on me   Darlingest Boy you say "Am I right"   I don't know it's what I think happened – darlint – but I don't know, I've never had any experience in such matters and I never discuss them with members of my sex as so many girls do therefore I suppose I'm rather ignorant, on such subjects but I'll tell you everything about it when I can look at you & you mustnt be cross with me darlint about getting up. I can't say I did know it was dangerous or whether I didn't, I just didn't think about it at all, I fought and fought with myself to make myself keep up & I think I succeeded, darlint. Put yourself in my place darlint & see how you would feel if

---

* Although it never affected her work, Edith's colleagues were surely all too aware that she was conducting an extra-marital affair (see also Letter 26).

you thought by stopping in bed and not making an effort a doctor would have been called in – would have said well what have you & I think he would – someone else not you would have taken both the blame & the pride for the thing they did not do.

I imagine how I would feel about it, I'm afraid darlint I would not have been able to keep silent. Please dont worry, darlint I'm alright really now – only a bit shaky – & I dont like the way you say "It was ridiculous for you to get up" etc because I'm not going to let you bully me so please take note monsieur & don't transgress again.

[...]

It is as if our thoughts & minds & actions were just one even tho' we are miles apart   Do you feel like that darlint I do when I'm doing anything by myself. I always think & say to myself that you are doing it & thinking it with me.

Darlint when you are home next time you must ask your sister to play that song* for you because it won't matter that she does know who gave it you then – will it – & I shall never be able to play it so darlint please do.

Fancy darlint you doing such a dreadful thing as to discuss those truly awful matters with me. I am ashamed of you [...]

Darlint is my letter to Bombay awaiting you on your arrival, or do you have to wait a week for it, I believe you do   This morning I think you arrive and you'll see Bill & I'll be thinking of & about you all this coming week,

* Presumably the one referred to in Letter 7.

darlint such a lot   I know you'll be careful you said you would

I want to tell you about a dream I had last week I received a letter by hand by Avis & the envelope was addressed in Harry Renton's* writing only inside was a letter from you

It wasn't your writing darlint it was a large round hand just like a schoolboy's   I read & read for a long time not recognising from whom it came until I came to the word Peidi & then I called out "Why its from my own boy"   I dont know if I did really, but I did in the dream.

Even now I can't determine in my own mind whether you sent the letter to him to send on to me, or whether he got hold of it somehow

Tell me what you think darlint. There's nothing but ordinary every day things to tell you darlint oh except one thing that I love you so much – but you know that dont you darlint. I wish you were here that I could tell you but you will be one day each day is gradually dragging on.

PEIDI.

* One of Edith's admirer friends, mentioned perhaps to keep Freddy on his toes.

14

Later Exhibit 16.

The depictions of Percy in this letter have a strong ring of truth. In her quick, lucid way Edith conveys the dogged frustration of a man veering between roles – 'the man of the house' determined to sleep in his own bed, the contrite breakfast-server who simply wants his wife back, the amateur private detective wielding his notebook. And, again, one both dislikes the man and feels pity for him.

Then, with regard to the material that would bring this letter to the attention of the Old Bailey... Quite a lot of it here.

The correspondence from late 1921, with its references to the 'wrong porridge' and so forth, has a straightforward defence: Edith was asking Freddy for help with an unwanted pregnancy, and was unable to explain this in court. But it is clearly impossible that, having managed to lose an unwanted baby in January, she was preparing to get rid of a second one in February. Therefore that defence – which some commentators seek to use in a vague, all-encompassing manner, to explain any and every request made to Freddy for something to be sent, or brought, or done – cannot, in early 1922, still apply.

In the following exchange (which incidentally shows how poorly conducted was her actual defence) Edith's junior counsel questioned her about a problematic passage.

'Look at your letter of 22nd February, where you write – "I suppose it isn't possible for you to send it to me – not at all possible, I do so chafe at wasting time darlint." What were you referring to when you wrote that?'

'Mr Bywaters had told me he was bringing me something and I suggested to send it to me, to allow him to think I was eager for him to send me something to do what he suggested. I wanted him to think I was eager to help him, to bind him closer to me, to retain his affections.'

Did Mr Frampton anticipate the possibility that Edith would reply in this flustered, confused and deeply damaging way? If he did not, he was negligent. If he did, why on earth did he not find a different way to frame his question?

Moreover: although Mr Justice Shearman was as hostile as a prosecutor, one has to admit that it was reasonable for him to intervene at this point and ask: 'But what was "it"?'

To which Edith replied: 'I have no idea. It was something he suggested.'

And one sees, with appalling clarity, why Sir Henry Curtis-Bennett had been so desperately keen to keep his client out of the witness box. Yet Edith had insisted on testifying. She did so, according to her counsel, because she was vain and obstinate; it might also be said that she did so because she was fundamentally innocent of the charges brought against her, and therefore did not fear the arc-lights of scrutiny.

Filson Young, one of the few people who pierced the mood of moral panic that prevailed against her, addressed this issue in his introduction to *The Trial of Frederick Bywaters and Edith Thompson*. 'I think if I had been in Sir Henry's place... I would have asked her to brief another counsel.' He also expressed polite dismay with her defence, saying:

> It seems to me that Sir Henry Curtis-Bennett lost one of the opportunities of his lifetime when, after the confused and uncertain opening of the Solicitor-General, he did not for once do what counsel are so often telling juries they are doing, but, in fact, so seldom do – leave the prosecution to prove its case and attempt no positive defence.

Exchanges such as the one above demonstrate how right he was. Young perceived both the essential weakness of the case, and the way in which Edith herself invited it to strengthen. Had she instructed her counsel to say that she had known nothing about the killing, and that anybody who claimed otherwise should go and find some actual evidence, then – Young again – 'I do not think you could have found a British jury to convict her.'

As it was, a censorious old judge was able to seize upon the phrase 'this thing I am going to do' and state, in his summing-up: 'It is said that the meaning of that is, "If I poison him is it going to make any difference to you afterwards"; that is what is suggested is the plain meaning of the words.'

The truth is that there was no plain meaning to the words. Instead there was an arena in which almost every person present believed in the writer's imprecisely defined guilt, interpreted the words accordingly; then said that they had found their 'meaning'.

❦

Mr F. Bywaters, P&O, RMS *Morea*, Port Said
Postmark: London, 22 February 1922, 5 p.m.

Darlint, I've been beastly ill again this week – only with a cold tho, but it was a pretty rotten one, pains all over me I caught it from him, I asked him when he had his if he would sleep in the little room and he said "No, you never catch my colds, I always catch yours" so we remained as we were and I caught it badly

Darlint in a hundred years you'd never guess what happened on Sunday – I'll tell you, but you mustn't laugh – I was given my breakfast in bed, I think he was feeling sorry about not sleeping alone when I asked him, so did that

Darlingest boy, it is four whole weeks today since you went and there is still another four more to go – I wish I could go to sleep for all that time and wake up just in time to dress and sit by the fire – waiting for you to come in on March 18, I dont think I'd come to meet you darlint it always seems so ordinary and casual for me to see you after such a long time in the street, I shall always want you to come straight to our home and take me in both your arms and hold me for hours – and you can't do that in the street or a station can you darlint. I think Bill is leaving Bombay today, I wonder if you have played any matches and I wonder and want to know so much who has won

Darlint, did anything happen in Bombay – or did any kind of conversation happen whatever referring to me at all. I felt terribly lonely all this week, darlint – a kind of "don't care, can't bother to fight" sort of a feeling.

I'm just waiting for a gorgeous long letter from you when will it come, I suppose not for a long time yet, I do so want you to talk to me today, I keep on looking at you [his photograph] to make you talk, but no words & not even thoughts will come I am looking now darlint, hard at you and I can hear you say "dont worry Chere" to Peidi.

Darlint, pleased, happy, hopeful and yet sorry – that's how I feel, can you understand? Sorry that I've got to remain inactive for more than another whole month, and I had thought by that time I should be seeing you for just as long and every time you wanted me   However, for that glorious state of existence I suppose we must wait for another three or four months*   Darlint, I am glad you succeeded   Oh so glad I cant explain, when your note came I didn't know how to work at all – all I kept thinking of was your success – and my ultimate success I hope.

I suppose it isnt possible for you to send it to me – not at all possible, I do so chafe at wasting time darlint

---

* Another obscurity. Why did they need to wait three or four months before attaining 'that glorious state of existence'? The best guess is that Freddy – in an attempt to dampen down the more dangerous fires within this correspondence, which at the same time he was merrily feeding – had told Edith that the substance he hoped to obtain would not be immediately available to him.

He had a cold last week and didnt go in, but came up to meet me about 5   Of course I didn't know he was coming and it was funny – our Monkey was on my desk – which must have been and I'm confident was noticed

Miss Prior told him we had not worked after 5 since last year and he mentioned this to me – as much as to say "How do you account for saying you worked late some weeks ago" I didn't offer any explanations.

On the evening that I told you we had words – about you – he asked me for your address which I gave him and which he wrote in his note book, he also asked me what had happened to the Xmas greeting letter* you sent and when I said I kept it he said "Why, you never do keep letters from people" so I answered "I kept it for bravado, I knew you'd miss it and know I had kept it and one of these days ask me for it."

He also said "Have you anything whatever belonging to him – anything mind you" (I knew he meant our monkey) "I have nothing whatever belonging to him" I said – darlint it wasn't a lie was it, because the monkey belongs to us doesn't it and not to you or to me, and if it was a lie I dont care, I'd tell heaps and heaps and heaps to help you even tho I know you don't like them

Darlint that reminds me you said in one of your letters "It was a lie and Peidi I hate them", about something I had or had not told you and I forget which, but I am sure I told it to help us both

---

* See note to Letter 7.

That hurt ever such a lot when I read it darlint, it hurts so much that I couldn't talk to you about it at the time

Darlint, do you think I like telling them, do you think I don't hate it, darlint I do hate this life I lead – hate the lies hate everything and I tell so many that's what hurts – it hits home so hard – if only I could make an absolutely clean – fresh start – it would all be so different – I'd be so different too darlint and we're going to start a new fresh clean life together soon darlint, arent we tell me we are, tell me you are confident – positive we are, I want telling all the time – to make me hope on

Darlingest boy, this thing that I am going to do for both of us will it ever – at all, make any difference between us, darlint, do you understand what I mean   Will you ever think any the less of me – not now, I know darlint – but later on – perhaps some years hence – do you think you will feel any different – because of this thing that I shall do

Darlint – if I thought you would I'd not do it, no not even so that we could be happy for one day even one hour, I'm not hesitating darlint – through fear of any consequences of the action, don't think that but I'd sooner go on in the old way for years and years and years and retain your love and respect. I would like you to write to me darlint and talk to me about this.

15

Not put in evidence.

Interesting for its depiction of Edith in her Everywoman guise. The reference to the agonizing resumption of her periods shows again the quotidian courage of the female, battling one's body with its susceptibility to pain and pleasure, keeping up the scented façade... And then the quotidian life with Percy, that other façade, the dance parties and whist parties and helping with her husband's accounts, which a part of Edith had no desire to bring to an end.

The reference to the SS *Malwa* is also of interest. Although this was not brought out at the Old Bailey, a man named Arthur Newbury, chief clerk in the P&O Pursers' Department, had given a police statement about Freddy Bywaters during his term of employment on the *Malwa*. At the start of 1921 Freddy had been suspended, having jumped ship at Tilbury docks.

It was a serious offence. The obvious inference is that it happened for reasons connected to Edith, whom of course he already knew. But why did he need to jump ship on her account?

More likely he was compelled by a sudden rush of blood to the head. The action could have ruined his prospects forever, yet he did it. He was a young man replete with good qualities – above all bravery – but he had an inflamed streak of wildness that flourished separately from Edith; she knew this, and although she reached out to Freddy's finer self, she found it attractive.

The person who helped Freddy out of this deep hole was, oddly enough, Percy Thompson, who received poor reward for his intervention. The son of the Thompsons' sitting tenant, Mrs Lester, was also a P & O employee; Percy asked him if he could find Freddy a berth on the SS *Orvieto,* which he did. Freddy was taken on as a baggage steward and remained with the *Orvieto*

---

* As, for instance, in Letter 3, when she pulled him up for his reference to a 'native' woman. Hers, here, very much the contemporary voice – with Edith these reactions were instinctive.

from February to June 1921, receiving a 'VG' (very good) for both conduct and ability.

※

Mr F. Bywaters, P&O, RMS *Morea*, Marseilles
Postmark: London EC, 6 March 1922, 6.15 p.m.

My Darlingest boy,

I was so pleased to get letters from you last Monday I hadn't expected any – as I got that note after the Port Said letter & thought it must have been posted at Aden   Darlint if you were 1½ hours out from Port Said how did you post it?

In your letter you say you felt I had been ill, darlint I told you not to worry & you mustn't when will you do what I ask you?

I suppose I have been ill probably more so than I thought but I wouldnt give way because I wanted to keep that illness all to ourselves thinking that helped to keep me up.

I certainly did receive your cable in time to got [sic] you an answer, but darlint, it never entered my head that you would expect one   I am so sorry if I disappointed you it was not intentional.

You see darlint, I had told you in my Marseilles letter about it. I thought I could write in full in my Bombay letter & what could I put in a cable darlint only "Dont worry better" & you would still have worried   I hope you are not now anyway there is no need.

On Sunday I was ill – as usual – & I did feel really ill darlint, I think it was worse than before what happened

The only effects I feel of anything is a languid lazy sort of feeling – no energy – just pale & limp but all that will be altered when you are in England   I didnt stop away from 168 [Aldersgate Street, her place of work] because I thought of your letters and I knew they would forward them to 41 [Kensington Gardens] if I was not there so I managed to get in every morning & went early & then Mater got ill* & I had no time to think of myself.

Darlingest boy dont talk or think about losing me that will never happen will it? if I go you will too won't you? You say "I must let you know of all those things that you ask me & I have forgotten"

Darlint, do I forget to answer anything I dont remember forgetting anything & I try not to forget anything that we ever say to each other or do with each other or ask each other.

Tell me what I have forgotten & I'll answer everything. Darlint you say you realise what it was for me after Aug 5th† I am glad you do, in a measure, it was & still is too awful, I daren't think too much I should always be weeping & that wouldn't do, would it? because you told me to dance – only sometimes to dance is much harder than to sit & think.

Do you remember the cutting I once showed you – where tell me? "Eyes that tell of agony untold Lips that quiver with unuttered pain. A heart that burns with misery" & grief etc

---

*   Mrs Graydon's flu is mentioned in Letter 10.
†   The day that Freddy left 41 Kensington Gardens.

Darlint do you remember anything happening to me on Nov 7th° I do & I think you will. We have just got the Doctor's bill in for it here & he has charged 10/6d so Heaven knows what he will charge for Friday Jany 20th I dont know whether to offer to pay or let 168 pay, what would you do?

I have bought "the Red Planet" by W. J Locke & am reading it but am disappointed in it & I think it is the one that you have read & which you thought was "The Rough Road" anyway it is a war story and I'm not very keen.

Do you remember I told you I had been ill with a bad cold well I managed to shake it off a bit – but last Sunday brought it back again – so I slept in the little room of my own accord, last Saturday I went to see "The Co-optimists"† at the Palace Theatre & was awfully disappointed in them. I had heard them raved about & suppose I expected too much.

Darlint I'm beginning to think that I expect too much always of people & things in fact too much of life altogether do you think I do? darlint if you do think so do you think I always will? I have enclosed you a sheet of sketched Millinery that we had done. I had to write 100 of these how would you like the job?

Twelve of us, mostly Stamford Hill people & Reg & Bess [Akam] went to a private dance at Shoreditch Town Hall

---

*   The day that Edith fainted at work.

†   This variety revue, which opened in June 1921 and helped launch the career of Stanley Holloway, was indeed a hot ticket.

last week, he came too   Darlint I enjoyed it – do you know it hardly seems possible that I could to me & I'm sure it does not to you   I enjoyed it dancing with Reg. & Mr. Philpot – they are both good dancers & now he wants us to make arrangements for 8 of us to go to the Nonstop March 16, 22. I suppose I shall go   I shall have to, but I wouldn't if you were in England would I? [...]

I suppose you left Bombay on Saturday for England only 3 more weeks   By the way I heard that a boy from the "Malwa" knocked Mr Moore right down a ship's gangway & rather hurt him. I didn't hear what he did it for.

To-day I finished the "Turkish Delight" its all gone now & I'm sorry I was so greedy but I know I'll get some more soon. Enclosed is a cutting that reads as if it might be you? What do you think?

Last Saturday we went over to Tulse Hill – to Mr Manning's – I went to his office and helped him [Percy] with his books until 5 p.m & then met Mater & Dad. Avis & we all went together. None of us this time managed to carry away a prize (it was whist) it is unusual as one of us usually manage to take one. There was no mail in on Monday this week – perhaps there will be later in the week – I do hope there will be   I'm longing to hear you talk to me, but darlint longing much more for you to be here to see you, for you to hold me tight so tight I cant breathe

Au revoir darlint.

PEIDI.

16

Not put in evidence.

Hard to understand the 27th reference here, especially as by 27 March Freddy would be home on leave. The postmark must be correctly transcribed, as the note has been sent to Marseilles. So: another small mystery.

꙲

Mr F. Bywaters, P&O, RMS *Morea*, Marseilles
Postmark: London EC, 7 March 1922, 12.30 p.m.

27th

You know all & everything I wish you darlingest & myself.

I was very very sorely tempted to buy myself a birthday present from you today. They looked so lovely everywhere you go you see them now, but then I thought next birthday you will be in England to buy them for me so I refrained, altho' it was hard

Good bye darlint you have all my love PEIDI.

Not put in evidence.

A shame, really, as the rather touching picture of Edith going into the City to buy chocolate for Freddy hardly squares with her Messalina image. One might even describe the action as maternal; and this of course sits conveniently with the eight-and-a-half-year age difference, the childless marriage and the expression of disappointment after miscarrying a baby.

At the same time, and in direct contradiction, Edith often took a girlish role in the relationship – as if she were the younger of the two, although this was also a form of flattery to Freddy's alpha male ego (I need a strong man to lean on darlint...). And she was not, on the whole, the motherly type: she was far too fascinated by herself. Nor is it necessarily the case that women without children seek an alternative outlet for the maternal impulse, the toy dog or the toy boy, according to taste.

More likely, Freddy's youth appealed for reasons both simple and complicated. He was straightforwardly gorgeous, in an era when people grew old far more quickly and her husband, at thirty-two, had the aspect of a middle-aged man. And then, perhaps, he allowed her to dream, to play the part of the woman she longed to be, in a way that would have been more difficult with an older man. The affair would have assumed a realistic aspect, which was not at all what she wanted; and which (she wrongly believed) it need not do with this romantic-looking boy who was almost never there, with whom she could curate her image and conjure alternative lives, and who – although he might sometimes fancy an easier ride – would remain under her womanly spell. No girl of his own age would have treated him with this absolute concentration, relentless and serious, whose slow, sensual pulse can still be felt.

So in that sense he *was* her plaything, because he let loose yearnings that were in the end all about Edith; that existed most powerfully when she sat alone at her desk, or in the bathroom at 41 Kensington Gardens, writing herself into a different world.

Mr F. Bywaters, P&O, RMS *Morea*, Plymouth
Postmark: London, 14 March 1922, 5 p.m.

Je suis Goche˙ darlint & disappointed I said in my previous letter I was sending 1 large & 1 small parcel.

I have only sent 1, the large one.

Lunch time I went to Queen Vic. St to get some "Toblerone" to send with the tissue paper (a small pcl) but finding "Toblerone" is out of stock for a few days, therefore I've not sent the tissue, but I'll give it you when we meet.

Au revoir darlint, I'm consumed with impatience. PEIDI.

---

* Perhaps she means something like *j'ai tout gaché*, as in 'I screwed up', but this is very obscure.

18

Later Exhibit 20.

The length of this letter, and its ongoing references to the desire to read the letters written by Freddy – even though he was two days away from arriving in Britain – shows oh-so clearly how passionately Edith inhabited the world of words: she 'talks' on the page in a way that was surely not replicated in physical meetings and, however much she craved Freddy's living presence, her imaginative longing – which was for something more than just him – was still more intoxicating.

But there is a sense within her words, vivid and palpable even now, of the ship docked and the man on his way to her. No feeling quite like that one.

Meanwhile, Percy again... The absurd little incident in which he accepted an invitation then refused to go; such power struggles – ridiculous to outsiders, all-consuming to the protagonists – occur in happier marriages than the Thompsons'. Nevertheless it brings one back to Avis Graydon, and her description of him as a man of 'peculiar character'.

And there is something else to suggest that Percy may have had another reason for changing his mind, as recounted (it also makes one wonder about Edith's *en passant* remark that he came home late). In her letter to Bonar Law, Avis wrote: 'His case was just the same as my sister's which you can see by the letters, not produced.' This was an oblique reference to the fact that Percy had started a little romance of his own.

His 'girlfriend' was a Miss Tucknott, a stout young woman some ten years his junior, who worked in the same office, and whom, perhaps, he had wanted to take out in preference to spending an evening with Edith's clan. There is nothing whatever to suggest that Percy was conducting an actual affair. Far more likely is that he was boosting his flailing ego and – although he did not tell Edith what was going on – relishing the revenge on an errant wife. But really: what a towering shame he did not break through the barrier of convention and run off with this far more suitable life partner, who sent a wreath to his funeral then disappeared from view. A shame, too, that his little dalliance was not referred to during the trial. The general view would have been that Percy was justified in his behaviour, as indeed he was; nevertheless the mere fact of Miss Tucknott would have chipped away a little at the image of the Thompsons as a saint married to a scarlet whore.

The letter contains an unusually intense example of Edith's capacity for engagement with books. *The Slave* is by a writer she adored, Robert Hichens (also read by the young Jean Rhys), 'popular' but not absolutely without stylistic merit – even though the plot of *The Slave* does read like something dreamed up by Elinor Glyn at her most excitable: a young woman marries an old man in order to obtain an emerald, which her former lover steals in order to reclaim her. Edith identified powerfully with this situation and her observations, within the stream-of-consciousness scattiness, are perceptive. One notes, especially, the phrase: 'Not English at all'. *A Pin to See the Peepshow* is explicit about how Edith's 'Englishness' was part of what condemned her. Her fictional self makes a trip to Paris where her life-affirming sensuality is allowed to bloom free, and is straightforwardly appreciated rather than feared and resented.

Of course one might say that to analyse *The Slave* in this profoundly – indeed naively – absorbed way was to give it an importance that it did not deserve. No doubt Edith's taste in novels was a factor in causing a prominent member of the literati, Rebecca West, to say in late 1922 that she was, 'poor child, a shocking little piece of rubbish and her mental furniture was meagre... I am not asking for sympathy for Edith Thompson. She is a poor, flimsy, silly, mischievous little thing.'

So much for the sisterhood. And how interesting to see that the doctrine of free love, deemed noble when practised by West and H. G. Wells, was rendered apparently contemptible by a woman who acted, not according to high-minded modernist principle, but on unconsciously liberated instinct.

Mr F. Bywaters, P&O, RMS *Morea*, Plymouth
Postmark: London EC, 14 March 1922

Don't you think this is funny darlint? Mr. Lester, the old
man, is failing fast, and hardly knows anyone now

He doesn't know me   Avis was over to tea the other day,
and was toasting some Sally Lunns in front of their fire,
and he said to her – "I don't know who the lady of this
house is, but she is a beautiful woman, and such a good
woman to her husband"   I don't know whether I feel
honoured or otherwise

He is moving to new offices in Eastcheap next week, and
henceforward will use Fenchurch Street Station˙   More
bad luck darlint, we never seem to have any good, do we?
I've got 10/- each way on a horse to-day, it's supposed
to be a cert, but I don't expect it will win, because I've
backed it. Before I forget – can you let me know about
what time you will arrive in London on 18th   We are
going to a party at Mrs Birnages on that day, and if you
were in early I might squeeze an hour to be with you.

On Sunday the 19th we and Avis are going to Stamford
Hill [John and Lily Laxton] to dinner – we shall arrive
at L'pool St at 12.22 and catch the 10.37 or 11.7 p.m back
from Liverpool St. at night   Darlingest boy, when you
do get to London – if I don't see you until you want to
see me – you won't do as you did before, will you? please,
pour moi. We'll want all the spare money you have to

˙ The same as Edith herself, meaning that it would make after-work rendezvous with
Freddy more difficult.

"celebrate" at least I'm hoping we will. You're not going to do anything this time, without me are you? You can't imagine how I'm looking forward to the first time we – not, quarrel, but are cross with one another – then 'the making up.'

You are going to love me always aren't you – even when you're cross with me, and when you are I'll ruffle all your hair lots of times until you have to melt – and smile at me – then you'll take me in both your arms and hold me so tight I can't breathe, and kiss me all over until I have to say "Stop, stop at once."

Why do you say to me "Never run away, face things and argue and beat everybody." Do I ever run away? Have I ever run away? and do you think I should be likely to now? That's twice this trip, something you have said has hurt. You will have to kiss all that hurt away – 'cos it does really hurt – it's not sham darlint.

I'm not going to talk to you any more – I can't and I don't think I've shirked have I? except darlint to ask you again to think out all the plans and methods for me and wait and wait so anxiously now – for the time when we'll be with each other – even tho' it's only once – for "one little hour" – our kind of hour, not the song kind.

and Just to tell you

(PEIDI) Loves you always.

Since finishing my letter to you I have a confession to make.

To-day I've been into the Holborn Restaurant* – no don't be cross darlint, not to lunch –

I got off the 'Bus at Southampton Row to go and pay the piano account and ran into Mr. Derry outside the Holborn Rest. Do you know whom I mean? The "White Horse"† man. He wanted me very much to have lunch with him there, and I only got out of doing so by saying I had mine. However I consented to go into the buffet with him and had a guinness with a port in it, and two ports afterwards so with nothing to eat since 9 p.m. last night you may guess how I felt when I got back here, oh I forgot to say I had a lb. of French almonds as well – he knows from previous experience that I don't like chocolates. You're not cross are you darlint? No, you musn't be, not with Peidi.

*****

A note from you this morning darlint, it bucked me up ever so. I can't say for certain that I shall be at 168 any time after 5.30. It depends on how busy we are. If you wire me "Yes" I will go to Fenchurch Street and wait until you come. If you wire "No" I'll wait until I hear further from you – perhaps you could 'phone me – Bill got home at 3 p.m. – perhaps you will too – I'm impatient now – if only I could shut my eyes and then open them, and find it was Friday night.

I have sent off to you to-day two parcels one small and

---

* On 22 June 1921, Freddy and Edith had lunched together at the Holborn – a splendid arena, high-ceilinged and gilded – and talked properly for the first time about her marriage
† Possibly the White Horse on the Broadway in Ilford.

one large* per pcls. post. Let me know if you receive them, I wasn't expecting you to get in early – or I could have posted them a day before.

Oh darlint, even the looking forward hurts – does it you? every time I think of Friday and onwards my inside keeps turning over and over – all my nerves seems like wires continually quivering.

The "non-stop" for Thursday is off   Thank God or anybody   Reg has gone to Derbyshire and Avis's partner is down with the 'flu, I am glad – even so – at any rate I shan't be tired to death when I see you – all Wednesday – all Thursday and all Friday and then – The Fates – our luck will decide

Remember how I've been looking forward and when you remember – you'll be able to wait just a little longer, eh darlint?

This is Friday and on Monday I'm expecting a huge mail from you – you'll have had all my letters – and if you are not able to talk to me darlint, at least you'll be able to answer all my questions – now just keep up to scratch or I'll be cross, no I won't, I don't think I could be somehow – "cross" wouldn't be the right word – it would more often be "hurt"

When we were at Mrs Manning's [a friend of the Graydon family] her sister asked him to go over there the following Sat. and when she asked me I hesitated, so she said I've already asked Percy, and he said "Yes," so of course I did.

---

* A typical Edith mystery – in the previous letter, postmarked the same day, she wrote that she had only sent one parcel.

I've mentioned this to him in front of all at 231, and he didn't question it, but a few days later said "he wasn't going" – he wouldn't have me making arrangements to go anywhere without first consulting him, and obtaining his consent   The next morning I sent Beatty a card saying it was impossible to keep our promise to see her on Sat In the afternoon I went home and had a general clean up everywhere.   The sun was shining in the windows beautifully it was a typically English spring day and I did so want to be in the park with you darlint   He didn't come home till 5 30 p m darlint I do hope you don't mind me relating to you all these trivial little incidents that happen I always feel I wanted to talk to you about them

[...] I have heard darlint that the Stoll film Syndicate have secured the rights to show "Way down East"* in Suburbia – so we may be able to see it together after all   We're going to Bessie's to dinner this Sunday and then follows Monday, when I shall hear from you, such a big budget I hope. I'll write again after the week end darlint

Au Revoir

PEIDI.

*****

I saw Bill on Friday darlint   He looks very thin I think – in the face. Bombay and you were not mentioned at all – that horse I backed lost of course. Will you tell me how many letters you have got at Marseilles. Wed. the last day for posting was fearful here – gales and snow storms,† and

---

*   A 1920 film starring Lillian Gish.
†   1922 was unusually cold – snow persisted even into April.

I believe the next day no Channel boats ran at all   I hope nothing went astray   I wrote three letters and one greeting, posted separately   Enclosed are some cuttings that may be interesting   I think the "red hair" one is true in parts – you tell me which parts darlint   The Kempton cutting may be interesting if it's to be the same method*   Altho' it's Monday darlint, the mail from Marseilles is not yet in, I'm expecting it every moment, I wish it would hurry up and come   I will put this away now until you have talked to me, and then I will be able to talk to you for another long time.

The mail came in 12 noon, and I thought I would be able to talk to you after then – but I don't think I can. Will you do all the thinking and planning for me darlint – for this thing – be ready with every little detail when I see you – because you know more about this thing than I, and I am relying on you for all plans and instructions – only just the act I'm not. I'm wanting that man to lean on now darlint, and I shall lean hard – so be prepared.

In this case I shan't be able to rely wholly on myself, and I know you won't fail me. I can't remember if I only sent one letter to Port Said, if it was a very long one perhaps there only was one, but even if there wasn't – it doesn't matter much, does it? There would be no identification marks in it either for you or me, and the loss of one letter seems such a small thing when you and I are looking forward to such big things darlint, this time? Yes! About "The Slave." I didn't know what to make of that girl – yes I think she is possible – perhaps and apart from being happy with her body – he was quite happy seeing her with those jewels. They were 2 similar natures – what pleased him – pleased

* See Exhibit 20a.

her – not English at all, either of them. She stooped low – to get back that Emerald – but darlint wouldn't all of us stoop low to regain something we have loved and lost. I know hers was without life, but that was because she had never lived herself and she didn't live did she? not in the world as we know living – she just existed in her casket of "live things," as she knew them. I don't know if you will understand this, it seems a bit of a rigmarole even to me. I asked you in one of my letters it seems ages ago, whether I should send you a book to Norwood [his mother's house], or keep it for you – you never told me. When you read my letters do you make a mental note of all the questions I ask you. I don't think you do, because I seem to have asked you heaps and heaps of things that you never mention. Darlingest boy, when you get my letters and have read them are you satisfied? Do you feel that I come up to all your expectations? Do I write enough? Just don't forget to answer this and also don't forget I won't, I won't, I won't let you bully me.

Why not go to 231 darlint, I think you ought to go as usual, it would be suspicious later if you stopped away without a reason known to them and there is not a reason is there? You haven't fallen out with Bill have you? What about Dr. Wallis's case – you said it was interesting but you didn't discuss it with me. Darlint, about making money – yes we must somehow, and what does it matter how – when we have accomplished that one thing – we are going to live entirely for ourselves and not study any one except ourselves? Of course I'd not like to sacrifice any one that has been or ever still is dear to me – but I've no other scruples darlint – except actually robbing my own flesh and blood and perhaps one or two persons that are even dearer to me than my own flesh and blood. Yes. It must be done – we must get up high darlint not sink lower or even stop where we are – I'd like to see you at the top – feel that

I'd helped you there – perhaps darlint in my heart right deep down I don't want to stop in a hat shop always – if things are different. If they were to remain as they are now – yes I should – it takes me out of myself but when we are together – I'll never want to be taken out of myself because myself will be you as well and we can't ever be parted can we? If we have to be in person we shan't be in mind and thought. About that flat I'm afraid its going to be difficult to get one unfurnished – they all seem to be furnished – I've been looking for a long time now. Darlint could I get a furnished one at first until you come home next time and look for an unfurnished one in the meantime. I don't want to furnish it all by myself I want you to be with me, everything we do must be together in future and you see darlint it would have in it everything I like and perhaps lots of things you don't like   That musn't be – If I want something I like and you don't then for that one thing... you must have something that you like and I don't   This is right, isn't it? It must always be "give and take" between us, no misunderstandings about trivial things – darlint plain words perhaps hard ones but nevertheless plain ones they're always the easiest to fight and then we're pals again

[Part of letter missing here]

not over the object "jewels" but over other things, take for instance Ambition – social and otherwise   Yes, I can imagine her real – but Aubrey – I could shake him – no go – no initiative of his own – just standing and looking on at other people calmly taking what could have been his, away in front of his eyes – oh an ass – nothing more [...]   I think Sir Reuben – you seem hard on him for his spite on Caryll – over his first wife – but I suppose its natural darlint – I suppose all of us right down deep would like to hurt someone when we have been hurt.

Exhibit 20a.

Extract from the *Daily Mail*, 10 March 1922, page 7, column 7. With headnote:

'Girl's Death Riddle.
'Tales of London Night Life
'Beautiful Dancer Drugged.
'Visit to a Chinese Restaurant'

Then follows a report of the inquest held on the 9th of March in the course of which Mr Oswald, the West London Coroner, addressing the jury on the opening of the inquest, said that it was suspected Miss Kempton died from cocaine poisoning, and he had been also told there was a suspicion of cyanide of potassium.

The inquiry was adjourned till 17th April for an examination of the contents of the stomach to be made by Dr. Spilsbury.

19

Not put in evidence. Undated, but obviously written during Freddy's leave of 16–31 March – almost certainly Monday 20th – and therefore sent to Lilian Bywaters' house at Norwood.

The couple had met for the first time since 19 January on the 18th – 'Saturday': a working day for Edith, but they probably lunched together and perhaps had tea at the nearby Fullers, which would feature prominently in the days before the murder.

The last line is a mystery.

Oh darlint I do want to thank you so much, heaps & heaps, heaps for everything – you're much too good to me darlint in that way really you are

At any rate I'll be able to think of you every morning & every evening because I'll be able always to wear silk now, & the beads no darlingest boy I cant say "thank you" enough – everybody wants me to leave them to them in my Will – I feel proud ever so proud when anybody admires anything you have given me.

The lilac set I like best of all, I told you this before, but I must tell you again, they are for Thursday first & then only for the first & last times I am with you. I dont think you can possibly know how much I thank you, but I dont mind if you dont know, because I know how much.

Darlingest boy, I got your note this morning, if you felt it was awful on Saturday & you wanted to die, how do you think I felt? its indescribable, all the pain that this deceit and pettiness causes

Yesterday I thought was too awful to bear, I dont know how I got thro the day, my mind and thoughts I had to make frozen, I daren't think, not about anything, I should have run away, I know I should, I felt quite sure.

Saturday at 5.30 it was terrible, every time I see you, the parting is worse, on Saturday it was awful, so bad I couldnt B B [be brave] any longer, I had to cry all the way to 41. I keep on asking myself "Will it ever be any different" things seem so hopeless, do they to you?

You said in your note "What am I saying don't let this make you too miserable Chere." Darlingest nothing that you say like that can ever make me feel more miserable than I do, just try & think darlint that Peidi always feels as badly about things as you do perhaps worse, circumstances always have to be considered & remembered.

Will you think this always darlint perhaps it will help. I am going to see you tonight arent I, just for that "very little while," its the only few minutes of the day that is worth living.

When you shook hands on Saturday I felt sick with pain, that that was all you & I could do, just imagine shaking hands, when we are all and everything & each other, to each other, two halves not yet united.

Have you thought any more about that "leave it at night" for

PEIDI.

20

Not put in evidence. Undated, but again written during the March leave.

According to Proust there is no love without jealousy, and Edith, in the first line of this letter, says almost the same thing. Lovers are compelled to check that jealousy is all present and correct; what they forget is that it then has its own ideas on how to behave.

In this instance, the jealousy game has a tame feel: a sense that it is being played within garden walls. During Freddy's March leave, Edith decided to get worried about a girl whom he had known in Australia (where he would return in the summer), and asked to see the letters that he had received from her.

Of course Freddy was able to attract young women on his travels. The 'girl in every port' cliché might easily have applied to him; although because he was – like Edith – innately desirable to the opposite sex, he did not have to pursue brief encounters in order to prove himself. The encounter in Australia, however, *was* something more – perhaps an enhanced version of his relationship with Avis Graydon, which would doubtless have developed into a 'courtship' had Edith not distracted Freddy from that worthy pathway. The point about Edith was that she could stay in his mind when he was away from her: that was a woman's gift, not a girl's.

Nevertheless, and for all that Freddy airily dismissed her concerns about the 'Australian girl', at the same time he had clearly stoked them up – just as Edith did, with her pinprick references to Mr Birnage, to Mr Carlton, to Mr Derry, to the man who invited her to the Chapter House for a glass of wine. Or, indeed, with her references to *him*: the immutable Percy, demanding his husbandly rights. Dripping fuel on to the flame of jealousy, looking for proof of 'love' – it was a game, but it could be a dangerous one: the last line of Edith's first paragraph says as much.

Darlint, I did have a doubt about Australia – doesn't doubt show great love sometimes? I think it does, its that sort of doubt I had – perhaps "doubt" is the wrong word – its fear more – fear of losing you – a woman is different for a man – a man says "I want it – I'll take it" – a woman wants to say that – but an inborn feeling of modesty is it? makes her withhold her action perhaps you'll not understand this   Men are carried away on the moment by lots of different actions, love, hate, passion, & they always stand by what they have done.

Darlint, Australia frightens me – memories, with faces, return – & humans cannot control their own Fate

Supposing Fate has it written down that you & I are never to be happy, you'll fight against it, but you'll have to give in & perhaps you'll come back, perhaps you wont Darlint I'm going to forget there is such a place from the day you sail this time, till the day you return

On the evening you said to me "Au revoir" in January – you told me you still had something – something in connection with Australia. All the time you were away I wondered why you mentioned it what made you remind me about it

Darlint before you go this time send me everything connected with Australia & when you come back to me from Australia I'll give them all back to you, to do with what you like

Whatever you think about this will you talk to me about it please darlint.

Nothing, nothing on this earth over will make a teeny scrap of difference to our love

Darlint, it is real & for all time too large – too great – too grand for anything to destroy it.

I'll keep those things, at least for you to see the first time, but darlint if its possible for us to go out this Thursday [probably 30 March], I'm going to wear one set [the beads that he gave her], & on the day you come home I'm going to wear the other set   Yes, you want me to? or not?

Why and how was I a "little girl" – darlint I always feel that I want you to take care of me, to be nice to me, to fuss hold me always in your 2 arms, tight, ever so tight, & kiss me, keep on doing it darlint

An organ outside now, playing "Margie."

Darlint I'll try not to be cynical, hard   I'll try always to be just a "little girl" a tiny little girl that you call

PEIDI.

21

Later Exhibit 50. Undated, but clearly written soon after Letter 20 and just before Freddy sailed on 31 March.

There is nothing especially damaging about this letter, even though it was selected for reading at the Old Bailey; Edith writes about going away with Freddy as a way out of the impasse of her marriage, which is hardly suggestive of husband-murder. However, the passage that begins 'After tonight I am going to die' and ends 'unless things are different' was interpreted, thus, in the opening speech for the prosecution:

> In that letter, two possibilities are presented. I suggest that the phrase 'if things are the same again' means 'if my husband is still alive, and I cannot be with you except by leaving him, I will go with you'. In the other case, how were things to be different except by the destruction of her husband's life?

The talk of 'failure' recurs in letters from this period; when questioned as to its meaning, Freddy answered: 'The failure to get a separation, and the failure to take her abroad' – Edith, he said, had talked of working in 'a millinery business' overseas. This explanation was no less plausible than that of the prosecution, which read the word 'failure' as an attempt at poisoning that had not come off. When, and with what? It is all astonishingly vague.

But the key point, surely, was that if Edith Thompson had truly wanted rid of her husband she could have got on with poisoning him herself, as other discontented spouses had done – without badgering Freddy to act as a drug smuggler or indeed anything else – and that the fact of her desire to involve him was, in itself, the truly significant thing: a means to intensify their bond, just as the talk of pregnancy and miscarriage had been. But then, of couse, her lover did indeed kill Percy. And therefore the legal minds had their justification for interrogating her words.

The court would also not have liked the phrase 'Pride of possession', with its implication that Edith belonged to her partner in adultery rather than to Percy. Nor, one imagines, would it have cared for the image of Edith, asleep in the godly marital bed, with Freddy's letter beneath her.

෫

Darlingest Boy, This will be the last letter to England – I do wish it wasn't, I wish you were never going away any more, never going to leave me – I want you always to be with me

Darlint, about the doubt – no I've never really doubted – but I do like to hear you reassure me   I like you to write it   so that I can see it in black and white and I always want you to say, "Please do believe darlint that I don't really doubt"   its just a vain feeling I have to hear you say things to me – nice things – things that you mean – which most people don't   I wonder if you understand the feeling – perhaps you don't – but I always say and think and believe nobody on this earth is sincere – except the one man – the one who is mine

Pride of possession is a nice feeling don't you think darlint – when it exists between you and me.

I sent you the books darlint, all I felt were worth reading... I hope you'll think of me when you're reading them and I hope you'll talk to me about them.

After tonight I am going to die   not really   put on the mask again darlint until the 26th May – doesn't it seem years and years away? It does to me and I'll hope and hope all the time that I'll never have to wear the mask any more after this time   Will you hope and wish and wish too darlint pour moi

This time really will be the last you will go away [a few words of text appear to be lost here, although the meaning is clear enough] like things are won't it? We said it before darlint I know and we failed, but there will be no failure next time darlint, there mustn't be   I'm telling you   if things are the same again then I'm going with you wherever it is   if its to sea   I'm coming too and if its to nowhere – I'm also coming darlint   You'll never leave me behind again, never, unless things are different

I've sealed up your envelopes and put them away   I did not look at them – except at a small slip of paper I found in one of the small packets. I did read that – and then put it with the other – did you know it was there darlint – it was about a chase – a paperchase I think and a request not to be wakened early.

I'm beginning to think I'm rather silly to have asked for them because you do love me – I know that – Do you think I am silly?

I slept on your letter last night darlint unopened I had no chance to read it but got up at quarter to six this morning to do so. Darlint you can't imagine what a pleasure it is for me to read something that you have written. I can't describe it   Last night darlint I didn't think of you (Because you once told me not to) but I hope you were thinking of me. Its much harder to bear when you're in England than when you're away. This must be au revoir now darlint in the flesh at all events not in the spirit   Eh! We are never apart in that.

Here's luck to you in everything especially in the thing concerning two halves – one of whom is

PEIDI

I always do and always will love you whatever happens.

22

Later Exhibit 17, this letter – written in fits and starts, like Letter 3 – is the longest that Edith wrote, and one of the most significant: she was now reaching the peak of her heightened emotional state. As will be seen later, this may have had consequences for her actions, as well as her words.

Percy cannot have been unaware of his wife's state of voluptuous restlessness. Did he suspect that he had slept with Freddy's words in his bed? Surely not, but he would have been on high alert throughout the March leave. Lily Vellender – one of Edith's few female friends, who worked with her at Carlton and Prior and knew some of what was going on – was surely trying to convey a warning with her account of a dream, in which Percy sought to murder Edith because she had spent the night away from home. Lily sensed danger, although she mistook the quarter from which it came. Although who knows – perhaps Percy, too, had been capable of murder, if caught in a certain mood.

And Edith did come close to spending the last night of the leave in a hotel. Something had stopped her – the proscriptions of class, the fear of entering reality – and held Freddy back also. But the hours of passionate unsated congress were still heaving through her body as she wrote. He, too, must have been high on frustration: part of the reason why he could never get enough of this woman was because, quite simply, he never got enough of her.

The night of the 30th had bloomed for them both, making the fact of imminent parting almost unbearable; not least because there is a sense, in the letters, that the leave up to that point had been faintly disappointing – as was surely inevitable. Edith had turned this young man into the recipient of all her complex and numinous longings. He himself could not possibly compare with what she had made of him. The reference to the Kensington flat says it all, in a way. She *could* have taken it on, separated from Percy and waited for him to divorce her. It would have been a scandal, as well as financially risky – there was also the question of the house in Ilford, which she did not love but absolutely treasured. She knew, however, that Mr Carlton would have been extremely reluctant to lose her, and would have helped her find alternative employment if need be (she was very good at her job). She could have bitten the bullet and taken the flat if she had *really* wanted to – but it was not, in fact, quite what she wanted.

Lilian Bywaters had said as much to Freddy, when she told him that there was nothing to stop Edith leaving her marriage. And she turns up here again, still refusing to soften her stance. During this leave, Freddy and his mother had an almighty row – all about Edith, of course – whose effects diminished but did not entirely go away; indeed Lilian spent part of her son's last year on earth in a state of semi-estrangement from him. He, as tends to happen in these situations, had taken the side of his lover, although his very vehemence leads one to suspect that he recognised the truth in his mother's misgivings.

The last passage of Edith's letter reads uncomfortably. Not so much the stuff about electric light bulbs and gas, but the words: 'Don't keep this piece'. Again there is that sense of caution, of foresight. She believed that he was keeping none of her words, but about 'this piece' she wanted, in the words of Macbeth, to make assurance double sure.

The reference to 'Dan', however, strongly indicates something else: it suggests that whatever Edith was writing to Freddy, she was getting the same kind of thing back from him, and that this made a mockery of the notion of incitement.

In his closing speech for the prosecution the solicitor general, Sir Thomas Inskip, showed himself less than interested in such niceties. 'I am bound to say to you that this letter of 1st April is one that deals entirely with this idea now occupying so much of her attention, that her husband must be got rid of. The passage is full of crime.' This was entirely typical of the prosecution, whose method was to seize upon a part, an aspect, then – in a way defiant of both logic and justice – allow it to infect the whole. The 'passage' at the end of the letter could, for sure, be described as 'full of crime'. The letter itself is nothing of the kind; no honest analysis could say that it 'deals entirely' with the idea that Percy 'must be got rid of'. By merging the two as he did, however, the solicitor general was making an assertion that nobody listening would have dreamed of challenging. It sounded plausible, therefore it had to be true.

Freddy was questioned about this letter, and testified that he had brought a drug – quinine – when he came home on leave in March, which he then gave to Edith. 'It was in the form of five-gram tabloids, white.'

Asked why he had given her this substance, he replied that she had talked of a desire for the means to commit suicide; he had obtained quinine for her because he knew it to be harmless. It has been suggested, by commentators, that the quinine was really wanted as an abortifacient – which is surely impossible – or perhaps as a contraceptive. although given Freddy's nervousness about having full sex ('say no, Peidi') during the leave, this too seems unlikely.

In fact there was another explanation for the 'quinine', offered by Freddy a couple of weeks before his death; as will be seen.

He was also asked about this line at the end of the letter: 'he puts great stress upon the tea tasting bitter'. The solicitor general said:

'What did you understand by the passage?'

'That she had taken quinine and it had tasted bitter.'

The solicitor general read the sentence again and, with exaggerated patience, asked: 'To whom did it taste bitter?'

'Mrs Thompson.'

'Do you suggest that, Bywaters?'

The absurd reply, firmly delivered, was: 'I do.'

Walter Frampton, junior counsel for the defence, would later ask Edith about the incident of the tea, and her own responses carry greater verisimilitude.

'Was there ever any time when your husband complained to his mother about the tea tasting bitter?'

'Not to my knowledge.'

'Was this an imaginary incident then that you were recording?'

'Yes.'

Mr F. Bywaters, P&O, RMS *Morea*, Bombay
Postmark: London EC, 1 April 1922, 2.30 p.m.

I believe I insufficiently stamped the first Marseille letter
I sent. If I did darlint I [sic] ever so sorry. I hate doing
anything like that. You know dont you.

I think Thursday [30 March] was the worst day and
night I ever remember. All day long I was thinking of the
previous Thursday, and contrasting my feelings, one day
with the other – the feelings of intense excitement and
those of deep depression, and then when night came it
was worse – it was awful. I was fighting all night long to
keep your thoughts with me darlint   I felt all the time
that you were not with me – didnt want to be   Just
had withdrawn yourself, and try as I would I couldn't
bring you back   Darlint, tell me what was happening on
Thursday   I cried and cried and cried, until I eventually
went to sleep, but I had heard the clock strike five before
I did so, and then Friday morning I saw your sister' and
she just gave me one of those looks that are supposed to
wither some people and then I felt that the whole world
was up against me and it wasn't really much good living
Still, that fit of depression is on me and I cant shake it
off   Perhaps on Monday when the mail is in I shall feel
bucked up a bit; also I got your complaint badly since
Thursday – all my teeth ache and my head and neck   Is
yours better now darlint? I hope it is   Lily had a dream
the other day that the Birnages came to 168 to warn me

---

* Freddy had two sisters, Lilian (b. 1901) and Florence (b. 1905), as well as a younger
brother Frank (b. 1912). It is unclear to which sister Edith is referring here – all three
young women knew each other by sight.

that he was going to murder me – as he had found out that I had been away from home for a night with a fair man (her expression).

She didnt know any more than this as she woke up   On Wednesday I met Harry Renton and he told me he was giving up his flat and going to live at Woodford – did I know any one that wanted it –

Darlint it is just the thing we wanted   I do wish I had been able to take it just three rooms unfurnished 35s. per week including electric light, in Moscow Court, Kensington. Its a very nice one I practically chose it for him myself two years ago   That boy's fearfully ill really The Doctor has ordered him to live in the country else consumption through his shoulder wound, will take hold of him   We went to lunch at "Manchester," but I only had one hour darlint, and a wretched man sat near me who absolutely reeked of scent   It was overpowering I can understand a woman using such a lot, but a man – oh! its beastly   To-day I'm going home to entertain Dad He is coming to dinner and to help him with a job after and Mother and Avis are coming up to tea   Darlint, this writing is awful I know   I hope you will understand it I know you'll understand me, and how I'm feeling   Ive got to get thro that weekend again.

Au revoir until Monday darlint I wish you could say "I love you cherie"

Thank you 20 times darlint – the mail is in and I've got such a budget. I wish we weren't quite so busy – Its Easter week – and usually the busiest week in all the year and it seems as if its going to live past its reputation this year

*****

Before I talk to you about your letters darlint, I want to say one or two things that I forgot last week, When Avis came over on Wed. although it was 11.30 before she went he insisted on seeing her to the tram and when I offered to come with him he was most emphatic in his "No." I expect he wanted to ask her about you – had she seen you? Did she know if I had etc? I didnt ask her anything about it and she volunteered no information   Also, you remember her telling me you had a diamond ring on – she added "on his engagement finger." I said, Why, is he engaged? and she said "Probably. He was always knocking about with some girl or other before he knew me, and now he doesn't see me and he probably does the same."

I do laugh at some of the things that are said. A thought has just struck me – may I ask you? Yes, of course I may. Darlint, has your head "turned again to its proper place"? I thought of the expression "she has absolutely turned your head," and really darlint I can't possibly imagine anyone "turning your head" if you didn't want it to be turned – let alone me – therefore the only conclusion I have come to is that, if it is turned, you wanted me to turn it and only I can turn it back again. Do you want it turned back again?

I saw Molly this morning – darlint if you saw her you say at once – the same as you did about the girl in the "Strand"   Do you remember? What is she doing to herself? She looked awfull – her face and lips are rouged terribly and thick black lines pencilled under her eyes – and her face is fearfully thin fallen in under the cheek bones   Perhaps its working in the West end   She certainly looks years older than her years and I shouldn't say she was pretty now – Oh darlint I do think it is a shame don't you?

Darlingest boy, I'm so sorry you thought I was silly – about those things from Australia – darlint – although I knew – I feel I am – I didn't want you to think so – but you do and I feel worse I feel small and petty and truly darlint I did not want them from any feelings of jealousy that I might entertain

I'm not jealous certainly not of her – darlint – I thought perhaps you wouldn't give them to me – I thought you might say "No I won't give them to you – but I will destroy them" and when you did give them to me I loved you such a lot – more and more and more every time I thought about it.

*****

About that Thursday – had there been anywhere to stop in Ilford – I should have said, "Take me there, I won't go home" and you would have said, "Yes I will" but darlint before we had arrived at the Hotel, I should have thought about things and so would you and I can hear you say just when we reach the door "Peidi, you're going home" pour moi   just this once darlint and I should have gone.

Darlint you're not and never will be satisfied with half and I don't ever want to give half – all, every ounce of me that lives, to you.

You say you're sorry for some things that happened. Yes! I suppose I am in a way but darlint, I feel I don't do enough. I want to show you how large my love is and when it is something you want and you do want it just at that moment don't you – I want to give it you – I want to stifle all my own feelings for you.

Darlingest boy you said to me "Say no Peidi, say No" on Thursday didn't you – but at that very moment you didn't wish me to say "No" did you? You felt you wanted all me in exchange for all you. I know this – felt this – and wouldn't say "No" for that very reason.

Half an hour afterwards or perhaps even ten minutes afterwards you'd really have wanted me to say "No" but not at that especiall moment.

Darlint I feel that I never want to withhold anything from you if you really want it and one of these days you're going to teach me to give all and everything quite voluntarily – arent you? Please darlint.

[...]

About the watch I'm so so glad it keeps good time and that you always wear it – I always want you to – go to sleep on it darlint, please pour moi – I always wear something you gave me now – both by day and at night What is it? do you know   I suppose in a way the barber was right darlint – he does know you better than I do – that part of you that lives on ships but I know you – the inside part that nobody else sees – or knows – and I dont want them to yet awhile at any rate

[...]

When I marked the paragraph about photos in Felix [by Robert Hichens], I certainly was thinking of my photo – dont be cross – altho you say you like them darlint I don't really – especially that one that I look so fat in   Tear it up please   To please me and then tell me you have done so. You can keep one I dont mind that one so much but I dont really like it and I hate the other one   Of course by now you will have finished Felix   You won't like Mrs. Ismay, although you said previously that you thought you would   You also say she wants to tell Felix she takes drugs but hasn't the courage to   You will also have found out by now that this is wrong That is the last thing on earth she wants to tell anyone

*****

Darlingest boy never mind about the news being ordinary   It is you talking to me and that is all I want and if it is ordinary it is interspersed with little bits that aren't ordinary that are for me only – such bits as "I love you" – always Chere" – and "I'm always with you in thought Chere" – that shows darlint that even though you write about ordinary things you are thinking of extraordinary things   My letters must always appear ordinary to you in most parts if you think like that, but I have to tell you everything that happens   I feel I must. I always want to and those things are always ordinary to me. Things are always the same – the same old round – unless you are in England and then it's a different world – a joyous world that hurts at the same time

[...]

Mother wasnt cross a bit about the Cigarettes* in fact she laughed it off as a huge joke and said I had three yesterday and they didnt hurt me [...]

Yes, you are a bully – but sometimes – only sometimes I like it. I like being told to do this by you   I didnt like you to bully me about a wet fur collar tho', darlint

---

* As explained in Letter 23, these cigarettes, brought back from Freddy's travels, were full of opium.

I read the copy to your Mother* and thought when I was reading it "what a pedestal he is on when he is writing this and I am the only one that can fetch him down" but when I came to the last two paragraphs I thought "this is more like the boy I know – not like the shell"   I'm glad you softened a bit

I have returned copy – thank you darlint   The part that hurt most was "that woman"

I could hear the tone in which it was said and it hurt such a lot – I had to cry altho I tried not to   Why didn't you tell me that on Thursday? there would have been time for you to kiss all that hurt away and now I shall retain it until you come back again

You didn't mention anything about what I wrote regarding your Sister   Why not?

Darlingest boy – is she your Mother any judge of whether "I'm no good", and if she is has she any right to judge me   Whether she or anyone I knew were good or bad I shouldn't judge them

---

* Freddy wrote to Lilian after their argument:
'Dear Mother,
    I am writing to you though at the cost of my dignity, to remind you of the foul, unjust and spiteful allegations you made against one, whom you do not know.
    You have a passing acquaintance and I suppose you conjure anything from that, anything that your mind may suggest; and without thought or reason but with unmitigated disdain, you slander.
    I ask you, I tell you, and warn you, not to interfere in any manner or form, with me or my private affairs.
    You do not seem to realise that I am now of an age when I live my own life – not a life to be mapped out and planned by you, though if it were, I know it would be done with the best of good intents.
    Mum, do please try and realise I am not Frankie.
    If you do want to answer Mum, please think about what you say or do.
    Your ever affectionate son, FEF, Frederick Edward Francis.'

Darlint I love you such lots and lots and the mail today made it more – by that mail I knew you loved me more – yet more than you did

It must be au revoir until Aden now   Je suis faché you have to wait such a long time to talk with me but darlint I am always with you wondering what you are doing and feeling and loving you every minute of always

PEIDI

Don't keep this piece.

About the Marconigram – do you mean one saying Yes or No, because I shan't send it darlint   I'm not going to try any more until you come back

I made up my mind about this last Thursday

He was telling his Mother etc, the circumstances of my "Sunday morning escapade" and he puts great stress on the fact of the tea tasting bitter "as if something had been put in it" he says   Now I think what ever else I try in it again will still taste bitter   he will recognise it and be more suspicious still and if the quantity is still not successful – it will injure any chance I may have on trying when you come home

Do you understand?

I thought a lot about what you said of Dan.

Darlint, don't trust him   I don't mean don't tell him anything because I know you never would – What I mean is don't let him be suspicious of you regarding that – because if we were successful in the action – darlint circumstances may afterwards make us want many friends or helpers and we must have no enemies – or even people that know a little too much. Remember the saying, "A little knowledge is a dangerous thing."

Darlint we'll have no one to help us in the world *now* and we musnt make enemies unnecessarily.

He says – to his people he fought and fought with himself to keep conscious – "I'll never die, except naturally – I'm like a cat with nine lives" he said and detailed to them an occasion when he was young and nearly suffocated by gas fumes.

I wish we had not got electric light – it would be easy.

I'm going to try the glass again occasionally when it is safe   I've got an electric light globe this time.

23

Not put in evidence.

Again, the portrayal of Percy here has a wonderfully convincing air – Edith is so on the money with her phrase 'injured air of mystery', her who-needs-punctuation rendering of his *sotto voce* gripes – although she did, perhaps, miss something. Was her husband at the theatre with Miss Tucknott on the evening of Freddy's last leave? Edith seems only to think that he was spying on her, but he may well have enjoyed the knowledge that he was – in his way – cheating on her instead.

And who could blame him if so? This was not a fair fight. It is clear, for instance, that Mrs Graydon was fond of the sexy, gallant, young Fred Bywaters – that she indulged his apparently harmless crush on the star of '231', her all-conquering Edie – and that Percy, although he was dutifully loved as a son-in-law, was basically unlovable. He would have been sensitive to this; he was not a fool. He was just married to the wrong woman.

With regard to what he might have known or guessed about 30 March... Edith had told him that she was at the theatre that night, and – to judge by Percy's targeted sniping – she had pretended to go with her friend Bessie Akam. It is not impossible that Edith and Freddy spent part of the evening at Bessie's house (although their sexual fumblings surely took place outdoors) and this, too, Percy may have suspected. Did he think that they were doing more than flirting and smooching? Of course he feared it. His mind must have been full of dark, unwanted images. But he may have told himself that Edith would never dare, that anyway where would she go to have sex, that deep down she preferred her comfortable married life – which was true, in a way – and, for all his constant policeman-like monitoring of her activities, he seems never to have pushed the situation too far.

Meanwhile Mr Graydon was probing tentatively and Avis prodding crudely, neither of which Edith would have particularly minded. Avis's inability to let Freddy go seems to have inspired no guilt in her sister, more a slightly contemptuous amusement at – for instance – her rampant mentionitis (also her pretence at having an evening appointment) mingled with irritable, irrational envy. Avis was free to pursue Freddy, even though he did not want her, whereas Edith must contend with a husband whom a part of *her* did not actually want to lose.

What Edith's parents thought about the relationship between Edith and Freddy is impossible to say. They were warm, easygoing people, and unlike Lilian Bywaters they certainly did not perceive danger: most probably their thoughts ran along the lines of 'it'll all come out in the wash'. Which at this point, with six months to go before the cataclysm, it could very easily still have done.

꙰

Mr F. Bywaters, P&O, RMS *Morea*, Marseilles
Postmark: London, 4 April 1922, 6.15 p.m.

First of all darlingest about Thursday [30 March]. He knows or guesses something – how much or how little I cant find out. When I got home & went upstairs I found him not there.

As I was getting into bed a car drew up outside & he came in looking, well you know how with that injured air of mystery on his face attempted to kiss me and then moved away with the expression "Phew – drink." He had been to a Theatre – he had a programme – what I imagine is – waited for me on the 11.30 found I wasn't on it & caught the next – of course was surprised to find me home. If he has any sense he could easily put 2 & 2 together   Your last night last time & your last night this time I went to a theatre on both occasions.

He says he caught the 11 55 but there is no such train in my time table – there used to be

Tell me what you think about this please darlint

I must tell you this talking about rates [precursor of council tax] at 231 last night, Avis said "if you don't pay they'll take you to prison"   He said "No they won't I'll see to that." Avis "Well they'll take your wife." He (under his breath altho I heard it) "A good thing too" He's never even said "What did you see or how did you enjoy yourself." Oh its a rotten spirit   Avis came over to tea on Sat & said "The last time I came Bess & Reg were here." He Bess is supposed to be here to-day – but she doesn't know she hasn't been asked (I asked Bess to come down for the week end as Reg would be away – but she replied by Thursday to 168 that she couldn't come as he was coming home at noon Sat)   He didn't ask me if we enjoyed ourselves or if Bess was coming so I didn't mention it

After Avis had gone I said "A remark you passed at tea time about Bess what do you mean by it I want to know." He "You want to know do you – well you shant you can just imagine how much I know & how much I dont & I hope you'll feel uncomfortable about it"

I'm afraid I let go then & said several things in haste perhaps it would have been better had I held my tongue & finished up with "Go to Hell" – you can only keep good tempered when you [are] getting what you want – a case of sugar for the bird & he sings. I was told I was the vilest tempered girl living & "you used not to be, but you're under a very good tutor" now it seems. That was Saturday I went to bed early & how I got through Sunday I dont know living with banging doors & sour silent faces will turn me grey

*****

It was funny at 231 on Friday I didn't go down till 8.15 just had some tea in Lpool St. Buffet & read the paper. Mother asked me to have a cigarette almost immediately I got in & I said, "Where did you get these they look posh." She "Never mind I had them given me.

Me Well I dont suppose you bought them – where did you get them

She Fred Bywaters gave them to me

Me Has he been down here?

Dad Yes he's been 3 or 4 times

Me Oh I'm sorry I missed him next time he comes remember me to him & say if he lets me know when he's coming to 231 I'll come too.

Dad He's sailed now, went out today. By the way Have you had a row with him?

Me Have I no, the last time we met we were pals (this is right isnt it darlint).

Dad Has Percy had a row with him then

Me Yes – he did.

Dad & is it over yet. I thought it was when Percy came back to say good bye just before Xmas.

Me No, its not over & not likely to be – but still I'm sorry I didn't see Freddy. I should like to have done very much.

Dad Yes, I'm sure you would & I'm sure he would like to see you.

Mother What do you think of the fags.

Me Not much they are scented & I dont care for such posh ones.

Mother was quite indignant with me darlint & said "If they'd been given to you you'd like them," so I said "Would I" & smiled   Darlingest boy, you know why I smiled.

He came in then & mother offered him one – he looked & said "Amive" Oh they're doped cigarettes.

Mother What do you mean by doped.

He The tobacco is grown on opium fields.

Can you imagine me seeing the joke – inside me – all by myself – when are we going to see the joke together darlint. Oh mother said something about "By the way he spoke" – I said to Avis, he must not have seen Edie (meaning you)˙.

Avis came to tea Sat. as I've already told you & went again at 7.30 to keep an appointment she said.

---

* This little bit of reported speech is somewhat convoluted. 'By the way he spoke' is a direct quote, referring to Freddy. The rest is what Mrs Graydon then went on to say – i.e. she had mentioned to Avis that Freddy had apparently not seen Edith during his leave.

In the afternoon we went shopping together & she spoke about you a lot. She seemed to be quite friendly with you.

She mentioned she saw you on the station every morning & what a lot it must cost you for fares & it would be cheaper she thought if you lodged in East Ham & then they would be able to see more of you.

Also you had on a diamond ring & seemed to have plenty of money altho "I know writers don't make more than £5 per trip" she said – she also told me you asked after Peggy & that she told you all about it & that she went round & had a drink with you she didn't see why she shouldn't as you could be pals (her interpretation) if nothing else.

She said lots of small things connected with you which aren't important & I didn't remember.

*****

Darlint what a poor quality Mail card this time – not a bit like the usual.

Are you Oxford or Cambridge, the former I expect – men nearly always are. Well they didn't win & I'm glad because I'm Cambridge & I won 5/- on Sat. over it.

By the way I had 5/- e[ac]h. way on Leighton on Saturday for the Newbury Cup & the meeting was abandoned owing to the course being covered with 6 inches of snow.

Au revoir darlingest boy.

24

Not put in evidence. How terribly wrong that seems, reading a delicious letter like this one: the product of a young woman full of life despite her discontentment, with its butterfly-flitting and chattering inconsequence and bursts of imaginative intensity, as when Edith asks Freddy how he feels when his ship moves out of dock. A letter that is not 'full of crime' but utterly devoid of it – crime-free indeed. Yet it played no part at the Old Bailey in contextualising the rest.

The 'fainting fits' that had alarmed Freddy (did he think that she could possibly be pregnant again?) were surely a symptom of Edith's gynaecological issues. If a woman suffers from endometriosis, the pain can be so intolerable as to cause light-headedness; and if *this* woman had recently suffered a miscarriage, which had not been medically treated in any way and which led (see Letter 38) to considerable blood loss, then the fallout would no doubt be still greater pain and weakness. Edith had in fact been ill, on and off, since January, and would continue to be so. Her constitution was fundamentally sound, but her resilience seems to have been in some measure impaired (no doubt it would have returned in time, had there been that time). This argues against the miscarriage being an invention (see commentary to Letter 9), which anyway is extremely unlikely; that said, any kind of menstrual problem – cumulative by its very nature, and a century ago even less treatable than today – can lead to general debilitation.

※

Mr F. Bywaters, P&O, RMS *Morea*, Marseilles
Postmark: London EC, 5 April 1922, 2.30 p.m.

I didn't get your letter first thing in the morning darlint. I felt a wee bit disappointed but supposed you'd been too busy with work that must be done, & I was prepared to wait till next Monday to hear from my own man, but at 12.15 just as I was going to leave your letter came. It bucked me up such a lot I thought to myself well it will help me to get thro the "inevitable weekend" & it did help me darlint. All the time I felt miserable & downhearted I was thinking to myself "when you go to 168 on Monday you'll have a real letter to read again." I shall read it every morning until I get another one from you just as I say "good morning" to you. No not to you but to your picture & ruffle your hair & make you cross first thing in the morning (Is this right). Darlint that ache which you and I share & you speak about – yes its awful – not a sharp stabbing pain that lets you know it is there & then goes – but just a numb feeling a feeling of inactivity – like a blind that is never more than half raised, just enough to torment you with the sight of a tiny bit of light & sunshine.

About what you told me* – No I dont think it will worry me – but I can't help thinking about it can I? after all darlint – but for me it never would have happened   I'm always the cause of pain to you & perhaps to myself as well – but always to you ever since you just knew me you've never been really happy, & perhaps had you known me less you might have been

Darlint I dont think you told me everything that you & others said on that Thursday – you didn't because you thought it would hurt, but if I promise it wont hurt, will you write & tell me please. I want to know everything. I do tell you everything that is said about you don't I?

Why didn't you recognise your sister† on Thursday you must darlint pour moi – you know what you promised to

* This refers to the quarrel with Lilian Bywaters.
† Probably Florence, who had become involved in the quarrel with Lilian and taken her mother's side.

do for me & she's my sex – forget she's your sister think she's me when you meet her & be courteous   I'm ever so sorry you didn't recognise her whatever is ever said or ever happens connected with them & me don't forget this. Does this sound like a lecture? I dont what [sic] it to be, I just want you to remain as I know you now, not to revert to you I knew last year

Of course darlint I love all you've said about me, about giving up what people cherish most for me, about those horrid thoughts that people have that you will stamp out I love all that darlint I feel proud when I read it that you say it about me – proud that I have someone that thinks so much of me – its so nice darlint   I've never had anyone quite like you (like you were once, yes, but not as you are now). When & if you do write to your Mother I want a copy of the letter please, yes I do & you must send me one, you've not to ignore this subject or dismiss it in the usual manner [...]

Darlingest boy I received a telegram from you on Friday "G.M.M.C. always stop – dont worry" Now am I very dense or are you a little too vague, because I dont know what "Always stop" means   Please tell me darlint   I can only think you mean we will always stay together is this it?

I'd like you [to] tell me darlint just how you feel when you move out of dock – what are your thoughts when you begin to move when you must realise that you'll not on England [sic] or anybody connected with you & England for 2 whole months

You told me you were sailing about 2 & about that time I began thinking how you were feeling if you were hopeful and not too downhearted & I thought about everything connected with the last fortnight, some things I was sorry about & some things pleased. How did you feel? [...]

I don't want to give in darlint oh I do want to have you so much & if we give in people will only laugh & think us failures & we're not are we – tell me we're not going to be – we're going to succeed you & I together even tho' we fail in "Our Glorious Adventure"

We'll fight to the last while there's an ounce of strength & will power left – fight to live our life, the life you & I will choose together – we're not cowards to shirk & hide behind a cloak of previous misfortunes – we'll take the bull by the horns shape something good & clean out of something bad.

I cant help this paper being another colour – its the only pad the stationer had in stock

A lady has just come in whom I have not seen for 5 years nearly, she has since been married & had 2 children one of which & her husband has died   She says I don't look any older – but I'm sure by the way she said it, she doesn't think it   I wonder why people will pay doubtful compliments they dont mean

Today is April 4th & the snow is falling in thick lumps & laying in some places – the weather has stopped trade & made everybody miserable   What poet was it [Browning] who wrote "Oh to be in England now Spring is here"   I wish he were alive & feeling miserable as I, on this nice English Spring Day.

Dont forget darlint when you are reading the books that the Shulamite comes first   The "Woman Deborah" after

I wonder if you will notice anything in "The Woman Deborah"   I await your remarks

Jim fetched my case from Barking & left it at 41 for me, he was going down to Ilford.

Darlint the Turkish Delight is lovely this time much better than the last lot.

Enclosed is one that you sent me, it is a fortnight today hasn't it kept well   I have tended this one especially to send you – cut its stalk and given it fresh water with salt in every morning.

Darlint tell me you love me & how much – keep on telling me make me feel all the time you do, its a long time 2 months darlint & I want telling heaps & heaps of times, no, not because I doubt but because I like to feel that you're always thinking it

Darlingest boy I do love you – yes, always, while this life lasts so much – oh so much, I cant tell you – but you must know you do know darlint, that there never has been anyone I love at all, only just you, there is such a difference – Good bye until Bombay.

(Good luck) PEIDI.

****

---

* *The Shulamite* and *The Woman Deborah* were both by the husband-and-wife writing partnership Claude and Alice Askew.

145

Darlingest boy,

11.45 am 5/4/22 – I've just read your cable – it came first thing this morning I believe – but I didn't feel up to the mark – so I didn't go up until 11, & then I was besieged by people wanting this done & that done.

It was nothing much darlint just a few fainting fits one after the other, nothing whatever to worry about so please dont.

I notice it says "Good afternoon" so you quite expected me to get it on the 4th but it wasn't recd in London until 7.48 p.m.

Anyway – whatever time it came I was pleased to get it. Pleased to know that when you sent it you were thinking about me.

I've got to post this to-day darlint, I dont suppose you'll get this one till Friday but I hope when you do you'll feel its all you want [...]

PEIDI.

25

Not put in evidence.

🜨

Mr F. Bywaters, P&O, RMS *Morea*, Bombay
Postmark: London EC, 12 April 1922, 1.30 p.m.

I just wanted to write a few lines to you darlint, before we close here for the [Easter] holidays – from Thursday 1 oc till Tuesday 10 oc

Friday – Saturday – Sunday – Monday – 4 whole days darlint with nothing whatever to do but think, & only you can know what those thoughts will be

If I only had all that time to spend with you darlint can you imagine what it would be like – I cant & can't possibly imagine such a long time – I suppose it would only seem like 4 hours – instead of which it will now seem like 4 years – but perhaps it won't always be like it, eh – I'm going on hoping so – hoping hard – are you too? You haven't given up yet, have you? please dont darlint?

We're fearfully busy here – I was here till 7 the last 2 nights & still we have such a lot to do before the holidays –

Darlingest boy – I love you such a lot & want you such a lot oh so badly – why aren't you here to hold me tightly & make me feel how much you love me – its such a starving sort of feeling darlint – just living on a picture

I do want you so much – I want comforting darlint & only you can do that for PEIDI.

26

Later Exhibit 18.

And now Edith was back to giving the Old Bailey what it wanted, although the passage about the lightbulb is so ridiculous that it is hard to believe even the solicitor general could, in his heart, have taken it at face value.

As for the Aromatic Tincture of Opium episode, which almost reads as though Percy had sinister plans of his own... Avis was questioned about it at some length.

She had – as she testified in court – been at the Thompsons' house during the day on Easter Monday, out in the garden with Percy, where (ever the handmaiden) she was helping him to demolish the case of the grand piano. This odd task sounds like something conjured by Percy to get him away from Edith, who was seated by the fire. When he hit his finger with a hammer (temper?) and asked Avis to go upstairs and find a bottle of what he called 'New Skin', she saw the opium – about half a pint of it. Avis then advised her sister to 'nip up and get it'; and, when she returned the New Skin to its place upstairs, she found that the opium had been removed. It was now standing on the sideboard in the drawing room.

Avis told the court:

> I said, 'I will do away with this, so there can be no more trouble,' and I took the bottle and went to the scullery and poured the contents of the bottle down the sink. I then put the bottle in the fire in the morning room.

So what on earth was all that about?

Opium (of which there is a surprising amount in this story) was then taken for heart problems, which Percy seems to have believed himself to suffer from. Possibly this bottle of medicine was what had caused the episode in February (Letter 12) when he woke his wife to complain of feeling ill. Edith had told her sister about this incident, so perhaps Avis had thought to avoid a repeat when she poured the stuff away?

Or – just conceivably – her reasoning was less easy to define. She knew that the Thompson marriage was not happy, and one can only imagine the atmosphere in the garden when she and Percy were swinging their hammers while the lady of the house remained indoors. Her poor opinion of Percy, as expressed after the event, may not have been quite so low in Easter 1922. On the other hand, perhaps it was. She was only too aware of Edith's increasing closeness to Freddy, and unsure as to how much Percy knew – or how he would react if he knew more. In other words the situation was a loaded one, which Avis may have felt was not improved by the presence of a half-pint of opium.

It sounds highly dramatic to suggest that this level-headed girl thought anything along these lines – it sounds, in fact, a lot more like her sister. But, as shown by Edith's collection of cuttings, the newspapers were full of tales of domestic poisonings; indeed the solicitor Herbert Armstrong had just gone on trial for dosing his wife with arsenic. In the vaguest possible of ways, Avis may have felt that it was simply better not to have temptation lying around.

A final point: Avis's statement that she poured the opium away, which is surely true, means that Edith's claim to Freddy – that she 'took possession of it' – was a lie.

🙞

Mr F. Bywaters, P&O, RMS *Morea*, Aden
Postmarks: London EC, 24 April 1922, 5.30 p.m.; Aden, 7 May 1922

I think I'll tell you about the holidays darlint – just what I did – do you want to know? or will you say its all ordinary common place talk – I suppose it is – but after I have discussed the ordinary things, I may be able to really talk to you   On Thursday we left at 1 and I went to the Waldorf to lunch and stayed on until the dance tea – I only danced once – a fox trot – I don't feel a bit like dancing darlint – I think I must be waiting for you. We left the Waldorf at 6.20 and met Avis at 6.30 and went with her to buy a costume [suit] – getting home about 9.

On Friday I worked hard all day starting that "Good Old fashioned English housewife's occupation of spring cleaning," not because I liked doing it – or believe in it, but because I had nothing else to do and it helped to pass the time away. I started about 9.30 and went to wash and dress about 20 to 6

Dad took us to the E H. [East Ham] Palace to the Sunday League Concert in the evening and we stopped the night at 231

In return for this I booked for us all at Ilford Hippodrome on Saturday   The show was good and a girl – in nurses uniform appearing with Tom Edwards sang "He makes me all fussed up"

Of course Avis remarked about you and the song also Molly was sitting behind us with another girl and a boy – is she affected in her conversation? She was very much on Saturday and I wondered if it was put on for my special benefit

Avis came back to stay the rest of the holiday with us Bye the way, we, (she and I) had a cup of tea in bed on Sunday – we always do when she is stopping with us

Mother and Dad came over to me to dinner – I had plenty to do. On Monday Mr. and Mrs Birnage came to tea and we all went to the Hippodrome in the evening Bye the way what is "Aromatic Tincture of Opium" – Avis drew my attention to a bottle of this sealed in the medicine chest in your room.

I took possession of it and when he missed it and asked me for it – I refused to give it him – he refuses to tell me where he got it and for what reason he wants it – so I shall keep it till I hear from you.

I used the "light bulb" three times but the third time – he found a piece – so I've given it up – until you come home

Do you remember asking me to get a duplicate of something* – I have done so now

On Sunday we were arguing about the price of "Cuticura" [ointment]   Avis is quite certain when she bought it, not for herself, (her own words) it was 10½. Mother said when she bought it for you it was 1/- and I said the same

The remark was passed – "you all in turn seemed to have bought it for him"

I had another mysterious parcel this Easter – a large gold foil egg filled with chocolate about 2 lbs by the weight – still with no word or even a name attached, posted in the City E.C 2. to 168   I suppose it's from the same source as the Xmas parcel† but I haven't and shan't acknowledge it...

Darlint, do you like this term of endearment   I shan't tell you why I ask, but you'll probably notice it one of these days, "Carissima."

[...]

I had a funny dream the other night darlint – you had

---

* The following letter may offer a (semi-)explanation as to this reference.
† One of Edith's admirers, presumably, but there is no clue as to whom.

taken me out somewhere and saw me home and persisted in coming in.

Eventually you and I slept in your little bed – in the morning I woke early and went into the big room and found Harold was sleeping with him – you were unbolting the front door in your pyjamas to get out quickly when he came down the stairs, so you went into Mrs Lester's room. She didn't like it a bit and you thought you had better make a clean breast of it and came up to him and told him what had happened – there was a fight – I don't remember how it went on – Dad and Mother were there with him and they had been discussing things and wouldn't let me stop there I don't know what became of me or of you

*****

I've been reading a very very interesting book, darlint. I want you to read it after me and give me your opinion – not just a few lines and then "Dismissed" – but your real opinion of every one of note in the book. Read and remember it carefully will you? pour moi.

It's called "The Fruitful Vine"* by Robert Hichens, and it's very very nice and the subject is interesting – not lovely like the "Common Law" or "The Business of Life" – it's too sensual for that but "the one act" in the book would lead to hours and hours of discussion – even now I have finished it – I am not sure whether she did right or wrong and I am not sure which man I really liked [...]

You must tell me everything you think about it, it's rather long 500 pages and there are several passages that I have

* A more detailed analysis of this novel is in Letter 50.

marked – some I have queried for you to answer others I have just marked – because they have struck me as being interesting to us, or to me, I'm very anxious to know what you think of it, what shall I do with the book? – send it to you?

I think I have never found it so difficult to talk to you before all the times you have been away – I am just dried up waiting to see you and feel you holding me

It is Friday now and altho I had a mail in from you – about 11.30 – I still don't feel like talking darlint, I'm not disappointed – not a little bit – in fact I'm pleased – ever so pleased – at the difference when I read all you say to me I feel you are with me [...] so different from before and I wonder if its going to last and shall I have a letter from Plymouth saying "I'm not going to answer your questions Peidi and I don't mind if you are cross about it" Youre not going to say that any more are you? – darlint please don't, I said I wouldn't ask again didn't I, but I'm doing so [...] I must go on asking and asking not minding whether my pride is hurt – always asking until you consent

Darlint do you remember being very proud once? I remember and I gave way first – write and tell me if you remember the incident and what it was[*]

Its not going to happen again tho' is it? Mr Carlton said to me at 11 30 to-day – "I have news from your brother for you"– I wasn't thinking of the mail being in and

---

[*] This refers to the fact that on 27 June 1921, when Freddy was lodging at the Thompsons' house, it was Edith who took the Duchess of Malfi's part to assure him of her interest – she, the supplicant, went to his room and the couple had sex for the first time.

said "How have you got news?" and he just gave me your envelope. I thought the remark rather strange and can't quite make out if he really thought it was from my brother – or was being sarcastic. You get into Bombay today – just 5 more weeks – I wish they'd fly.

I had a doctor's bill in yesterday – I took it in myself as it happened so of course I kept and shall pay it myself – without saying it is even in and then there can be no question of who's to pay it can there

You want me to pay it, don't you darlint – I shall do so

Why that passage in your last letter   The last time we met, we were pals, weren't we Chere? why the question darlint if you had wanted to write it, you should have said it as a fact

Of course we were pals, we always are and always will be, while this life lasts – whatever else happens and alters our lives – for better or for worse – for either or for both of us we shall always remain that darlint – don't ask me the question again – it hurts

On Saturday we went to the dinner party at the Birnage's – it was a very posh affair for a private house – full course dinner and she cooked everything herself – I think she is awfully clever

Yesterday I thought I should have gone mad with faceache – I took 24 Asparins [sic] – in 6 lots of 4 during the day and made a pillow of thermogene at night – I didn't get a scrap of sleep tho'

Has your pain gone darlint? I think you must have left it with me, I thought I might get a letter from Suez to-day otherwise I wouldn't have come up to town to-day.

I think I want you here to take care of me – it seems more than ever before – shall be so glad when we get nearer the 26th May, just that darlint nothing more

PEIDI

27

Later Exhibit 10, and a very damaging letter.

Edith, who never missed a day's work, was ill again – this time with a sore throat – but surely it was nonsense for her to suggest that she was pregnant again. If she was, then Percy was the father; her visceral reaction to the novel, *The Woman Deborah*, implies that she was sleeping with him, while Letter 22 made it clear that she and Freddy had stopped short of having full sex on 30 March. But in truth the whole passage gives the impression that – as in Letter 5 – she was hinting, softly nudging, in order to strengthen her intimate connection with Freddy, to remind him of what they had done together and might do in the future; it also, once more, raises the faint possibility that the entire November–January pregnancy was a phantom.

Of course the reference to 'herbs', which here were almost certainly abortifacient in property, could not be properly explained in court. Nevertheless the inference was there to be made, and anybody with more than one brain cell at the Old Bailey would have done so. In that arena, however, it would merely have added to the choking atmosphere of prejudice against Edith, rather than opening up the possibility that not everything she wrote was literally true or to the point.

Without that understanding, with only the settled belief in Edith's guilt, this letter reads appallingly. No question.

It would not have mattered to the court that 'big pieces' of lightbulb, had these in truth been administered, would have caused Percy a) to notice their unexpected presence in his food; and b) to be hospitalised immediately. Then there is the more complicated fact that this letter was very plainly a reply, part of a fervid and erotically charged dialogue; and that, had Freddy's letters also existed, he would have been seen to be engaged in it as deeply as Edith herself – the 'finger marks' line is just one example of this. But Freddy's guilt was already – in many quarters, reluctantly – priced into the trial. What mattered was the woman, and the need to bring her down for what she represented.

And so, the pure gold of what she had written here: the police must have swooned in ecstasy when they read it.

꩜

Mr F. Bywaters, P&O, RMS *Morea*, Port Said
Postmark: London EC, 1 May 1922, 6.15 p.m.

Darlingest Boy I know,

If you were to hear me talk now you would laugh, I'm quite positive and I should be angry – I've got practically no voice at all – just a little very high up, squeak.

It started with a very sore throat and then my voice went – it doesn't hurt now – the throat is better but it sounds so funny. I feel like laughing myself but altho you'd laugh darlint you'd be very kind wouldn't you? and just take care of me. I know you would without asking or you answering – but you can answer because I like to hear you say it.

About those fainting fits darlint, I don't really know what to say to you.

I'm beginning to think its the same as before – they always happen 1st thing in the morning – when I'm getting up and I wasn't ill as I should have been last time, altho' I was a little – but not as usual.

What shall I do about it darlint, if it is the same this month – please write and tell me I want to do just what you would like.

I still have the herbs.

"I like her she doesn't swear."

This is what you write – do you like her because she doesn't swear or was that bit an afterthought. I'm wondering what you really think of a girl – any girl – even me who says damn and a few stronger words sometimes – or don't these words constitute swearing as you hear it.

[...]

Talking about "Felix" darlint can't say I was disappointed in the end because I didn't expect very much of him. You say you expected him to do a lot for Valeria – I didn't – he was too ordinary – too prosaic to do anything sensational – he'd do anything in the world for her if it hadn't caused comment but when it did – he finished [...]

Darlint isn't this a mistake "Je suis gache,˙ ma pauvre petite amie." This is how you wrote it.

I was glad you think and feel the same way as I do about the "New Forest" (by Horace Smith). I don't think we're failures in other things and we musn't be in this. We musn't give up as we said. No, we shall have to wait if we fail again. Darlint, Fate can't always turn against us and if it is we must fight it – You and I are strong now We must be stronger. We must learn to be patient. We must have each other darlint. Its meant to be I know I feel it is because I love you such a lot – such a love was not meant to be in vain. It will come right I know one day, if not by our efforts some other way. We'll wait eh darlint, and you'll try and get some money and then we can go away and not worry about anybody or anything.

---

* This refers back to Edith's 'Je suis Goche' in Letter 17, but remains inexplicable.

You said it was enough for an elephant. Perhaps it was. But you don't allow for the taste making only a small quantity to be taken. It sounded like a reproach was it meant to be?

Darlint I tried hard – you won't know how hard – because you weren't there to see and I can't tell you all – but I did – I do want you to believe I did for both of us.

You will see by my last letter to you I havn't forgotten the key* and I didn't want reminding – I didn't forget that – altho' I did forget something last time didn't I altho it was only small.†

We have changed our plans about Llandudno – it is too expensive we are going to Bournemouth July 8th, and while Avis was over last night he asked her to come with us. The suggestion was nothing to do with me – it was his entirely and altho' I wouldn't have suggested such a thing for the world – I'm glad – because if things are still the same and we do go – a third party helps to make you forget that you always lead the existence we do.

Au revoir for the week end darlint.

*****

The mail was in this morning and I read your letter darlint, I cried – I couldn't help it – such a lot – it

* This may relate to the 'duplicate' that Edith mentioned in the previous letter. A key to what? The obvious suggestion is a receptacle in which to hide a nefarious substance. Again, very damaging – to Freddy also, who (see below) had clearly asked about it – although, as usual, there is no proof that Edith ever actually did the thing that she is describing.
† This reference is obscure, but again does not read well.

sounded so sad I cried for you I could exactly feel how you were feeling – I've felt like that so often and I know.

I was buoyed up with the hope of the "light bulb" and I used a lot – big pieces too – not powdered – and it has no effect – I quite expected to be able to send that cable – but no – nothing has happened from it and now your letter tells me about the bitter taste again. Oh darlint, I do feel so down and unhappy.

Wouldn't the stuff make small pills coated together with soap and dipped in liquorice powder – like Beechams – try while you're away. Our Boy had to have his thumb operated on because he had a piece of glass in it that's what made me try that method again – but I suppose as you say he is not normal, I know I feel I shall never get him to take a sufficient quantity of anything bitter. No I haven't forgotten the key I told you before.

Darlint two heads are better than one is such a true saying. You tell me not to leave finger marks on the box – do you know I did not think of the box but I did think of the glass or cup whatever was used. I wish I wish oh I wish I could do something.

Darlint, think for me, *do*. I do want to help. If you only knew how helpless and selfish I feel letting you do such a lot for me and I doing nothing for you. If ever we are lucky enough to be happy darling I'll love you such a lot. I always show you how much I love you for all you do for me. Its a terrible feeling darlint to want – really want to give all and everything, and not be able to give a tiny little thing – just thro' circumstances.

You asked me if Deborah [in *The Woman Deborah* by Claude and Alice Askew] described her feelings rightly when she was talking about Kullett making love to her.

Darlingest, boy, I don't think all the feelings can be put on paper because there are not words to describe them. The feeling is one of repugnance, loathing not only of the person but of yourself – and darlint when you think of a man and a woman jointly wrote that book it's not feasible that the words used would be bad enough to express the feelings. The man Author wouldn't allow the woman Author to talk too badly of Kullett – do you think? I still think that nobody can express the feelings – I'm sure I couldn't – but they are there, deeply rooted and can never be plucked out as circumstances now are unless they (the circumstances) change.

Did you notice any similarity in 2 girls names in two books that you recently read and the utter dissimilarity in their natures (I don't think I spelt that word rightly). I didn't know that you would be in London a month this time – altho I had a little idea.

That month – I can't bear to think of it a whole four weeks and things the same as they are now. All those days to live thro for just one hour in each.

All that lying and scheming and subterfuge to obtain one little hour in each day – when by right of nature and our love we should be for all the 24 in every day.

Darlint don't let it be – I can't bear it all this time – the pain gets too heavy to bear – heavier each day – but if things were different what a grand life we should start together. Perhaps we could have that one week I could be ill from shock – More lies – but the last. Eh darlint.

Do experiment with the pills while you are away – please darlint.

No we two – two halves – have not yet come to the end of our tether.

Don't let us.

I'm sorry I've had to use this piece of paper but the pad was empty – I sent the boy for a fresh one and they will have none in until tomorrow.

We have started on the 5th week of your absence now – each week seems longer than the last and each day the length of two

Do you know darlint that the Saturday I usually have off when you are home is Whit Saturday and I shan't be able to see you nor on the Monday following

Three whole days – and you so near and yet so far – it musn't be darlint – we musn't let it somehow.

Good bye now darlint I can't write any more   You said you have a lump – so have I in fact its more than a lump now

Good bye until Marseilles next week. I do always love you and think of you

PEIDI.

28

Later Exhibit 21, although it held little to offer the prosecution case. Instead, there was such vitality in the first paragraph – such a sense of all that would be taken from Edith: her straightforward animal joy in living, which palpated continually amid all the mournful numinous yearning for something 'more'.

As for the unconscious foreknowledge with which she parades in the widows' hats... what novelist would have dared fabricate a scene of such blistering irony?

Again one notes the sisterly snap against Avis in the needling game that they played over Freddy Bywaters; Edith fairly revels in her own sense of superiority while resenting – and fearing – the one thing Avis had that she did not: freedom.

The reference to Mr Birnage – so persistent in his attentions, perhaps because he was a man of means, able to place Percy just a little in his debt – is of particular interest here, as it raises the question of insurance. Speaking to the police after the murder, Mr Birnage, who must have been shocked to the core, stated that he and his wife had visited the 'affectionate' Thompsons about six times (no mention of the separate encounters with Edith), but amid all these anodyne remarks he said one thing that caused detective ears to twitch: Percy had asked him to 'effect an insurance on his life. I did so, the account being for £250 at death.'

This was really not relevant to Edith's situation, who was a solvent working woman. The prosecution's contention was that, as with Dr Crippen[*] and other such 'classic' crimes, she had sought to avoid the financial and social perils of divorce by simply eliminating the unwanted element from her life; if, therefore, she had got away with murder, there would have been no pressing need for £250. She would have lost nothing except the nuisance husband. Nor was any

---

[*] Convicted at the Old Bailey in 1910 for the murder of his wife, Cora, whom he had poisoned with hyoscine. His lover, Ethel le Neve, whose air of demure fragility aroused public sympathy rather than prejudice, was acquitted of all charges.

financial motive alluded to at the trial; although very late in the day, when the question of a reprieve was being debated, and the authorities were doing everything in their power not to weaken, a Home Office memorandum decided to throw £ s. d. into the mix.

'The Appeals were dismissed in the most scathing terms,' wrote Sir Ernley Blackwell, a senior civil servant, on 28 December 1922. 'The Lord Chief Justice said it was a squalid and rather indecent case of lust and adultery in which the husband was murdered in a cowardly fashion, partly because he was in the way and partly, it would seem, because the money he possessed was desired.'

This last, if not a downright lie, was certainly a piece of inspired speculation. But it was made with a very specific aim, in order that Sir Ernley should emphasise his most important point: if money were any part of the motive, then a *crime passionnel* became instead a long-planned plot – cool of head as well as lustful of body – which indubitably justified the death penalty.

⚜

Mr F. Bywaters, P&O, RMS *Morea*, Marseilles
Postmark: London EC, 15 May 1922, 5.30 p.m.

My very own darlingest boy,

I received the mail this morning – but am not going to answer it yet – I've got several other things I want to tell you, and talk to you as well. I had no time to read your letter alone, so what do you think I did darlint. I got on the top of a bus – back seat by myself and went to Hyde Park Corner in my lunch hour and read it. I couldn't stop in in the lunch hour – it was such a glorious day in fact it has been a beautiful week end warm and sunny – quite warm enough to wear very thin clothes and not feel cold I do love this weather – it's not too hot yet – but even when it is I'm not going to grumble – this winter has been terribly long and cold, *and* lonely   Do you know darlint I won 30/- on Paragon in the City and Sub[urban, run at Epsom] and lost 20/- in each of the 2000 gns. 1000 gns. and the Jubilee. Money was never made to stop with me.

When you've been in England have you ever seen "Les Rouges et Noirs." They are all ex-soldiers – running a concert party – like the Co optimists and impersonating girls as well as men.

Men usually dressed as women especially in evening dress look ridiculous – but these were splendid – very clever and very funny – I did laugh such a lot – it was really dancing through the hours. We went with Mr. and Mrs Birnage. He has made him an agent for the Sun Life privately and now draws commission on any policies he gets – it has been about £750 premiums up to now and he draws 1% on some and ½ % on others   Miss Prior's sister lost her husband quite suddenly and as I happen to be her stamp – Miss Prior asked me to go up west and buy some mourning for her – a costume – a silk frock and a cloth frock – jumper – shoes stockings and gloves It was a nice job, and when I got back – there were some widows hats with veils at the back and nobody including Miss Prior had the pluck to try them on – they all say it is unlucky – so because of it being unlucky to them I thought it might be lucky to me and tried them all on.

I think they all think terrible things are going to happen to me now – but darlint I am laughing. I wonder who will be right, they or I? Talking about bad luck – Mother came over to hang some clean curtains for me and in moving the dressing table the cheval glass came off the pivot and smashed the glass in a thousand pieces – This is supposed to mean bad luck for 7 years – I am wondering if its for us (you and I) or her. What do you think about it?

Darlint I've bought a skirt – cream gabardine – pleated to wear with a sports coat – It looks lovely – are you pleased?

Do you know the skirts are going to be worn longer?

I shall have to wear mine a wee bit longer – if I don't want to be hopelessly old fashioned – but it won't be very much, will you mind? On Friday Mr Birnage came up and took me out to lunch again. I left him at 2 and was astonished when at 4 p m they said a gentleman wanted to see me upstairs – and on going up found it was him waiting to take me out to tea   I went – but I didn't really want to – I shan't go too often darlint   You said you were home for a month this time – does that mean that you are going to sail on the 23rd June

Darlint I hope not – I do so want to be with you – even if its only for a little while on June 27th 1922   Our first real birthday   Are you getting in on the Friday again this time?

You mentioned about a boy and a girl and a chocolate incident in one of your letters – you said "I smiled and thought a lot" what did you think – you didn't tell me and I want to know

Darlingest boy – I like Montelimont as well as Turkish Delight   "Cupboard Love" did you say? I am glad you didn't like Waring – I thought perhaps you might – just a little – I didn't a bit   I was cross with Deborah – several times darlint – especially for sending him away that first time but I admired so much the will power she had to do so – didn't you? You say "Deborah" was more natural than "Maria"   No I don't think so – they were two very different types – but both were absolutely natural according to their mode of living. Deborah was primitive

– Maria civilised more – but both natural – darlint don't give "Maria's" place in you to anyone else   Admire others as much but not more, pour moi – I loved Maria and I admired Deborah

I don't know whether Avis liked the books or not – but if you asked her why she did or did not she couldn't say, could she do you think – she couldn't discuss each character as we do – she wouldn't remember enough about them – she would only remember the general theme of the book – so why ask? [...]

In a book I have just read* which I am going to lend you there are two characters – whom you and I must copy – only if things are never got to be right darlint if they are always as they are now – I want you to remember what I have written   I shall be like and do what

Dolores does and you must do what Cesare does – Of course what I do will be from a different motive from Dolores and you must fight like Cesare [...]

You will probably wonder what I am rambling about – I shan't tell you I shall wait until you read the book and then you will find out for yourself. To-day its 3 weeks before you're in England – I'm trying to get thro the time – without letting it feel too hard – only I hope you will hurry to England

and PEIDI.

---

* *The Fruitful Vine by* Robert Hichens.

Exhibit 21a.

      Extract from *Daily Sketch*, 13 May 1922, columns 1 and 2.
      With headnote:

      'Holiday – Then Death Pact.
      'Passionate Farewell Letters in Seaside Drama.
      'Women's Sacrifice.'

The newspaper reports proceedings at an inquest held on George William Hibbert who was found dead in a gas-filled room at Brighton and by his side lay Maud Hibbert, wife of his youngest brother, unconscious.

29

Later Exhibit 22.

This was sent one week before Freddy's ship docked on Thursday 25 May. It contains one of Edith's most characteristic – and beautiful – observations, in response to her lover's complaint about a novelist whose conclusions seemed to him unsatisfying: 'Forget the ends lose yourself in the characters and the story and, in your own mind make your own end.'

Books were not just real to her; she entered their reality. And this, once more, would become a means to attack her, when her profound engagement with Robert Hichens' novel *Bella Donna* was probed at the Old Bailey.

Of course the quotation at the top of this letter looked extremely bad.

Moreover, the romance at the centre of the book was uncomfortably transgressive. The eponymous heroine, older than her husband by six years, falls beneath the spell of a seductive Greek-Egyptian. So what, asked the solicitor general, did Edith think that Bywaters would learn from *Bella Donna*?

She replied: 'The book was really about Egypt, and I thought he might learn something in it about Egypt.'

At which point Mr Justice Shearman, beyond outrageously, interrupted. 'I should like to clear this up. Is not the main point of it that the lady killed her husband with slow poisoning?'

Edith said: 'Do you ask me that question?'

'Yes,' the judge replied. 'It is plain to me—'

'I was going to deal with it in cross-examination,' said the solicitor general, but the judge was not to be stopped: 'Although I never like to take part in it you know it must come out... Possibly some of the jury might not know it, and I thought it ought to be cleared up.'

Having been thus helped along the way, the solicitor general later returned to this point. 'There is a plot,' he stated, 'which is really the plot of the story, to poison her husband, without anybody finding out what she was doing?' With a flash of her old spirit Edith answered:

'It is a matter of opinion whether that is absolutely the plot, is it not?'

'Anyway, that is an important incident in the book?'

Despite her terror, she fenced again. 'At the end, yes.'

When her junior defence counsel, Walter Frampton, dealt with *Bella Donna*, he asked very simply: 'Did you know what digitalin was?'

Edith replied: 'I had no idea'.

'Why did you write and ask Bywaters "Is it any use?"'

'I wanted him to feel that I was willing to help him; to keep him to me.'

The defence went on to remind the court that Edith herself bore no resemblance to the character of Bella Donna, a woman whom she would describe, in her wholehearted way, as 'abnormal – a monster'. But the judge, who had a gift for timing his interpolations, had done his work, and the rest was merely white noise for many of those in the room.

The idea that a person's life could hang in the balance, and that the content of their reading matter could actively influence the decision whether or not to execute them, is the stuff of dystopias; it is also, of course, ludicrous; yet again it seems that almost nobody was able to recognise the fact, nor listen to what they were hearing.

※

Mr F. Bywaters, P&O, RMS *Morea*, Marseilles
Postmark: London EC, 18 May 1922, 2.30 p.m.

'It must be remembered that digitalin is a cumulative poison, and that the same dose harmless if taken once, yet frequently repeated, becomes deadly.'

Darlingest Boy,

The above passage I've just come across in a book I am reading "Bella Donna" by Robert Hichens. Is it any use.

In your letter from Bombay you say you asked a lot of questions from Marseilles. I hope I answered them all satisfactory Darlint. I want to. I want to do always what will please you. I can't remember all you asked. I have nothing to refer to everything is destroyed [his letters] – I don't even wait for the next arrival now. About the Co-Optimists, I remember the song quite well and darlint, if you can only be practically true to me, I'd rather not have you at all and I won't have you. What's more now I'm the bully aren't I? but it's only fun darlint – laugh. Yes a lot pour moi. I've heard nothing at all from your Mother I've seen your sister several times. Darlingest boy you must never question me being still here. However hard (even the hardest you can possibly imagine) things are, while you still say "B B [be brave] Peidi" I shall hang on – just because you want me to and tell me to. Don't ever question me again. You have often said a thing as a question when you have known it is a fact. Why is that Darlint? Don't ever doubt. I'll always love you – too much perhaps but always, and while you say stay I shall.

I shall ask you about the laugh in the Buffet, but when shall I? I'm not clear about what you write   Do you mean me to ask you when I see you this time or to wait until things are perhaps different. You say "I'm not bullying I'm deciding for you Chere" Darlint, that's what I like. Not that hard tone 'You must, you shall'   But the softer tone I know you can use especially to me   Yes, I like you deciding things for me. I've done it so long for myself. Its lovely to be able to leave it all to someone I know will not go wrong – will do the right thing pour moi always. You will wont you darlint   I lean on you not on myself when you are here   Now I'll talk a bit about the books... I agree with you about [R.W.] Chambers endings darlint but the endings are not the story   The end is written to please nine out of ten people who read his books. You and I are the tenth and he doesn't cater for us darlint, we are so few   Do as I do   Forget the ends lose yourself in the characters and the story and, in your own mind make your own end. Its lovely to do that darlint – try it, and you must not be scathing about a particular author that I like. I wont have it you hear me – I'm bullying you now. I'll ruffle all your hair darlint until you're really cross. Will you be with me about anything ever?

Yes! we will be cross with each other and then make it up – it will be lovely. I shall have to stop for a little while now darlint. I have a ton of work to do. I do hope we are not quite so busy when you are home   Au revoir for now darlint

*****

One more day has gone by – I'm counting the days now darlint. What are you doing now, I wonder – its Thursday about 12 noon and I've squeezed 10 minutes to talk to you. Today is fearfully cold again and very windy – I hate wind. For the last 4 days it has been 82 shade and 112 sun and today shade temp is down to 52 – what a country to live in – hurry up and take me away – to Egypt if you like – but anywhere where its warm.

The book I'm reading "Bella Donna" is about Egypt – I'd think you'd be interested in it – although I don't think you would like the book – at least I hope you wouldn't – I don't

Do you remember telling me to do the "Scamp" for the Derby? Well I was rather hard up that week – so only put on 5/- each way   I got 20 to 1 price

Yesterday was the first time the "Scamp" came out and it failed miserably at a mile – the papers say it is a non-stayer [the Epsom Derby is run over a mile and a half] and made a very poor show and the price to-day is 33 to 1   What luck

I dont think I previously told you that old Mr. Lester – fell in the fire and gashed his head

He was taken to Hospital and is still there – that is 10 days ago   Reports at first said he wouldn't live through each night – but he has recovered after all   Don't some people exaggerate?

Darlint, I do feel so miserable to-day   I think I weather – it has been so bright and sunny and makes you feel quite cheerful and today is cold and dull and I feel cold too – not in the flesh – in the body inside I mean – that sort of feeling that only one person in the world can alter for me – why aren't you here to do it? I want you so badly to lean on and to take care of me to be kind and gentle and love me as only you can

Goodbye darlingest boy – I'll write again before the mail closes for Marseilles

PEIDI

Supposing I were to meet your mother in the street darlint, what should I do? What would you want me to do?

Answer this, please, particularly

When I asked you that question darlint I had already seen your Mother – but I really wanted to know what you would like me to have done

As it was – I hardly knew what to do – I couldnt pass her unrecognised without being absolutely rude so I just said "Let me smell, how are you?" and passed on, I didn't stop to shake hands. She had a large bunch of red roses in her arms and she had that tall man with her – I forget his name

Seeing her with red roses reminded me of you darlint, you like red ones don't you? – you told me so once – so do I, but not as much as one flower – they're all finished now isn't it a shame   I've taken the tussore to be made up darlint and was told that it was the best quality they have ever handled. I've also had a new navy costume made. I don't think you will like it because its a long coat – but I bought a cream gabardine skirt (not serge) to please you darling so I thought I could please myself this time. Am I right? I wonder if I shall wear the tussore costume with you darlint   I don't mean once or twice but always. I don't know, I don't feel even optimistic about things, I can't darling – not like I did before. That hand of fate is always held up at me blocking out the future. If I could only be certain? Darlingest boy pour moi be very very careful coming in this time. Things and people have become much more vigilant.   Understand? I don't want to lose any tiny minute of you, they will probably be so few, but even a few is so much better than none at all remember that darlint. I'm very very anxious to know if you are getting in on the Friday. I can't possibly wait over the week end – do let me know as soon as you can find out yourself. Bill got in on Friday darlint about 3 p.m. home and came up to tea yesterday. We had it out in the garden. He started the conversation about [word excised

– thought to be opium] and said if he knew where to plant it he would get some and we talked a lot about it. I wanted to change the conversation quickly but he would continue. On Saturday darlint I did something which you would have said made me look old – gardening all day   It passes the time away. Old Mr. Lester died last night   All their side of the house the blinds are drawn I havnt drawn mine and I'm not going to   I think they think I'm a heathen   "Will it be under the year" you say I wish I could be certain – feel certain – but I cant darlint I keep on saying to myself 'Yes! Yes! It must, it shall be 'Yes,' and I have that feeling deep down all the time that it will be 'No'   Your letter today made me feel miserable darlint, I felt how much I wanted to be with you, so that I could love you that 'Mothering feeling' came over me [...] By now darlint you will have heard from me several times. Yesterday you passed Suez and got my Port Said letters   I'm so sorry its a long time from Marseilles to Bombay, when you hear from me, but I can't do anything to help it can I darlint ? You'll be able to talk to me a long time this week to post at Marseilles because you'll have all my letters to answer   Yes darlint, I want you and love you such a lot just as much as you do   I want you to hold me and kiss me   Yes always   When you do see me darlint you will, you must, darlint   It doesnt matter where we meet, perhaps a Buffet but it musn't matter, we musn't think of other people being there we must just live for each other in that first minute   Dont forget darlint Dont just say how are you "Chere." It's so prosaic and we're not are we?

I dont know whether I'm sorry or pleased about you sailing on the 9th [June]   It's so hard to say now. If things are the same as now perhaps I shall be pleased   If we are successful I shall probably be sorry   I shall want you so much through that time I think   It will be awful to think of you miles away   Darlingest boy, get that ankle well quickly I do want to play tennis with you some time this year – dont bother about the blessed old football – it always makes it give out and isn't ankle spelt with a 'K' it looks so funny with a 'c.'

All June – all July – all August – you'll be home again Sept 9 [in fact Freddy did not return until the 23rd]. I wonder if we shall have that week together darlint, by the sea – Sept isn't too late is it?

I've got a real longing for you to take me to Tunbridge Wells. I've only been there once and I did like it so much.

Could you take me darlint for a week-end – or even for a day?

[...]

Goodbye darlingest boy – for now and Marseilles – the next letter to England – Hoorah! I do love you so much and miss you more than you can ever know – it's the whole of me – all my life – just all I live for now.

PEIDI.

29 (i)

Exhibit 22a.

Extract from *Daily Sketch*, 10 May 1922, page 3, column 3.
With headnote:

'Girl's Drug injections.
'Mysterious Death after Doses of Cocaine and Morphia'

Then follows a report of an inquest on Lilian May Davis, when evidence was given that she took injections of cocaine in the daytime and morphia at night for sleeplessness. Dr. Spilsbury gave evidence that he made a postmortem examination and could not assign the cause of death.

29 (ii)

Exhibit 22b.

Extract from *Daily Sketch*, 6 May 1922, page 15, column 5.
With headnote:

'Patient Killed by an Overdose.
'Woman Dispenser's Error of Calculation.
'Ten Times too Strong, Multiplied by a Hundred instead
of by Ten.'

The report refers to an inquest on Arthur Kemp, who died from an overdose of sodium antimony, prepared by a woman dispenser.

30

Later Exhibit 51. Postmark mostly indecipherable but evidently written on Monday 22 May.

It is unclear why this letter was considered worthy of inclusion at the trial, although it did offer Mr Justice Shearman another opportunity to demean Edith – a minor example, but telling of the mindset of this peevish old puritan. He had a cruel trick of reading out some of her words in order to make them sound as ridiculous as possible, and in this instance he ponderously quoted the phrase: 'A real posh car', before adding: 'Whatever that might be.'

Most unluckily for Edith, the judge belonged to the class of man who could not deal with her, and who therefore found a way of doing so by destroying what she represented.

It is interesting to note that Shearman had tried another case of 'joint enterprise' just a few months earlier, in July 1922. Elsie Yeldham, aged 22, had lured an ex-boyfriend to Epping Forest, where her soon-to-be husband – a year her senior – killed and robbed him. This sounded very much like malice aforethought, and both parties were condemned to death. However: a Home Office memorandum on the subject of female reprieves – compiled before Edith's execution, essentially in order to justify it – offered the view that 'the judge thought the woman acted under influence of the man'. This seems to have been an opinion rather than evidentially based. The inference is that Elsie (rather like Crippen's lover Ethel le Neve) displayed none of the more troubling aspects of Edith's demeanour, which led people to believe with such ease, and on so little evidence, that she was the 'real' killer.

Elsie was also luckier in her Home Secretary. Edward Shortt – a Liberal, a lawyer himself, and a man of some compassion – held the post until late October 1922, and accepted Mr Justice Shearman's analysis of the case. 'On this', concluded the Home Office document, 'and in view of her sex, it was decided to commute.'

Mr F. Bywaters, P&O, RMS *Morea*

The mail is in darlint, but I havent had an opportunity to read it yet. I'm fearfully busy. Miss Prior is in Paris and I've tons to do, but, darlint when I've read it I will answer it, even if I have to give it to you by hand I'm sure I shan't have time to do it today and I do want you to get something from me at Plymouth – even if its only a few lines. Friday [26 May], I'll see you shall I? Today to Friday four more days to live – no not live – exist thro. You are getting in Friday arent you darlint? do say 'Yes.' Are you going to answer my letters to you at Marseilles please do darlint. I dont want you to say what you did last trip. You wont darlint because I've asked you not to. On Saturday Mr. Carlton took me home by road. It wasn't his car but a friend of his. A real posh car you'd have liked it. I'm afraid if Miss Prior knew she might want to give me the sack. However I shan't tell her and I'm sure he won't. Also Bess and Reg came down quite unexpectedly on Sunday and we went for a ride from about 3 till 9.30 Bess asked after you. Darlint I had a terrible shock when the Egypt went down. Nobody said the name of the boat they just said a big P. and O. liner. Imagine what I felt can you? I have sent you a parcel to Plymouth containing 2 books 'The Fruitful Vine' and 'Bella Donna.' Read 'Bella Donna' first will you please whilst you are in England if possible and keep 'The Fruitful Vine' until we are parted again   Also in the parcel is something I forgot last time* I don't suppose you really want it but because I promised and forgot I got it this time. Forgive me for forgetting. You have, havnt you darlint? And there is a packet of

---

* There is no clue as to what this gift was.

Toblerone. I bought two. Sent you one and kept the other myself   Will you eat it Thursday and I will mine   Darlingest boy will you send the enclosed P C. as instructions attached in your name*   I have sent one in mine or rather in my 'used to name' that sounds funny doesnt it   After all whats in a name   Nothing at all except 'Peidi'   I saw your Mother again last Wednesday. I was with Harry Renton and behind her and purposely kept so

It has been frightfully hot this weekend. The sun has been fierce and I don't want a neck like I had at Shanklin I shall have to get a sunshade. What about Whit Saturday? We shan't be able to be together   He doesnt go in   I thought of asking for a day off, say Wed the 31st† what do you think? Bill brought Miss Ashley home. Did you know? He says she is very mean

I saw Carpentier‡ on the afternoon of his fight he was over the road at Pagets   The Police had to guard his car He looks very lined and old for his age   Young Mr Paget (you remember me telling you about him) says the fight was a frost and very unfair   Carpentier took an unfair advantage while the Referees were intervening

You wouldnt like me a bit today darlint "Why" did you say? Because Ive got my foulard frock on   Its so hot, and that reminds me the black frock with the white beads that I always wear when you take me out I thought I

---

* This was surely connected to Edith's plan, of which more later, to use the General Post Office on Aldersgate Street as an address for Freddy to send letters.
† Derby Day. Before 1995 the race was run on Wednesdays, and a popular day off for Londoners.
‡ The light-heavyweight champion Georges Carpentier had paid a celebrity visit to the sports shop, Pagets, on Aldersgate Street.

would wear it out for every day this Summer   It's too
conspicuous to keep for next winter and when I've got
some spare cash I'll buy another frock for you to take me
to dinner in, but I won't wear the blk and white until you
say I may, so write and tell me what you think also darlint,
let me know about Wed 31st because I must give them a
little notice as we are so busy.   On Sunday I cooked a
chicken my very first attempt at poultry   It was all very
nice – I think – stuffing and bread sauce etc. and then a
gooseberry pie   I thought about you the whole time and
wished I had cooked it for you. Dont be too disappointed
with this letter darlint, I havnt time to really talk to you,
but I will and give it you when I see you

It's been a fearful rush to get even this in, and I do hate
to rush when I'm talking to you. Au revoir darling for 4
more days. I love you such a lot – just as much – no more
than you love

PEIDI

31

Later Exhibit 23. Why? Of what earthly interest to the Old Bailey was this swift, swooping, impressionistic account of an ordinary/ extraordinary woman's daily life?

Was it the reference to the man who took Edith to Frascati's, an incident that might assist in bolstering her image as the world's worst wife, a feckless flirt unable to resist any sexual attention? She *did* enjoy flexing the delicate muscle of her allure – not a crime, although at her trial her very existence was a crime – yet this totem of carnality was strikingly chaste in her actual behaviour. She had absolutely no interest in a love affair with anybody except Freddy. She merely looked as though she had.

Was it the remark about being in a 'real live cage'? Or the fact that she had, in the eyes of those fearful of a future filled with emancipated women, a damn sight too much freedom – she could afford an expensive holiday, while Percy could not? An inverted gender pay gap, a century ago! One may well imagine how that was perceived.

Yet the real issue, surely, was *Bella Donna* again, and the clause 'you may learn something from it to help us' – a reference so brief and passing that one wonders anew at the way in which these letters were read. The dogged literalness; the absolute indifference to context.

As for the line quoted from the Koran – 'the fate of every man have we bound about his neck': it is scarcely bearable to read, not least because Edith had no real sense of what she meant by it – she was simply fascinated by fate, and alternated (sometimes within the same letter) between an energised belief that it could be conquered and a heavy, quiescent certainty that it had the upper hand. Perhaps what she was feeling was the strength of the *real* bars around her cage, the circumscriptions of gender and class that would, indeed, determine her story's ending.

Mr F. Bywaters, P&O, RMS *Morea*, Plymouth
Postmark: London EC, 23 May 1922, 3 p.m.

So it wasnt G.M.M.C. [Good morning ma Chere] it
was G.A.M.C. [Good afternoon] this time darlint, I was
surprised I got it at 4 20 pm, Monday...

Darlint, one day last week I went to Frascati to lunch and
took one hour and 10 minutes it was a fearful rush – it
was a man that I have known for years by sight but never
better until a few weeks ago   the usual type of man
darlint   that expects some return for a lunch.

However, that doesnt matter, this is what I wanted to tell
you he wanted to buy a box of chocolates and I said 'I'd
rather you didnt thank you'

He – 'Now what earthly difference is there in you
accepting from me a box of chocolates to a lunch.'

I – 'Oh its not that – its just that I dont like chocolates'

He – 'Good God, you're the first girl I've ever heard
refuse chocolates that she didn't have to pay for   Are you
sure you don't like them or is [it] a pose?'

Darlingest boy, what do you think of that? Can you
imagine me posing especially over chocolates   However
he ended up in buying me a pound of 'Marrons Glace'
Have you ever had them, they are chestnuts in syrup, I
really did enjoy them

Now about your letters   I cant say if you are right or
wrong about Molly   I dont know her sufficiently to say

and I do hate to judge other people by appearances   I'd much rather dismiss them from my thoughts altogether I had already sent you 2 books to Plymouth darlint, the only two I have read since you've been away. I'd like you to read "Bella Donna" first you may learn something from it to help us, then you can read "The Fruitful Vine" – when you are away. You say you think, [that] I think, you don't talk enough about books and things to me. Darlingest boy I'm not going to say anything at all about anything – I'm just going to be thankful for what I do receive – think to myself "I must not be impatient perhaps they wont always be crumbs." [...] You talk about that cage you are in   that's how I feel   only worse if it can be so   because mine is a real live cage with a keeper as well   to whom I have to account every day, every hour, every minute nearly.

"The fate of every man have we bound about his neck" (I dont know if I've got it quite right – you can tell me later on – but the meaning is right)

Have we darlint? have we the fate of one – or we two halves I dont know – I darent think   its like making sand pies at the sea-side   they always topple over. We havnt fixed up anything about Bournemouth yet   they are too expensive for Avis and him   I dont care personally   I'd sooner not have a holiday   I'm really looking forward with dread, not pleasure   I'll always be thinking first of Shanklin and then of our tumble down nook.

I'm going to post this now and risk whether it gets to you in time, wire me how many letters you receive – there should be two – then I should have answered all yours darlint and shan't have to give you anything by hand. I didnt like the idea   but thought that it would be force of circumstances   I've got a feeling inside me

of sinking   do you know what its like   it's a feeling of
great excitement   probable excitement but not positive
Au revoir for such a short time that will seem so long till
Friday

PEIDI

Later Exhibit 66. These telegrams were sent during Freddy's leave, which – owing to the rift with his mother – he spent at Shakespeare Crescent. Four months later, Mr Graydon would tell the coroner: 'He lived with me as a paying guest between his voyages.'

Office of Origin – Barbican, London City
Office Stamp – Tilbury, Essex, 6 June, 1922
Handed in at 10.36   Received here at 10.52
To – Bywaters, Steamer Morea, Tilbury Docks
'Failed again perhaps 5 o'clock to-night'

33

Later Exhibit 67.

Office of Origin – London
Office Stamp – Tilbury, Essex, 7 June, 1922
Handed in at 12.34   Received here at 12.45
To – Bywaters, Steamer Morea, Tilbury Docks
'Have already said not going 231 see you and talk six'

Later Exhibit 68. 'Fisher' was the name used by Edith at the General Post Office in Aldersgate Street, which she had decided upon as a safe place for Freddy to send his letters. In Letter 35, Edith would claim that Percy had threatened to stop any correspondence arriving at her place of work; in Letter 4 she had said that he might 'ring up and ask them to stop anything that comes for me'. It is hard to see how he would actually have done this. But he had already questioned Miss Prior as to what time the firm shut up shop (Letter 14) and Edith was wary of his mood, which was the kind in which spouses employ a private detective or create a damaging public scene. In fact Percy would almost certainly not have dared to do either of these things. Scenes were for behind closed doors. As has been said, he seems to have held back from truly decisive action – such as asking his wife, directly, if she was having an affair – in favour of the pleasureless pleasures of stalking and sulking. Nevertheless, Edith could not be sure of what he might do. In *A Pin to See the Peepshow*, her fictional counterpart is always alert to the fearful possibility of problems at her place of work – and she was always, unfailingly, punctilious about her job. The dream life with Freddy never bled into her professional commitments; she compartmentalised completely, this most feminine of women, in a way that is stereotypically associated with men.

Both Mr Carlton and Miss Prior had displayed an awareness of the mail that she received (one wonders if he, at least, was also aware of the concentrated scribbling that went on during her work breaks). This did not matter in itself – unless they mentioned it to Percy – but Edith may have thought it borderline unprofessional for such letters to be arriving at her office. So she took the decision to use the GPO; which would generate its own complexities, as will be seen.

Office of Origin – London City
Office Stamp – Tilbury, Essex, 8 June, 1922
Handed in at 9.35   Received here at 10
To – Bywaters, Steamer Morea, Tilbury Docks
'Send everything Fisher care GPO call Monday.'

Later Exhibit 24, dated four days after the end of Freddy's leave.

As usual, the longed-for reappearance of Edith's darlingest boy had been almost anti-climactic. The difficulty of arranging meetings, the demands of family members and her job, above all the omnipresence of *him*... and Percy was especially on the alert during this late spring interlude. The Whitsun weekend of 3–5 June offered no opportunities, and no doubt left Edith in a fractious state that would have given her husband a grim and knowing satisfaction.

But after this, and with the sense of her lover's imminent departure pressing upon her, Edith sprang into action: she sent the telegrams as above and the couple met on the 6th, 7th and 8th. With the consequences set out in her letter? Not quite. This document is particularly interesting, in fact, because the mixture of truth and fabrication that it contains can be weighed with near-certain accuracy.

The first episode – when Percy claimed to be having a heart attack on the night of 8 June – did happen, as Edith testified openly to her defence counsel. Although on trial for her life, she was unable to keep a note of contempt out of her words: 'I knew when he had a heart attack; it was entirely different. The scene which took place on the night before Bywaters sailed was entirely due to the fact that I had been out that night and did not return till late.' Not perhaps the best way of putting things, but undeniably honest.

What did she mean, though, about Percy's heart attacks? Again, the victim presents something of a mystery.

During the trial, Mr Justice Shearman referred to his 'weak heart' as if it were a matter of record; although, if the judge had absorbed any of the post-mortem report prepared by Bernard Spilsbury, he would have known that this was not the case. Spilsbury referred (as has been mentioned) to 'slight fatty degeneration of the heart muscle', but to use the word 'weak' was frankly emotive. Richard Thompson told the police that his brother's heart 'had been affected since his birth'; again, however, this was not really backed by Spilsbury's findings.

Percy had passed his medical when he volunteered for the 14th Battalion, the London Scottish, in late 1915. Quite soon afterwards, however, he was hospitalised with a suspected cardiac issue. After six months he was discharged from the army and went on a belated honeymoon with Edith.

The facts are not entirely clear. Percy looks perfectly hale in photographs but his early years, spent in dank lodgings just a few steps from the Thames, may have generated physical weaknesses that his adult lifestyle – he was always a heavy smoker, possibly a drinker – did nothing to improve. The story was that, when he began army training, he increased his cigarette intake to around fifty a day in a deliberate attempt to bring on breathing problems and be deemed unfit, too ill to serve his country. Clever, really; although other young men had to fight in his place, and by 1916 they were assuredly just as reluctant as he. It has also been suggested that Percy boasted in the success of his ruse at avoiding obliteration at the Front, thus causing a degree of friction with his new father-in-law, whose eldest son Newenham had served in France.

Is the story true? It came from somewhere – presumably from the Graydon family and their supporters – so there is surely truth in it, as they were not the kind of people to invent such a thing.

Therefore it would seem that, although Percy's heart was neither perfectly healthy nor dangerously defective, the real question is what *he* thought about its condition. Was he a hypochondriac, faking illness when it suited him, or was he genuine in his fears? Most likely he was somewhere in between the two. In support of the more generous interpretation, Mr Graydon told the coroner's court that he 'had always, as long as I had known him, complained of his heart'. The sitting tenant Mrs Lester (no member of the Percy fan club) tended toward scepticism, saying to the police: 'Occasionally he had heart attacks, or I should say what I was told were heart attacks.' Like Edith, she used the term 'heart attack' to mean something milder than would be the case today, a 'funny turn' rather than a life-threatening event. Both the Thompsons were prone to fainting; with Edith, the cause was clearly gynaecological, but with Percy it is impossible to say, as the only actual evidence – the post-mortem – revealed almost nothing.

With regard to the incident on 8 June, however, it is safe to say that there was nothing wrong with Percy except rage. Edith's account of him in this letter – his ludicrous displays of 'manliness' (how threatened he must have felt in that regard), his spying and quizzing of the man 'Booth', his fierce attempts to prevent his wife from sleeping in another bedroom, his pathetic frustrated misery, which could see no satisfaction beyond that of making Edith miserable too... it all rings completely true.

As, indeed, does the incident in which Percy marched round to '231' and attempted to engage poor Mr Graydon in his cause.

Except that when Sir Henry Curtis-Bennett quoted from the letter, and asked Mr Graydon whether there was 'any truth in those two paragraphs', he received the reply: 'None whatever.'

If the denial itself were true, and there is absolutely no reason to think otherwise, this unequivocal tribute to Edith's powers of imagination constituted one of the most significant answers given at the trial; accordingly it was completely overlooked.

Avis, too, gave a firm statement that the incident was an invention. There is a faint possibility that she herself had invented it. Edith wrote that the account came from Avis, which is an unusual piece of elaboration. And the younger sister was – of course – deeply attracted to Freddy, almost certainly to the point of nurturing dreams of marriage; might she, therefore, knowing how much Edith adored their parents, have played the family card in a despairing attempt to stop the affair with Freddy in its tracks?

Not that Avis would have thought it was an affair. Fond though she was of Edith, she really did not know her at all; and more than anything she was astounded by the letters. The sound of shock was still in her voice when, in 1973, she said to an interviewer: 'I just couldn't believe that my sister... could have lent her name to anything like this. I – *disbelieved* her writing the letters.' This was the reaction of the woman in the street, impossible to comprehend today; one can imagine the contemporary equivalent of the furore caused by Edith's words, but not a replication of the shame. 'I couldn't lift my head up. I couldn't believe it. It knocked me back to such an extent.'

That is what Edith Thompson represented to the society of 1922.

Avis was on her side – staunchly, unswervingly, from the moment of Edith's arrest; although the sixteen months that led up to it had seen the sisters' relationship gravely complicated by the handsome Freddy Bywaters. And the end of this letter does not show Edith in a good light. There was Avis's heart laid quivering on a plate – 'she said she could hardly realise it' – and Edith, blithely dismissive, feeling nothing but her own feelings, scribbling a coda of sublime and childlike selfishness: 'Darlint its not an infatuation is it?'

A last point: her relief that she and Freddy had been seen on the 7th, rather than the 8th, implies that on the Thursday (the day that Percy sought to control) they had been physically close, perhaps kissing, in a not entirely private place. The following letter further implies that they had sex – where, who knows, but on a warm night they would most likely have gone to Wanstead Park – and that when Edith returned home that night, with a secret elusive glow upon her, the effect upon her husband, both staged and nothing of the kind, was a 'heart attack'.

❧

Mr F. Bywaters, P&O, RMS *Morea*, Marseilles
Postmark: London EC, 13 June 1922, 4.30 p.m.

Darlingest Boy,

I'm trying very hard – very very hard to B.B. I know my pal wants me to.

On Thursday – he was on the ottoman at the foot of the bed and said he was dying and wanted to – he had another heart attack – thro me.

Darlint I had to laugh at this because I knew it couldn't be a heart attack.

When he saw this had no effect on me – he got up and stormed – I said exactly what you told me to* and he replied that he knew thats what I wanted and he wasnt going to give it to me – it would make things far too easy for both of you (meaning you and me) especially for you he said.

He said he'd been to 231 and been told you had said you were taking a pal out [ie, as a cover story] and it was all a planned affair so was the last Thursday you were home and also Tuesday of last week at Fenchurch Street – he told them at 231 a pal of his saw us and by the description he gave of the man I was with it was you.

Thats an awful lie darlint because I told him I went to F St. for Mr. Carlton and saw Booth and spoke to him and I asked him the next day if Booth mentioned me and he said no – nothing at all.

We're both liars he says and you are making me worse and he's going to put a stop to all or any correspondence coming for me at 168. He said "Its useless for you to deny he writes to you because I know he does" – hence my wire to you regarding G. P. O.†

He also says I told him I wrote to you asking you not to see me this time – he knows very well I said last time – but I think he has really persuaded himself I said this time.

---

* Presumably Freddy had instructed Edith to ask for a separation – she may indeed have said 'exactly' what he told her, but she may also have written this in order to flatter him. That said, Percy's reported reply does sound very characteristic.
† In other words, Edith was asking Freddy to send his letters to the anonymous repository of the General Post Office.

I rang Avis yesterday and she said he came down there in a rage and told Dad everything – about all the rows we have had over you – but she did not mention he said anything about the first real one on August 1st – so I suppose he kept that back to suit his own ends   Dad said it was a disgraceful thing that you should come between husband and wife and I ought to be ashamed. Darlint I told you this is how they would look at it – they dont understand and they never will any of them.

Dad was going to talk to me Avis said – but I went down and nothing whatever was said by any of them. I told Avis I shd tell them off if they said anything to me I didnt go whining to my people when he did things I didnt approve of and I didnt expect him to – but however nothing was said at all.

Dad said to them "What a scandal if it should get in the papers" so evidently he suggested drastic measures to them.

On Friday night I said I was going to sleep in the little room – we had a scuffle – he succeeded in getting into the little room and on to the bed – so I went into the bathroom and stopped there for ½ an hr – he went downstairs then and I went into the little room quickly – locked the door and stopped there all night – I shd have continued to do so – but even a little thing like that Fate was against us – because Dad was over on Sat. and asked me if he could stay the night   I suggested he should sleep with him in the big bed – but Dad would not hear of it – so sooner than make another fuss I gave in.

On Saturday he told me he was going to break me in somehow – I have always had too much of my own way and he was a model husband – and in future on Thursdays the bedroom was to be cleaned out

He also told me he was going to be master and I was to be
his mistress and not half a dozen mens (his words) I don't
exactly know how to take this – Darlint, do you know
Avis said to me – Miss M'Donald saw you with Freddy
last week – of course I denied it – but she described my
frock – anyhow it turned out to be on Wed – so of course
it was all right – but you see – we are seen and by people
who know us and can't hold their tongues   Avis said she
was upset because you had gone for good – she said she
could hardly realise it   She also said that he said at 231
"I thought he was keen on you (Avis) but now I can see it
was a blind to cover his infatuation for Edie"

Darlint its not an infatuation is it? Tell me it isnt

I dont think there's anything else heaps of little things
were said that I can't remember but you can judge what
they were – because you know me and him

I'm writing a letter to Marseilles darlint – this is only a
summary of events

36

Later Exhibit 53. The 'I am doing something just a little for you' passage relates – fairly obviously – to a sexual encounter at the end of Freddy's leave (as hinted at in the previous letter). What is fascinating is that the tone, the wording, the erotic push–pull could just as well be describing the yearning to obliterate Percy.

It will be seen that Edith's scheme to send letters via the local GPO had run into difficulties. She was a genuinely capable businesswoman, but it is quite remarkable how silly she could be in other matters. It seems to have amazed her that the post office would refuse to hand over letters to a person who merely claimed to be Miss P (for Peidi) Fisher.

She extricated herself from the problem, but not without the involvement of the young Rose Jacobs, 'Rosie', something of a protégée of hers at Carlton and Prior. Here, too, Edith was airily heedless of consequence.

'Some time in June,' Rose would later tell the police, 'Mrs Thompson and I were in the basement. She said, "Would you mind writing a letter for me and address it to Miss Fisher c/o Carlton and Prior." I wrote at her dictation – "Dear Miss Fisher, I beg to call your attention to our next Committee Meeting which will be held on Friday (and a date I can't remember) and your presence will be required. Yours truly, R. James." Mrs Thompson sealed it in an envelope and kept it. I've no idea what the letter meant...'

The GPO 'solution' continued to be complicated, and later Freddy began writing to Carlton and Prior again. As the driver James Yuill told the police: 'About once a week – on the average – either a registered or ordinary letter arrived for Mrs Thompson, which I always put into her desk. They generally have foreign post marks. I do not know the contents.' Jim may have suspected a boyfriend, but he continued: 'I have known Mrs Thompson since she has been with the firm. I also knew her husband. He has called at the shop for her, and I have also seen him at the annual outing of the firm. They always appeared very affectionate [that word again], and I thought them a very happy couple.'

The real issue with this letter, as far as the Old Bailey was concerned, was the reference to ptomaine poisoning. Thrown in by Edith between the adventures of Miss Fisher, memories of the Isle of Wight and the evening from hell with her husband's relations.

※

Mr F. Bywaters, P&O, RMS *Morea*, Marseilles
Postmark: London EC, 14 June 1922

Darlint Pal,

I've come to the conclusion that you and I do absolutely mad things especially I.

I never have a thought about having those letters sent to G P O   I called there on Monday and was told that unless I could prove I was Miss P. Fisher I couldn't have them

I thought, this is a devil of a mess and wondered what to do

Eventually I decided to have some cards printed (this cost me 6/6) dont laugh, darlint and I also got Rosie to address an envelope to me at 168 in the name of Fisher

The card and envelope I showed to the man at the G P O today – fortunately it was a different man from yesterday Darlint I think it would be best to address all letters there until I tell you otherwise, dont you?   The watch I received quite safely darlint – you say in your letter it goes 10 minutes a day fast this isn't right is it? It should be slow

However yesterday I took it back and they promised to put it in order for me   I shall probably send it to Sydney

– is this what you wish   Also the cheque* I received
but not until today of course – I will try and cash it
tomorrow and let you know the result   In any case I will
put the money on the Hunt Cup [at Royal Ascot that
week] for you and for me   The Oaks money has not
been paid out† – I dont think we shall get it – at all – Jim
tells me the man got 7 days for obstructing the Police and
he (Jim) can't get hold of him now   Have also sent what
you asked me for – hope you got it safely

Darlingest boy, don't forget to answer the note I gave you
on your last night in England. I'll feel much happier if I
know. I'm so glad you're not sorry this time, no I'm not a
bit. I really begin to feel that I am doing something just a
little for you – not exactly doing something for you but
giving you something – a part of me, for you and no one
else – write and tell me that not only are you not sorry
this time but you're glad really glad because I am.

Mr. Carlton likes my hair cut – he noticed it, and told
me so immediately he saw me, I told you nobody but Lily
did didn't I – do you? you never said.

I wonder how my own pal is feeling – I'm feeling very
blue myself – an inactive sort of drifting feeling, that
can't be described – I suppose its really reaction – I'm
longing to hear from you next Monday – I hope its a lot.

On our birthday [27 June] you will be left Aden on
your way to Bombay – you'll be thinking of a girl whose
best pal you are in England won't you – I'll think of

---

*   Freddy had sent a cheque to pay for some racing bets, as listed at the end of the letter:
    the flat season was now reaching its height and much of the public would have been
    following it.
†   Edith had backed the winner of the Oaks at Epsom with a dodgy bookmaker.

you – all day every little minute – and keep on wishing you success as I can't be [sic] – Perhaps you can and as you are still hoping darlint – so shall I. Time hangs so dreadfully and just because I want to work it away we are not busy this week and are leaving at five. I suppose we shall thro the Summer now. Darlint, how can you get ptomaine poisoning from a tin of salmon? One of our boys Mother has died with it after being ill only three days.

One year ago today we went for that memorable ride round the island* in the char-a-banc do you remember? Last night when I went to bed I kissed you goodnight in my mind because that was the first time you kissed me.

Darlint this month and next are full of remembrances – arnt they?

I went to 49 [Seymour Gardens]† last night and sat and listened to ailments for about 2 hours – its awfully exhilarating especially when you feel blue. I also had a small row with them. He asked why Graham‡ never came to see us and I said "Why do you ask for him to come round when you know he's not allowed to."

This led to words of course and I was told that neither his mother nor his Father would tell him not to speak to me – my retort was that I know his Father would not but it would take more than any of them to convince me his

---

* A reference to the Isle of Wight holiday, always fixed in Edith's mind as a paradisiacal interlude.
† The Ilford home of her brother-in-law Richard.
‡ Graham was the son of Kenneth and Lily Chambers, who appear also to have attended this deadly gathering. Edith had provoked the 'words', as she called them, but my goodness who can blame her.

mother would not, and I wish to God I didnt have to go there – I feel really bad tempered when I come away.

I was taken faint in the train this morning – I didnt quite go off though – On Saturday I'm going to see a Doctor, I think it is best that I should – I dont like doing these silly things in public places – I've got my costume home – it looks very nice – I'm ever so pleased with it – but I dont want to wear it – I wish you could see me in it – what would you like me to do? Next week I'll be writing to the other end of the world to you darlint – I wish you didn't ever have to leave England, even if I didn't see you I should feel happier and safe because you would be near – but the sea and Australia sounds years and years apart, I do so much want my pal to talk to and confide in and my own man to lean upon sometimes.

*****

Have just come from the Bank, they cashed the cheque for me after a difficulty – asked me if I was F. Bywaters – I thought it best to tell the truth – as they might ask me to write [a] signature, so I said, "No." "Did you endorse the back?" "No" – "Just write your name on this paper please"   I did so, and they then asked me what authority I had from F. Bywaters to cash the cheque   I had your letter with me – showed it them – and they paid out. So much for that incident – What a mess we do get into!

I shall have to close now darlint, goodbye until Sydney – I always loved my only Pal and I do love so much my own boy – think of this all the time you are in Australia – I shall be thinking of you and wishing you were with

PEIDI

Written in pencil on plain envelope:

𓅓

Darlint,
We must give up horse racing
We have lost between us
30/- each way Scamp
20 /- " " Montserrat
10/- " " Pondoland (£6)
and won about 10/- on Craigangower* on which I had
2/6 each way for luck.

[...]

Don't send me any more money please darlint.

Goodbye and good luck –

always,

PEIDI

---

* Craigangower was third in the 1922 Derby, which Edith had briefly considered attending with Freddy.

Not put in evidence, and undated, but the reference to Marseille – and to 'our birthday' – means that it must belong around here.

❧

Darlingest boy I know always and ever, after all I shant be with you on our birthday – darlint I shall think of you such a lot & you will too eh?

I want to leave every little thing to you darlingest boy, I know you will decide and do what is best for two halves, only I should like to know all your thoughts & plans darlint, just to help me bear up & live, no exist thro this life, until it is time for us to be joined together. Could you write to me from Marseilles & tell me everything. Am I selfish? I believe I am because I am always thinking of myself & yet right deep down in my heart I want to do what is best for you.

Its fearfully hard to decide, thats why I want you to pour moi & whatever you say or do I shall accept without fear or doubt or question, & think all the time, even if it seems wrong to me, that you know it will, at some indefinite period be, best for us. This is right isnt it?

It gets harder and harder every time doesnt it. I seem to have lived years & years in that little one from 27.6.21 to now.

Goodbye darlingest [...]

PEIDI

Later Exhibit 25, this letter is yet another of minimal relevance to a court of law – it is beyond absurd that it should have featured in a murder trial – but it contains a great deal of fascinating material.

Firstly, Mr Graydon. Why was he spending so much time at 41 Kensington Gardens? There may have been nothing to it – they were a close family and it was normal, more so than now, to be in and out of relations' houses. There is certainly no suggestion that he wanted to get away from his own marriage. Was he, therefore, keeping an eye on his daughter's? He may have been trying to act as peacemaker and get things back on track (as when he refused to share a bed with Percy and insisted on Edith doing so). Or was his presence an expression of something more like concern, a desire to look out for his daughter's wellbeing? In her 1973 interview, Avis spoke very bluntly about Percy's 'violent' temper, and said: 'If my father had the least inkling that this was going on, he'd have gone and taken her away and he would have applied to somebody, to see that he didn't molest her!' Mr Graydon did not take Edith away, but was he on the scene to prevent any need for doing so?

As has been said, it is extremely difficult to assess these statements made by Avis, which are corroborated only up to a limited point. Unwelcome though such a view will be today, by the standards of 1922 it is possible to portray Percy as a liberal husband, who gave Edith a great deal of freedom that she frequently abused. So this question remains unresolved; not least because, although the mystery of other's people marriages is an eternal one, the institution of marriage has changed so much in the past century.

Secondly, the visit to the doctor. Although Edith was more than capable of making up at least some of these details, the assumption is that the incident did happen as described. For a start, it seems wholly credible that a 1920s doctor would have prescribed Burgundy for anaemia. It is well-known today that (contrary to the reported assertion) young people *can* suffer from the condition, especially women who suffer heavy monthly bleeds, but this doctor clearly – and almost certainly rightly – suspected a miscarriage, and had a shrewd idea that it may have been self-induced (a far more common occurrence than the pearl-clutchers would have dared admit). Did Edith really believe that she might be pregnant again? She had missed a period (the doctor prescribed pills to be taken 'until I am ill'); but, given that she and Freddy did not have full sex at the end of March, any baby growing inside her would have been Percy's. And why would she be pregnant by Percy, having avoided such an occurrence for some six and a half years of marriage? Why would she even be writing about it? Her allusion, instead, was to whatever had happened between her and Freddy on 8 June. In other words this ongoing talk of conception, although perhaps an indicator of Edith's confused ignorance, was really a reference to the act that might have generated it: once more she was wrapping a dark veil of intimacy around her lover.

As to the question of whether Freddy was 'disappointed'... Edith knew, of course, that he was not, that the last thing in the world he wanted was a baby. She knew it still more the following day, when she bustled off excitedly to pick up her letters. Freddy had already fobbed her off with a note sent from Dover, saying that he would write from Marseilles. Now she found another note, another semi-ghosting, saying that he would write from Port Said.

Even now, there is an almost unbearable wish that she had, at this point, let the whole thing go.

Freddy had sailed on 9 June and would be away for an unusually long time. He saw this, quite clearly, as an opportunity to distance himself from Edith. Had he spoken to his mother, to a friend? Had Avis said something to him? It is possible. She would have been discreet, of course. But something along the lines of 'Oh, Mum and Dad are ever so worried about Edie' (bearing in mind the faint possibility that she had said such a thing to Edith herself; see Letter 35) would have stuck in Freddy's mind. He was fond of the Graydon family; the parents whose lives he wrecked were like an aunt and uncle to him. Perhaps he was even trying to persuade himself to shift allegiance back to Avis, the good and simple girl, whose role in this story is nonetheless a nuanced one.

He had not broken his attachment to Edith. It was more

that he was trying to do so. And he may have needed no outside intervention. He knew, deep down, that the affair (such as it was) had no real future, that he was a very young man in a wide world full of wonderful things and pretty girls, that the words written by his lover had no meaningful application to real life. He may have wanted to rid himself of the frustration and sheer oddity of the whole business, the pathetic husband with whom Edith went about so tamely, even as she wrote about leaving him, asking him for a separation, poisoning him. As Freddy sailed away he seems to have resolved to act upon all this: to push aside the tangled magical webs that had been woven around him, and call a halt.

Therefore there is, thirdly, the end of the letter, which is heavy with the intimation of rejection. How easily it could have marked the end of the story; yet it seems never to have occurred to Edith to get her blow in first and sever the relationship. Her investment in it was too great. Like her lover, she had a life full of other things – a vast capacity for pleasure, a good job, a marriage that she could have improved or, in the end, abandoned – yet she had poured everything that she valued in herself into the vessel of this relationship, to the point where she felt herself unable, quite simply, to cope with its sudden shutdown.

'When Bywaters was away from 9 June until 23 September this year,' she was asked by Sir Henry Curtis-Bennett, 'were you getting as many letters from him as previously?'

'No.'

'What did you think from that?'

'I thought he was gradually drifting away from me.'

'Did you still love him very much?'

'Yes.'

And so, over the next fifteen weeks, she exerted herself to keep the 'love' alive, by means of the letters that were, of course, the heart of the matter: the metaphor for her other self.

Mr F. Bywaters, P&O, RMS *Morea*, Sydney
Postmark: London EC, 20 June 1922, 1.30 p.m.

Darlingest Boy I know,

This time last year I had won the sweepstake for the Gold
Cup [Royal Ascot], this year I have lost £1 10/- e[ac]h
way Kings Idler and the result is Golden Myth at 7 to
1, Flamboyant 20 to 1, and Ballyheron 8 to 1   I'm not
going to bet any more – even in horse racing the fates are
against me.

You get into Marseilles tonight I wonder how you're
feeling darlint, very blue – or not feeling anything at all –
just drifting – its hard either way isn't it?

I wish you had taken me with you darlint – I don't think
I will be able to stay on here all alone – there seems so
much to contend with – so long to "dance" when you'd
rather die and all for no definite purpose   Oh I'll pack
up now, I can't talk cheerfully – so I shan't talk at all
goodnight darlint.

It's Friday [16th] now, darlint nearly time to go, I am
wondering if you remember what your answer was to me
in reply to my "What's the matter" tonight of last year.*

I remember quite well – "You know what's the matter, I
love you"   but you didn't then darlint, because you do
now and its different now, isn't it? From then onwards

---

* During the holiday to the Isle of Wight, when Edith and Freddy were sitting alone
together on the verandah of their boarding house.

everything has gone wrong with our lives – I don't mean to say it was right before – at least mine wasn't right – but I was quite indifferent to it being either right or wrong and you darlint – you hadn't any of the troubles – or the worries you have now – you were quite free in mind and body – and now through me you are not – darlint I am sorry I shouldn't mind if I could feel that some day I should be able to make up to you for all the unhappiness I have caused in your life – but I can't feel that darlint – I keep on saying to myself that "it will – it shall come right" – but there is no conviction behind it – why can't we see into the future?

When you are not near darlint I wish we had taken the easiest way* – I suppose it is because I can't see you – can't have you to hold me and talk to me – because when you are in England I always want to go on trying and trying and not to give up – to see and feel you holding me is to hope on, and when I can't have that I feel a coward. The days pass – no they don't pass, they just drag on and on and the end of all this misery and unhappiness is no nearer in sight – is anything worth living for?

There are 2 halves in this world who want nothing on earth but to be joined together and circumstances persistently keep them apart – nothing is fair – nothing is just – we can't even live for ourselves – can we?

I suppose the week end will pass somehow – the only thought that helps is that you will talk to me on Monday.

Goodbye darlingest boy – I do wish you were here.

---

* A reference to the suicide pact that Edith sometimes mentioned in a low mood, as here.

Its Monday [19th] now darlint, that day you came up and took me to lunch at the Kings Hall [in 1921] do you remember?

Things are very quiet here and Mr. Carlton has taken 2 or 3 days off this week. He told me he would come up about Thursday – to fix up the outing on Saturday – that was the day last year that you and Avis came to an understanding – I wonder if that's the right way to put it.

Nothing happened over the week end darlint except that Dad came up on Saturday and did not go home in the evening. It's becoming a regular thing now – I wonder why?

When you are in Australia – darlint you will tell me all you do and where you go – everything – I want to know.

I shall be in Bournemouth when you're in Australia think about me darlingest boy – it won't be the holiday I anticipated will it? I certainly shan't learn to swim neither shall I be playing tennis it won't be nice at all – because I shan't even be able to escape things and beings by going up to town each day – but it's one of those things that have to be gone thro in this life I lead and all the railings against it won't alter a tiny bit of it – so I must dance thro somehow. Are you going to see Harold [her youngest brother]? if you do, try and knock a bit of sense into him please darlint pour moi and write and tell me what he is doing, how is he getting on – everything – he writes such nonsense that you can't tell from a letter what he really is doing. He's written to Doris Grafton and tells her, he is sending over her passage money and she is to come out and marry him –

and a lot more of rot like that – darlint I'm sure he's not normal sometimes.*

See what my pal can do for me, please

Won't you have a long time to wait for a letter from me this time, Darlint? I have been looking at the mail card and see you do not arrive in Australia until July 22nd – I'm so sorry – I wish I could afford to cable you a long long letter to somewhere before Sydney, or better still, to be able to phone to you and hear you say "Is that Peidi?"

*****

I went to see a doctor on Saturday he asked me lots of questions – could he examine me etc – I said no – then he said are you enciente? [sic] to which I replied "No, I think not," but explained to him how I felt   Eventually he came to the conclusion that I have "chronic anaemia" – which will probably turn to pernicious anaemia if I am not careful

I asked him exactly what this was and he said, "all your blood every drop turns to water."

I also asked him if it was a usual thing for any one to have and he said "No" only much older people suffer with it; as a rule only younger people when they have had an accident and lost a lot of blood, have you had one? he said

---

* Harold was working in Australia. There were family connections with the country – had they really wanted to do so, it would have been feasible for Edith and Freddy to move there. One of Mr Graydon's sisters lived in Australia, and Bill Graydon (perhaps escaping the horrors that had befallen his family) would later do so. Harold returned to Britain, did not marry and died in Shrewsbury in 1978.

I said "No" – because it wasn't really an accident and I didn't want to tell him everything – he might have wanted to see my husband.

But I expect that's what has really caused this anaemia – because I lost an awful lot of blood.

The doctor says I must drink Burgundy with every meal – 1 glass a day – I don't know how I am going to do that – I hate the stuff

He has given me some medicine as well and a box of pills to be taken until I am ill

Darlint are you disappointed it is only that? tell me please

*****

I've just come back from getting the Marseilles Mail at the G.P O

What an utterly absurd thing to say to me "Don't be too disappointed"

You can't possibly know what it feels like to want and wait each day – every little hour – for something – something that means "life" to you and then not to get it

You told me from Dover that you were going to talk to me for a long time at Marseilles and now you put it off to Port Said.

You force me to conclude that the life you lead away from England – is all absorbing that you havn't time nor inclination to remember England or anything England holds.

There were at least 5 days you could have talked to me about – if you only spared me 5 minutes out of each day But what is the use of me saying all this – it's the same always –

I'm never meant to have anything I expect or want   If I am unjust – I am sorry – but I can't feel anything at present – only just as if I have had a blow on the head and I am stunned – the disappointment – no, more than that – the utter despair is too much to bear – I would sooner go under today than anything.

All I can hope is, that you will never never feel like I do today – it's so easy to write "try to be brave" its so much harder to be so, nobody knows but those who try to be – against such heavy odds.

It's more to me than anything on this earth – to read what you say to me – you know this darlint, why do you fail me? What encouragement is it to go on living and waiting and waiting

Perhaps I ought not to have written this – perhaps I ought to have ignored having a scrap only, altogether – but how I feel and what I think I must tell you always

Darlint I hope you will never never never feel as miserable as

PEIDI.

39

Not put in evidence.

⚜

Mr F. Bywaters, P&O, RMS *Morea*, Sydney
Postmark: London EC, 21 June 1922, 3.30 p.m.

Since I have posted the first letter to Sydney darlint
a whole night & a whole day has gone by & I've been
thinking & thinking such a lot & feeling so awful about
it – I couldnt sleep for one little minute – thinking about
you & what you would think of me & how you would
feel when you received it.

I am sorry darlint – but I wrote how I felt it was awful –
& sometimes when you feel so terrible you write & think
very unjust and bitter things your feelings at the time
carry you away they did me please, please, darlingest boy
forgive me.

Pals should never feel hard & cross with one another
– should they? & we are still pals in spite of that letter,
aren't we? do write and tell me it makes no difference –
I shant feel "right" with myself until you tell me it has
made no difference; I feel an awful beast about it: I wish
I had not posted it at once but kept it for a day then I
should have torn it up. Please forgive me & try to excuse
your pal. She did feel so awfully down in the world when
she found that or felt that the best pal a girl ever had had
forgotten or neglected her.

She'll try hard not to transgress again

40

Not put in evidence and not dated. Clearly sent during this long period overseas, because Edith refers to the possibility that Freddy will not be writing to her – or at least not as often. It is placed here as a best guess, because its nobly accepting tone seems to follow logically from the angry distress of Letter 38, and the morning-after-the-night-before damage limitation exercise of Letter 39.

❦

Darlingest boy I know, can I wish you all & everything you wish me

Here's luck to us both in "The Glorious Adventure" may our next meeting be real, darlint, real & true & happy I'll let you have your own way about writing darlint, if you think it really best & I'll quite understand.

Goodbye & good luck darlint, the very very best luck that could happen to you darlint and

PEIDI.

41

Not put in evidence. There was nothing incriminating about it. Instead it shows Edith – her spirit regained – at her most gloriously alive, kicking up her heels, transgressing only in the manner of a woman enjoying her sexy powerful youth. One can see from it why she was always judged, even before she stood before a court; one feels the luscious overflow of her personality and the reaction of those around her, those who couldn't get enough of it (Mr Dunsford, Mr Carlton) and those who disapproved, who would have whispered about her in corners and delighted in saying that she wasn't even that good-looking, who the hell did she think she was? People who, even now, would be threatened by a woman who is just a little bit *too much*.

Then – intriguingly, significantly – comes the mention of the 'white & jade frock' in the shop window, the dress that Edith coveted but could not afford. Yet by the end of the letter, it will be noted, she was wearing it. Plus accessories.

So had she succumbed, and spent the huge sum of twelve guineas, more than two weeks' wages, buying that gorgeous new dress as well as the pale mauve voile? If so, then she did it without mentioning it to Freddy (darlint, I couldn't resist, your pal is a hopeless case, etc., etc.). And that, alone, makes it almost inconceivable, with this woman who yearned to tell everything. What surely happened was this: having recalled the white and jade georgette in all its beauty, she was unable to resist clothing her dream self in it; and so clearly did she see the picture that she made – bursting into the fried fish shop like a goddess in white fur – that she conveyed that incandescent image to Freddy, and made it more real than reality.

How to explain that to the Old Bailey? Her counsel tried. In his closing speech Sir Henry Curtis-Bennett, who up to that point had not done the best of jobs, came into his own. Instead of fencing with the ghosts of the prosecution case, he was able to offer an interpretation of his enigmatic client that came very close to the truth, presenting her through the artistic prism of his own intelligence. He picked out the scattered fragments of incriminating material in the letters, so painstakingly stuck together in order to build a case, and said to the jury: 'It is suggested that those statements mean: "Murder him". Our answer is that it is fiction, as much fiction as *Bella Donna*.' It was a reading of the story ahead of its time, out of tune with the contemporary mood. Nevertheless he sought to flatter the jurors into believing themselves better than that.

> You have got to get into the atmosphere of this case. This is no ordinary case that you are trying... Am I right or wrong in saying that this woman is one of the most extraordinary personalities that you or I have ever met? Bywaters truly described her, did he not, as a woman who lived a sort of life I don't suppose any of you live in – an extraordinary life of make-believe... You have read her letters. Have you ever read, mixed up with criticisms of books, mixed up with all sorts of references with which I shall have to deal, more beautiful language of love? Such things have been very seldom put by pen upon paper. This is the woman you have to deal with, not some ordinary woman. She is one of those striking personalities met with from time to time who stand out for some reason or another.

How far he carried his listeners, before the solicitor general and the judge repossessed the case, is unknowable.

Mr F. Bywaters, P&O, RMS *Morea*, Melbourne
Postmark: London, 23 June 1922, 2.30 p.m.

> Today is Friday darlint by the day not the date the day you took me to lunch at the Holborn – first time when I let you see and told you some things that no one else knew. I wanted to ask you if you remembered anything about last Wednesday – I'm not going to tell you – just tell me if you do remember & what it is.

Nothing else of any importance has happened darlint since I talked to you last – we still argue about you & I suppose we always shall. Tonight we are going to a Garden Party & Fete in aid of the Seamens Orphanage at Wanstead.

Mrs Birnage & her people are on the Committee & she is partaking in the some [sic] of the amusements I believe & tomorrow is the outing – so perhaps this week end will pass a little more quickly   I shall still have to wait 5 days after Sunday to hear from you   Darlint I havent sent your watch on to you, because you have not told me what to do about it & I especially asked you so I shall keep it until I do hear.

It was rather funny on Tuesday Mr Dunsford offered to take me up in the Car and let me stand on the roof of it to see the Prince [of Wales] on the next day – of course I was rather bucked about it and told him on the Tuesday evening   He did make a fuss – said he objected & a lot more nonsense & asked how I was going to get on to the roof – I darent tell him Mr Dunsford was going to hoist me up – he would have been "terribly shocked" so I said I could climb up by a rope ladder at the side of the motor

However I went in spite of all objections & saw everything beautifully it was rather fun

Last week on one evening I went up West to buy a frock for the outing – I did so – I think you would like it – it is pale mauve voile embroidered in grey on the bodice & on the skirt & a sash of darker mauve ribbon   It was from the shop I saw the White & jade frock I told you about & I asked them if they had still got it – they had & showed it to me – it was lovely & so was the price – 12 guineas – so it had to stay in the shop

I was looking into a shop window up there & went to move away & found your sister & her fiancé* standing beside me, also looking in the window.

I suppose she was trousseau hunting   of course she's not coming to town after she is married, is she?

*****

Darlint, your own pal is getting quite a sport

On Saturday I was first in the Egg & Spoon race & first in the 100 yards Flat race & 3rd in the 50 yards Flat race

Everybody tells me I'm like a racehorse – can get up speed only on a long distance & my reply was "that if a thoroughbred did those things then I felt flattered"

Then I was M C for the Lancers† we stood up 10 Sets had some boys in from an adjoining cricket field   I sat on the top of the piano & made a megaphone of my hands & just yelled – nothing else – Mr Carlton said all that shouting was worth 2 long drinks afterwards so I had 2 double brandies & Sodas with him

We had a very good day indeed: In fact I think I enjoyed the actual outing better than last year – until we got to Lpool St coming home & then he started to make a fuss – says I take too much notice of Dunsford & he does of me & created quite a scene. I am really sick of this sort of thing – he gets jealous & sulks if I speak to any man now.

---

*   Freddy's older sister Lilian, who married later that year.
†   A square dance for couples. Presumably Edith, as Mistress of Ceremonies, called out instructions.

Darlint, if we're ever together for always & you get jealous I'll hate you – I shant be your pal

Im so stiff & sore today I can hardly move   I left the house 10 mins earlier than usual this morning – to make certain of catching my train: I was so stiff

This time last year you were able to rub me & gradually take that stiffness away do you remember?

It was rather fun on Thursday at the Garden Party – They had swings & roundabouts & Flip Flaps cocoa nut shies Aunt Sallies – Hoopla & all that sort of thing   I went in for them all & on them all & shocked a lot of people I think. I didnt care tho' & going home Mr Birnage said he'd like some fried Fish and potatoes – I'd got rather a posh frock on – wht georgette & tied with rows & rows of jade ribbon velvet & my white fur & a large wht hat, but all that didn't deter me from going into a fried fish shop in Snaresbrook [near Ilford] & buying the fish & chips

Getting it home was the worst part – it absolutely smelt the bus out: I didnt mind – it was rather fun   only I wished you had been with me: I think 2 halves together would have enjoyed themselves better than 1 half by herself

*****

Today is your birthday & our birthday – Darlint I wonder if you are thinking about it at all, I am

I sent you greetings by cable this time it was the only way I could celebrate darlint I wanted you to receive it on the exact day but I'm afraid you won't its not my fault darlint its the fault of that ship of yours not being within radio range of either Aden or Bombay on the 27th

Darlingest own Pal, I love you heaps & heaps more than yesterday and such a lot less than I shall tomorrow.

Miss Prior is going away tomorrow I expect I shall have plenty to do then until I go away

Only 2 more days before I hear you talk to me I hope its a lot – I do so want it to be.

Goodbye for now darlingest pal to

PEIDI.

42

Not put in evidence.

※

Mr F. Bywaters, P&O, RMS *Morea*, Melbourne
Postmark: London, 27 June 1922

June 27/1922

The birthday of the Palship of 2 halves

This is the real birthday darlint just the same as I always
wish I wish today & hope everything will not always be
in vain.

The birthday of the best pal a girl ever had.

Many happy returns darlint, may everything you
undertake in your life be successful

PEIDI

43

Later Exhibit 26. Edith's description of her cosy little late morning drinks with Mr Carlton may have been inserted in an attempt to incite jealousy, but they actually make one think – cynically – what a shame it was that she did not swop allegiance and have an affair with her boss instead; it would have represented a very different kind of escape, but escape nonetheless. Yet however much she enjoyed the zest of flirtation, the wink and clink of the glass, a Mr Carlton was not what she wanted. Which is to her credit, in a way, although such an anti-romantic course of action would have caused far less damage to all concerned.

Class, undeniably, played its part in her choice of lover (for it *was* a choice; however much Edith may have thought of it as fate, she had chosen Freddy). She never in her life met a man who could respond to what the writer Beverley Nichols, who attended the trial, called her 'innate quality of aristocracy'. The phrase had nothing to do with class in the narrow sense. What it described was the specialness in Edith that constantly sought an outlet, and that believed itself to have found one in her sister's 'beau', her brother's little school friend: like Percy Thompson, a boy next door. When she met Freddy again, at the start of 1920, he had of course begun to travel the world – while she, the woman of experience, still dreamed of Tunbridge Wells – and he carried with him an air of expansiveness and freedom. He was also, frankly, very good-looking, with that blend of the vulnerable and the hard-edged that is peculiarly desirable.

Yet it is significant, all the same, that Edith should have invested her soul in this penniless teenager, as though despite her desire to push outwards and upwards she lacked the daring to do so beyond Manor Park, the close circle of terraced streets in which she had grown up. Class, again. Edith had true refinement, even if she sometimes cut loose; Freddy was innately intelligent and gallant, he was able to appreciate an unusual woman, but he was still a very rough diamond when compared with the Mr Carltons and Mr Birnages. One notes how Edith often corrected mistakes in his letters (always doing it with care for his self-esteem) and sought to elevate him, probing towards the better part of him even as she inflamed the worst.

On 14 October 1922, eleven days after the murder, possessions found in his quarters on the *Morea* were opened at Limehouse Police Station, as reported by a detective:

> I opened them by means of keys found on prisoner Bywaters when he was searched... The trunk and brown paper parcel contained Clothing. In the ditty box I found 5 bundles of letters, some of which contained newspaper cuttings; an automatic pistol; 25 rounds of ammunition...

'I was,' Freddy wrote to the home secretary at the start of 1923, 'in the habit of carrying either a knife or a revolver.'

Beneath his aspect of a Rupert Brooke of the oceans, there lay, immutably, something of the thug. In an earlier age he might have been a highwayman, adored by the girls as he stood firmly on the gallows. Edith was such a girl, in her way, and a kind of sullen abasement pervades much of the letter at the thought that she might be losing her boy. Lilian Bywaters; the little woman in Ilford who asked after Freddy (was he *so* desirable, and to every damn female he encountered?); the GPO; the giggling idiots of Ilford – Molly and Mr Derry – to whom Edith was an object of get-her fascination; and of course Freddy himself, who again was pulling away from her, although he had not brought himself to stop writing altogether...

And Edith's answer to all this, a foolish and despairing one, was to ask why he was not 'sending' something. Having moved on from ptomaine, she suggested – for who knows what wild reason – bichloride of mercury.

'Does a laundry steward in a ship,' asked the solicitor general in his closing speech (and how one can imagine the hefty, gown-shrugging irony), 'even one interested in chemistry, study bichloride of mercury?'

Mr F. Bywaters, P&O, RMS *Morea*, Fremantle
Postmark: London EC, 4 July 1922

Darlingest Boy,

First of all last Sunday week a lady I dont know her name
– we all call her "2 jam pots high" asked after "that nice
curly headed boy". We met her in Ilford in the evening – I
said when I last saw you – you were quite well   I wasn't
by myself Darlint – he was with me

I felt quite jealous that she should remember you all this
time. Then last Wednesday I met your mother and she
cut me   I wasn't prepared for it either – I saw her coming
towards me and thought "as she spoke to me last time we
met that there is no reason why she shouldn't this time".
And as she came up I just smiled, bowed, said "How do
you do" – she just took no notice whatever and walked
on. I can't explain how I felt – I think I wanted to hit
her more than anything – things get worse and worse –
instead of just a tiny bit better every day

On Thursday afternoon I went to the G P O for the Port
Said Mail and encountered the first man that I saw before
– he handed me a registered envelope from you (which
contained the garters – thank you very much darlint)
and told me if I had an address in London I couldn't have
letters addressed to the G.P.O. – I told him I hadn't but I
dont think he believed me anyway he didn't give me your
Port Said letter and I hadnt the patience to overcome (or
try to) his bad temper.

I went again on Monday and got it, a different man was
on duty – when I read it I didnt feel very satisfied darlint

it didn't seem worth waiting all that time for – 24 days – however I won't talk about it – you ought to know by now how I feel about those things.

In one part of it you say you are going to still write to me because it will help, in another part you say – "Perhaps I shant write to you from some ports – because I want to help you" I don't understand – I try to – but I cant – really I cant darlint – my head aches – just with thinking sometimes

Last Friday last year – we went to see "Romance"* – then we were pals and this year we seem no further advanced

Why arnt you sending me something – I wanted you to – you never do what I ask you darlint – you still have your own way always – If I dont mind the risk why should you? whatever happens cant be any worse than this existence – looking forward to nothing and gaining only ashes and dust and bitterness

I'm not going to ask dad about you at all – I'm not going to say anything to anybody – they can all think the worst of me that is possible – I am quite indifferent

Miss Prior is on holiday and the only person in the world that is nice to me is Mr Carlton – I have had 2 half days off and am having another to-morrow afternoon – all this time off makes me think of last year – when you were with us – rushing home to see you

I've had a brandy and soda some mornings – about 11.30 and a half bottle of champagne between us other

---

* A film released in 1920, later remade with Greta Garbo.

mornings and I learn such a lot of things that are interesting too

This morning on the station I saw Molly – talking and laughing with Mr Derry – in case you don't remember the name – it's the little man in the "White Horse"

I've never seen her talk to him before altho she has passed me on the platform talking to him several times (me talking to him I mean). I bowed – said good morning to him as I passed and have since been wondering if they have told each other what they know about me.

Never mind, a little more bad feeling can't hurt – there is such a lot of it to contend with will you tell me if you'd rather I didnt write?

PEIDI

Have you studied "Bichloride of Mercury"?

44

Not put in evidence.

Again Edith was trying to reclaim her darlingest boy, although not this time by playing the old 'send me something' card. Instead she reminded him of their physical closeness: her periods had resumed and she had been terribly ill, although not in the same way as before. By that, presumably, she meant that she had not miscarried. No great surprise there.

Then she began to plead, with an abjectness that disdained cheap games such as playing it cool and that had, in an odd way, more dignity. For Freddy had gone one step further. He was now saying that he would not see Edith when he returned to England at the end of September. And he was trying very hard to hold to this position, although if he had absolutely meant it he could have simply cut off all contact; the fact that he did not do so gave her hope that she would win him back.

Incidentally it is hard to understand why, if Freddy was refusing to see her in the autumn, she believed that he would see her the following January. The fact that she did not leave it, that she instead refused to let him go, ensured another outcome altogether for that month.

※

Mr F. Bywaters, P&O, RMS *Morea*, Fremantle
Postmark: London, 12 July 1922, 3.30 p.m.

Darlint Pal,

I dont think Ive got anything to tell you just the ordinary things happen every day & I somehow don't think you want me to talk to you about those: I went to Henley last Thursday – with the Waldorf man – I previously had the invitation but refused on the plea of business – but on the Tuesday night Mr Carlton asked me if I'd like Thursday off so I rang up & made arrangements to go. We got there about 12.30 and had lunch at Phyllis Court at the invitation of an M.P. Mr Stanley Baldwin [who in 1923 became Prime Minister for the first time] – it poured with rain all the afternoon & was altogether miserable – I got home by 6 45 p m

I've had a lot of time off this fortnight – 2 Sats 3 half days & last Thursday & go [home] about 4 every day – I dont know what to do with myself – why are you not in England when Miss Prior is away – look what a lot of time we could have together   Last Saturday I was ill the first time since I told you about it last trip – in the evening I went to the Doctor & told him, he seemed pleased – I suppose because his pills had done their work. I felt terribly bad & could not have gone to business had I had to do so – fortunately I had the morning off

It wasnt the same sort of ill feeling that it was that time before tho

On Saturday we go for our holiday   Shall I call it? It won't be what I anticipated will it no swimming lessons or tennis or anything that I'd really enjoy. However I must make the best of it & dance – I'm so tired of it all tho – this dancing and pretending

I've not packed my peach sports coat. I dont want to wear it this time – so Ive left it behind.

This is the last day for posting mail to Fremantle & Ive not had your promised letter from Aden.

If it is at the G P.O lunch time perhaps I'll have some more to talk to you about before I post this

I'll leave it for a little while anyway.

Avis has just been round here & I was in the office having a brandy & soda with Mr. Carlton; he asked her to have one too – I think she feels very flattered – am I horrid I really believe I am – tell me – but everything in this world seems so topsy turvy – I'd give anything to be her – free I mean & I think she'd change places with me this minute if we could – but we can't – so I mustnt moan it'll become a habit.

By the way I told you about Molly & Mr Derry.

I think it was Tuesday he said to me "So you know that young lady I was talking to the other morning?"

Me. No, I dont know her.

He: But she knows you & all about you.

Me. Oh, probably. Lots of people know me & about me that I'd rather not know

He: I believe you're jealous.

Darlint, just try & imagine me being jealous of her talking to him of all people. I have to laugh right out loud when I think about it. Some men have such a high opinion of themselves & their charms that I'm afraid I can't climb up to them.

I wonder what "my only pal" is doing now & how he is feeling – when I try & contrast my feelings of going away

this year to those of going away last year* I really wonder
if Im living in the same world – I suppose I am – but its
not the same world to me darlint – that world last year
didnt contain a pal – just one only, to whom I need not
wear a mask – but this year does – altho he is still so very
far away that I go on wearing that mask to everyone I
meet – every day – I wonder if there ever will be a time
when I shall appear as I really am – only you see me as I
really am – the "pretence me" is my ordinary every day
wearing apparel, the "real" me is only visible for such a
very short time when you're in London. Darlingest Boy
– I cant bear to think of you being in England and not
seeing me – must we be so very strict & stern – cant you
imagine what your only pal – (no, not pal – I'm talking
to you darlint as the girl that loves you, I'm talking to my
veriest own lover not as & to a pal) will feel like knowing
you're in London, & expecting to see you at every turn
& really knowing deep down in her heart that she won't.
Must you be so cruel darlint? See me once – for one
whole day together for all that time & I won't mind if I
dont see you any more the whole time you are in London
I can't bear it if you go away without seeing me again –
nearly 4 more months after September – that makes it
January 1923 its too long to wait […]

Am I selfish? No I dont think its a selfish feeling cos its
for both of us – I'm fighting for our rights to break down
that reserve that you're going to build up against yourself
& between

PEIDI.

45

Later Exhibit 52.

It is clear, from this, that Edith was pushing through Freddy's attempts to pull away, and that these were anyway ambivalent on his part. On the one hand he was telling her, wisely, not to think about him. At the same time he was engaging in dialogues about *Bella Donna*... and here one sees Edith's detailed reflections upon the central character, who resembled what would become her own public image, and whom she herself disliked so much (as her defence attempted to explain to the Old Bailey – see Letter 29).

The passage about the age difference is fascinating and touching. Edith never shied away from her own vulnerability. Women are still susceptible to the fear of ageing – it remains a weapon that society uses against them, even (or perhaps especially) when they do not 'show their age' – and, in 1922, a woman of almost thirty was no longer young. In this letter she was not wielding power over the man who was her junior; she was admitting to the fact that she might lose it.

At the Old Bailey, Bywaters was asked what he thought Edith had meant by her words. He answered bluntly: 'Her age and mine. She was eight years older than me, and she felt it.' Even in such circumstances, that cannot have been an easy thing for her to hear. And those in the courtroom should have heard it properly too: it challenged the entire narrative of the case against Edith.

☙

Mr F. Bywaters, P&O, RMS *Morea*, Colombo
Postmark: London W1, 14 July 1922, 7.15 p.m.

Darlingest boy – you worry me so much – what do you mean you say "I want to be in England to look after you." I can understand that and I want you to be here also – but you then say "I want you to look after me too" What's the matter darlint, are you ill? is anything the matter that I could help you in at all. I do believe you've been ill – oh darlint why are you such miles away – why arent we together – so that I could help you. Would you like a pillow? the pillow that only Peidie can give you – I'd love to have you here now so that I could give it you. Do tell me what's the matter darlingest boy – I shall worry and worry all the time until you write and tell me. Its Thursday and I've just come from the G.P.O. with the Aden mail. Isn't it late this time darlint it's usually in on a Monday or at latest Tuesday. However I've got it and that's all that really matters   Darlingest boy didnt I say a long time ago "Don't trust Dan." Of course I didnt mean that in the sense you have told me he couldn't be trusted in [these circumstances are unknown] but my instinct was right wasn't it? You will be careful won't you darlint pour moi? I dont want to ever know or think that my own boy is in any predicament of that sort – because I'll be too far away to help won't I? The thought of anything like that makes my blood cold – I'll be always worrying. I'm writing this letter rather early to Colombo – because I'm going away tomorrow [to Bournemouth] and I shan't have an opportunity of writing to you again for a fortnight. Perhaps I could manage a letter card tho anyway you'll understand wont you darlint pal? I dont mind a bit pencil as long as its words on paper – it doesn't matter – because they're what you say and think and do – a letter darlint is like food only you have food everyday to keep you alive and I have a letter every how many days? 14 sometimes and I have to keep alive on that all that time. About Bella Donna – no I dont agree with you about her darlint – I hate her – hate to think of her – I don't think other people made her what she was – that sensual pleasure loving greedy Bella Donna was always there. If she had originally been different – a good man like Nigel would have altered her darlint – she never knew what it was to be denied anything – she never knew "goodness" as you and I know it – she was never interested in a good man – or any man unless he could appease her sensual nature. I don't think she could have been happy with nothing – except Baroudi on a desert island she liked [...] the luxury of his yacht the secrecy with which he acted all bought with his money – that's what she liked.

Yes she was clever – I admire the cleverness – but she was cunning there is a difference darlint, I don't admire that [...]

If she had loved Baroudi enough she could have gone to him – but she liked the security of being Nigel's wife – for the monetary assets it held

She doesn't seem a woman to me – she seems abnormal – a monster utterly selfish and self loving

Darlint this is where we differ about women.

I usually stand up for them against you and in this case its the reverse but honestly darlint I dont call her a woman – she is absolutely unnatural in every sense

You do say silly things to me – 'try a little bit every day not to think about me' – doesn't that 'trying' ever make it worse – it does for me always

About the 'age' passages in 'The Fruitful Vine' – I marked them because as I read they struck me as concerning you and I

Darlint I didn't do it with malice every passage in any book I read that strikes me as concerning 2 pals I mark – it doesn't matter what they are about

I hadn't mentioned the subject any more had I?

My veriest own lover I always think about the 'difference' when I'm with you and when I'm away sometimes when I'm happy for a little while I forget – but I always remember very soon – perhaps some little thing that you might say or do when we're together reminds me.

Sometimes I think and think until my brain goes round and round   'Shall I always be able to keep you' 8 years is such a long time – it's not now – it's later when I'm 'Joan' and you're not grown old enough to be 'Darby.' When you've got something that you've never had before and something that you're so happy to have found – you're always afraid of it flying away – that's how I feel about your love

Don't ever take your love away from me darlint – I never want to lose it and live

[...]

PEIDI.

46

Not put in evidence, this was a letter-card sent from Bournemouth. The meaning of M.H.R. remains obscure, as does the reference to Chorley, which is in Lancashire. Chorleywood, in Hertfordshire, was on the outer reaches of the Metropolitan line, so it is just possible that Freddy and Edith went there on 27 July 1921 – albeit that was a Wednesday, and by then she was back at work. So: a mystery.

❦

Mr F. Bywaters, P&O, RMS *Morea*, Colombo

27/6/21

Today is 27th M H R

Chorley today last year

PEIDI

Darlingest Pal,

I'm on the Boat that has been all round the I of W. landed at Ventnor – I'd rather go there than Cornwall I think: please take me – He says we're coming next year – are we?

Not put in evidence. This time the reference is self-explanatory: on Sunday 31 July, 1921, the couple had visited Kew Gardens.

꧁

Mr F. Bywaters, P&O, RMS *Morea*, Colombo
Postmark: London EC, 31 July 1922, 6.15 p.m.

29th

I am leaving for London today.

This day last year I was at Kew with my pal.

I shan't post this in B'mouth, probably shan't get an opportunity. I love you so much darlint,

I always shall.

PEIDI.

Not put in evidence, 'By the day', which meant the Friday of that week rather than 4 August, referred to the fact that Freddy had left the Thompsons' house on the 5th in 1921. With her willingness to confront bathos Edith wrote – as if of the Champs-Élysées – of their parting on the corner of 'Morris Avenue', a road very near the Manor Park church where she married Percy.

The paragraph about the 'coming year' is another example of the unconscious foreknowledge that can make these letters so painful to read.

As for the reference to the 'Russell case': this, yet again, raises questions about Percy (who must have been sorely tried by Edith and Avis during the gloriously described holiday – how one can picture the attempts to *épater* the *petit bourgeoisie* of Bournemouth and the relief of crossing the water to Ventnor – girl fun, pure and simple, in a life controlled by men).

A cause célèbre in 1922, the case was a divorce suit in which a wife, accused of adultery, made a counter-claim that her husband had subjected her to 'Hunnish' scenes and an attempt at rape. Did Edith mean, quite literally, that Percy was guilty of such things ('Hunnish' was never defined, but it clearly implied sexual violence)? Well: his insistence upon his 'rights' could well have escalated into a physical seizure of them – the episode in which he tried to prevent Edith sleeping in another bedroom (Letter 35) certainly implies such a thing. To a modern reader, for sure, this sounds appalling. At the same time one has to be scrupulous and admit another possibility, which is that Edith was exaggerating in order to get sympathy – and as a way to posit the familiar notion that she might escape from her husband, which by this time Freddy surely knew she would not do. If she had evidence that would help her in a divorce case, why not try to use it?

Mr F. Bywaters, P&O, RMS *Morea*, Bombay
Postmark: London EC, 4 August 1922, 4.30 p.m.

The bestest pal a girl ever had.

I wonder if you remember what today by the day is I keep on thinking about it & of you & wondering if you're thinking as well about leaving me all by myself at 41 for good, when Morris Avenue corner became one of the treasured spots in our memory   Last Tuesday was the memorable 1st [the day of the Bank Holiday showdown] such a lot seems to have happened in that little time – & yet such a little – everything that we wanted to happen hasnt & everything that we didnt want to happen has

However perhaps this coming year will bring us the happiness we both desire more than anything in this world – & if it doesn't? we'll leave this world that we love so much – cling to so desperately.

We are finishing at 168 at 1 p m today I don't know what the dickens I shall do with myself – everyone I know is away – I can't even get a lunch or a tea out of anyone – or even a few hours amusement.

Last holiday breaking up I had a Pal waiting for me – a Pal that really wanted to see me for myself alone & who really wanted to take me to lunch – for nothing

On Tuesday you're starting for home – how I shall count the days now & look forward so much – I dont know to what because you say you won't see me – but I shall hope & hope & hope that before Sept 23rd you'll melt just a teeny weeny bit towards your pal   I wonder if you've got anything to tell me or do you still feel very reticent about all your doings while you're away.

On Sept 24th I wonder if you would like to remember to her that it is Avis's birthday – I know she'd like to remember

Dont say I didn't tell you in time this year.

I am enclosing a piece of the evidence of the "Russell" Case

Have you read it all? I have found it very interesting & a portion of the evidence on enclosed slip struck me as being very similar to evidence I could give – does it you?

I've wished & wished all the time it has been on that she could be proved innocent but the jury have found her innocent in the case of the 2 co-respondents mentioned – but she will come up for trial again regarding the "man unknown." Write & tell me what you think about it please darlint

[...] I had an absolutely rotten holiday the Boarding house was terrible – "Ladies are requested not to smoke in the house" – no drink allowed indoors and not too much grub – even for ladies – I was sorry for the men

However we made the best of a bad job – there were 27 in the house & not a very sociable crowd either or rather they were too quiet. I think Avis & I managed to liven them up a bit. We did some mad things – climbed a tree in front of a row of Boarding Houses & had our photos taken up it (Avis & I I mean) everyone in the Bdg. Hses were watching us from the windows & had donkey rides up & down the front: the people stopping in our

Boarding Hse could hardly believe (they said) I'd been married as long as I had & I was the age I am: they said I only seemed a child   I felt glad they thought this pour vous – altho I really felt very old & miserable & lonely all the time I was away.

Bournemouth is a very stiff starchy place – not a bit like the Island – I'm very glad we didnt go there last year – that is one holiday I can look backward on & think I thoroughly enjoyed the holiday & myself in an impersonal way. You'd like Ventnor Darlint when we complained to the people there about B'mth being stiff – no smoking no drinking – (by the way there is only 7 licenses granted to the whole of B'mth & Boscombe & its a very big town 90,000 inhabitants) they said "There's nothing like that about Ventnor you can walk about naked if you like"   Thats the place for us we said & this man recommended us to a very nice Boarding Hse right on the front with 2 front lawns very like Osborne Hse [at Shanklin] last year.

We said to the Pier Master at Ventnor "I suppose you're going to dust us for 2d going off & 2d going on (they do in B'mth) as well" & he said "Oh, no, we want your Company here & not your money" & shook hands with us

Darlint I do so want a holiday with you next year please – I must do the wages now – last holiday you came with me to draw them didn't you?

Do you still love me as much? I do you – no more

PEIDI.

49

Not put in evidence, hence no mention of Miss Tucknott ever reached the Old Bailey. One notes the way in which Avis dragged her into the conversation, in defence of Edith and as a smart way of putting Percy on the back foot; the relationship between the sisters was close at this time. It may be stretching a point to think that this was because Avis had said something to Freddy in advancement of her own cause, and had hopes of him once more, but the overall impression is of a young woman behaving like Edith's happy equal.

Presumably the two books for which Edith was waiting had never actually been ordered by Freddy. As if to restore some balance to *their* relationship, she offered the story of the man looking for 'Romance': the old trick of trying to provoke, to arouse some jealousy.

Then Edith, who was full of the knowledge that Freddy had 'already started home', wrote the passage about her dreams; as if her unconscious self had intuited the forces of destiny moving towards her, with the gigantic indifference of the RMS *Morea*.

Mr F. Bywaters, P&O, RMS *Morea*, Aden
Postmark: London EC, 15 August 1922, 2.30 p.m.

Do you know darlint, I dont think I can talk to you very much – I dont feel like it a bit – I want to see you & feel you – not to imagine you & then talk, it's so awfully hard.

When I came back to 168 I went to G P.O. & got a letter & the discussion on the book from Bombay & a note from Colombo – I havent heard any more – I wonder if you have written to me since & when I shall get it if you have – it seems such a long time since you went, three or four times longer than when you go to Bombay, and now

you have already started home & I am writing to Aden –
a month is 12 when you're not in England & it will always
be the same darlint – that will never alter, whatever else
does

I meant to have mentioned before that the Turkish
Delight last time was stale – not a bit nice. Darlint, I'm
not ungrateful and I'm not looking a gift horse in the
mouth – as you might think, I'm just telling you this so
that if you liked you could tell the old chap from whom
you bought it, what you thought of him. I should want
to, I know & I think you will too. Dont be cross anyway
will you?

I've read one or two books while you've been away – &
I've not marked them – I've wanted you to find the
small things that interest us, out for yourself   I've got
the "House of Baltazar" [by William John Locke] now
& have just started it. The two you ordered for me, never
came in – the girl still says they weren't ordered there –
so I didnt bother – I didn't want to do it for myself – I
wanted you to do it for me – so I'll wait until you're in
England again

On Tuesday we went at 2 & I went to the "Waldorf"
to tea – & while waiting in the vestibule by myself
a gentleman came up to me – raised his hat & said
"Good afternoon, are you Romance?" I thought he was
mad & turned away & sat on a couch – he followed &
continuing the conversation said "Im sorry if youre not,
but I have an appointment here with a lady with whom
I've corresponded thro a "Personal Column," she calls
herself "Romance" & she was to wear a black frock &
a black lace hat." (I was wearing the blk frock with the
roses on it & the lace hat you like). Then he moved
away & later I saw him at a table with a girl in a blk frock

with steel beads & a black lace hat, so I supposed he was speaking the truth, altho at the time I doubted it

I think it was rather funny dont you? Darlingest boy, I've shown my beads [a gift from Freddy on his March leave] & said that Miss Prior gave them to me, do you mind? I did it because I can wear them more often now – they are very much admired

I think this is rather funny dont you? while I was away I wrote to 168 for Rosie's & the Dunsford's private addresses & he made over such a fuss about it – said I was too familiar & deceitful – because I couldn't say what I wanted to on a post card to him (Mr D) at 168. We had a right royal battle about it & I was told I was impudent & all sorts of things bad & that I must have a very good tutor – that is quite a favourite phrase and is often used.

Anyhow he sulked for 2 days and on the Sat. Avis came down and during the course of conversation she said to him, "My friend Bessie Hughes saw you in Lyons in Bishopsgate the other Friday evening." He "Oh did she, its quite possible." Avis Yes & you were with a short fat girl in a brown costume with a white stripe (This is Miss Tucknott). He Oh yes, I took her in to have something to eat as it was late after working at the office & it was my last night in town for a fortnight. I told him afterwards that I was not the only one who was deceitful, but he wont have it   We've been chipping him about Miss Tucknott ever since & I believe he thinks I'm quite jealous

Ever since I've been back in Ilford I've had most awful nights rest. I haven't been able to sleep for more than an hour together & even when I do that I dream – sometimes they're not very nice dreams. They are nearly always about you   One night I dreamed that you had married Avis – because she found out how much was between us (you & I) & threatened to tell everybody unless you married her – another night I dreamed I had been to a theatre with a man I know – I had told you about him & you came home from sea unexpectedly & when you found me you just threw me over a very deep precipice & I was killed, sometimes I've dreamed worse things than these & waked up in a fearful fright.

It reminds me of this time last year* do you remember. I didnt sleep hardly at all for 3 weeks then.

I think I [will] read your letter from Bombay thro again – destroy it & then talk to you about it for next week's mail & I'll also talk to you about Dolores† then.

I don't think I can now, I feel too sad – no not really sad – but I'm in a deep depression that only one person in this world can light.

Do you know who that is darlint? Just the best Pal of

PEIDI.

---

* When Freddy had left the Thompsons' house after his short time as their lodger.
† This character, from *The Fruitful Vine* by Robert Hichens, is mentioned in Letter 28.

50

Not put in evidence, not quite complete, this letter is all and only about Hichens' *The Fruitful Vine*. Mr Justice Shearman alluded to it in his summing-up, comparing it with Edith's analysis of the same author's *Bella Donna*. 'No doubt the letter about *The Fruitful Vine* was something similar; they write chiefly about so-called heroes and heroines, probably wicked people, which no doubt accounts for a great many of these tragedies.'

How *did* this judge get away with it? Here was a letter that formed no part of the trial, which had nothing to do with it, of which nobody knew anything; and he could not resist using it as a way to tip the scales of justice just a little bit further in what was, openly, his chosen direction.

The letter itself shows a tentative resumption of intimacy on Edith's part, in which analysis of *The Fruitful Vine* becomes a means to discuss their own situation without actually doing so. Edith identified, hungrily, with the character of Dolores ('I can feel with her & live with her'), who sleeps with another man to bear a child for the husband whom she loves. But she deliberately used this identification as a series of nudges to Freddy, pushing him towards the 'right' reading of the book, and towards appreciation of Dolores, who loves a man so much that she will make a 'supreme sacrifice' for him; who can separate love from mere desire; who has integrity and honour and a bold lack of conventionality... And where, runs the subtext, do you think you will ever find another woman like that? In Australia? At 231 Shakespeare Crescent? Of course Freddy knew that she was right, the question for him was whether it would be wiser – which *he* knew was right – to abandon this tricky, flattering, darkly sensual, essentially fantastical affair with a woman whose personality seemed to have no resting point.

There is a coda to Edith's profound engagement with the novels of Robert Hichens. Given the near-obsessive public attention that was paid to the Thompson-Bywaters case, it seems almost impossible that Hichens should not have known that his work featured as part of the evidence. In 1933 he published a novel entitled *The Paradine*

Case, whose central character – Mrs Paradine – is in love with a good-looking younger man and accused of the slow poisoning of her husband. She had, wrote Hichens, 'the secret inexplicable gift that here and there a woman possesses, and by its possession makes men do what are called "mad" things.'

In 1947 this novel was filmed by the man who had learned to dance at the school where the Graydons sometimes taught: Alfred Hitchcock. His Mrs Paradine, as played by Alida Valli, is not one of his doll-like blondes but an enigmatic exotic, who arouses her defence counsel to a hopeless self-destructive passion, and excites in her judge an eroticised desire to condemn her to death.

Mrs Paradine, incidentally, is guilty as charged, and hangs for something that she actually did. If Hichens had Edith in his mind when he wrote his novel – pure, but highly plausible, speculation – was that what he believed?

※

Mr F. Bywaters, P&O, RMS *Morea*, Aden
Postmark: London EC, 18 August 1922, 5.30 p.m.

I was reading the book & I could understand her so well – I should do the same exactly for the man I love – but you must love him darlint – real & deep & true [...]

You ask if it is sufficient reason that a good woman knows she is wanted, that she sins. Yes I think this right in a measure. A good woman who had no husband or lover – either had never had one or one that had died – would sin with a man whom she knew wanted her & she would willingly give herself [...] but a good woman who had a husband or a lover who really loved her & whom she really loved – would never sin with another man – because she felt that other man wanted her. Have I explained the difference, darlingest boy, I've tried to

I didn't like Theo myself – but I think he was a good man
& would have been a fine man if he had had a child   He
was terribly selfish darlint I know, but then every man is
selfish in life as well as in fiction, to be selfish is part of
their nature [...]

About Dolores darlint – I dont agree with you at all
about her not loving her husband. You think she loved
Cesare – because she gave all – darlingest boy she didnt
give herself in the true sense of the word   She loved her
husband so much that she would do anything in the wide
world – anything in her power – to give him pleasure
[...] She knew it was not thro her she didnt have a child
– it was thro him – he was the Fruitless Vine & she the
Fruitful & because of this she degraded herself in every
way for him.

I can feel with her & live with her darlint & I did

[...]

Had she have loved him – she would never have said or
written that – she would have gone anywhere with him –
to the ends of the world – she wasnt a woman who was
ruled by convention [...]

About the Mancelli darlint, you say you like her in one
breath & in another you say you quite understand Cesare
wanting to break away from her. These two sentences are
absolutely opposite.

I think you said you liked the Mancelli – to please me
– I think you thought "If I say I dont like her & could
understand Cesare's feelings in trying to get away from
her Peidi will be hurt – she will think of her position &
mine in relation to the Mancellis & Cesare's with regard

to age, so I will say I like her." Oh I hated her – she was a
beast a vampire – Oh I cannot bear her – darlint I should
have been much more pleased if you had said you hated
her

[...]

51

Not put in evidence, which is rather odd given the passage about 'attacks'. The phrase 'I know differently' could so easily have been given a sinister interpretation, even though it is – fairly plainly – the reaction of a woman who thinks her husband a contemptible hypochondriac. And then the line about the phrenologist at Boscombe (on the outskirts of Bournemouth) – that, too, could have constituted a little bit more grist to the prosecution mill.

It was, incidentally, the first time since early July that Edith had written anything of this kind. The prosecution assertion that she never let up in her efforts at incitement – whether insidious or blatant – was quite simply a lie. Nevertheless the Home Office memo by Sir Ernley Blackwell, dated 28 December 1922 and setting out the case against a reprieve (see commentary to Letter 28), stated it as a matter of proven legal fact. Referring to the failed appeal, he wrote:

> The Lord Chief Justice described the letters in effect as showing that continuously over a long period, beginning months before and *culminating at the time immediately antecedent to the commission of the crime* [his emphasis], Mrs Thompson was with every sort of ingenuity, by precept and by example, actual or simulated (it does not in the least matter which), endeavouring to incite Bywaters to the commission of the crime. There was a continual entreaty and hope that that which they both desired would be accomplished.

That 'does not in the least matter which' was a horribly clever catch-all phrase. If it meant anything, it meant that even if Edith had only been *pretending* to want Percy dead – the contention of Sir Henry Curtis-Bennett, who clearly should not have bothered – she was still guilty. It was all her fault because she should have known what her reader might infer from her writing. True enough; but was that any business of the Old Bailey?

The phrase also raised the issue of what Edith might have inferred from *Freddy's* writing, but nobody – except Avis Graydon, whose anguished common sense was not required in this world of logical illogic – chose to go into that, nor into the numerous implied remarks to which Edith was clearly responding (especially in Letter 27).

Incidentally this memo also made reference to Boscombe, using a holiday snap as a means to emphasise the duplicitousness of Edith Thompson; which, however much it was exaggerated and falsified by her accusers, seems genuinely to have terrified them.

'I was shown a photograph yesterday,' wrote Sir Ernley. '... It was taken at Boscombe this summer and showed Mr Thompson lying on his back on the grass with his head in his wife's lap, with both her arms round his neck clasping his wrists and both smiling out of the picture. I am told that about this very date Mrs Thompson was writing to Bywaters asking him whether he had studied bi-chloride of mercury and was it any use!'

Sadly inaccurate, old chap. The bichloride letter was dated 4 July. The Bournemouth holiday was for two weeks starting on the 15th. Again, nobody either noticed or cared.

The passage in this letter about giving Freddy a baby – a 'replica' – then absenting herself from the scene is ridiculous, of course, but Edith, who at the time was chock-full of *The Fruitful Vine*, was trying every trick that came into her unstoppably inventive head to keep her hold upon this man. It will be noted that he had suggested he might not even return home in September, but would stay in India. He, too, was trying everything; except tearing up her letters as if they had never been written.

Mr F. Bywaters, P&O, RMS *Morea*, Aden
Postmark: London EC, 23 August 1922, 1.30 p.m.

Thank you for your wishes on the 27/6/22* darlingest boy.

It seemed such a strange day to me, I did want to wish
you "Many Happy Returns" for yourself first – then for
we two darlint – in person that day – but I couldn't – so
I sent the "Radio"†

Darlint, tell me what you thought when you were first
told there was a message for you – before you knew what
the message was. I thought about you such a lot that
day & wondered if I did right in sending it   I thought
perhaps it would give you a shock – that perhaps you
would think it was something to do with "Health" either
mine or his

About Dolores darlint – you say "Forget her romance in
connection with you."

I said it would be as her case with me darlint, because I
felt it would be so good to do something for you – to
give you something to live for & cherish all your life –
you could be happy then darlint – I know you'll say you
couldnt – but think a little – I'm sure you could – you
could live in a memory and with a replica

---

* The time lag on letters was usually six weeks, so Freddy does seem to have been dilatory
with this greeting.
† A radiogram. Post-war technology allowed these to be sent by private citizens – quite
expensively.

However, while you still tell me to hope – I shall forget about Dolores.

*****

Talking about "Scamp" darlint, Im a bit fed up with him   While I was away he ran in the Steward's Cup at Goodwood [29 July] & I made sure he would win it especially as I was away & couldn't back him – so I thought about it & sent a wire to Rosie to do £1 each way for me & then the wretched thing didnt win.

Darlint remember when the "Morea" is due in England, both 231 & 41 will [be] sure to try & find out if you are still on her or if you have stayed in India as you said.

I went to the Regent Palace to tea the other day darlint with Lily [Vellender]. I'm trying to overcome that horror of the place & she asked me to go & I didnt want to say No, I felt very uncomfortable all the time I was there tho', & I did try hard not to think of previous experiences there.*

It's rather funny sometimes at 41 The attacks continue so I am told of course I know differently – but I say nothing & laugh all to myself right deep down inside. They always happen after "words "or "unpleasantness."

A Phrenologist at Boscome [sic] told him he would live to be quite an old man.

Darlint, I've used all my perfume, shall I buy some myself, or shall I wait for you to do it for me.

---

* This reference is unclear.

I'd really like you to do it best but I'll do just whichever you tell me to do.

Goodbye for another week darlint Pal I do hope I shall hear from you soon – I've had nothing since Colombo – & I'm starving now   You havent forgotten your Pal in England have you? her name is

PEIDI

52

Later Exhibit 63. The '5 years' reference is to the suicide pact that she and Freddy had made (see also Letter 3), which Edith had dated back to their 'anniversary' on 27 June 1921, whose premise was that they would kill themselves five years thence if nothing in their situation had changed.

Having told the Old Bailey that he never considered this pact seriously (as if either of them did), Freddy was asked some more about what he understood from Edith's words. His replies, which show his sense of self unimpaired by the shadow of death, came close to admitting the unreal basis upon which their feelings – real feelings – had rested.

The solicitor general said:

'Did you tell your learned counsel that you read her letters as melodrama?'

'Some.'

'What was it you understand as melodrama?'

'She had a vivid way of declaring herself; she would read a book and imagine herself as the character in the book.'

'Do you mean that you read her reference to poison as melodrama?'

'Some as melodrama; some as general knowledge.'

'I don't understand that. What did you understand when she mentioned a particular poison?'

'To what are you referring?'

'Are you aware, or do you remember, that she mentioned several times a poison in her letters?'

'Yes.'

'Did that suggest to you a dose of poison that might kill her husband?'

'No.'

'Did you not read those letters as meaning that the idea was in her mind?'

'No.'

Mr F. Bywaters, P&O, RMS *Morea*, Port Said
Postmark: London EC, 28 August 1922, 6.15 p.m.

Darlingest boy, today is the 27th and its on a Sunday, so I am writing this in the bathroom, I always like to send you greetings on the day – not the day before or the day after.

Fourteen whole months have gone by now, darlint, its so terribly long. Neither you nor I thought we should have to wait all that long time did we? although I said I would wait 5 years* – and I will darlint – its only 3 years and ten months now.

Many happy returns and good luck darlingest boy – I cant wish you any more can I? every day I say 'Good luck to my Pal' to myself.

PEIDI.

---

* A reference to the suicide pact.

53

Not put in evidence. Freddy was still maintaining that he would not see Edith on his return home.

❧

Mr F. Bywaters, P&O, RMS *Morea*, Port Said
Postmark: London EC, 29 August 1922, 3.30 p.m.

Darlingest, I got a letter from you last Thursday, from Fremantle I think, I don't think there was anything in it that I can talk to you about – you say you are longing for that letter from me that you will get in Sydney – well darlint, I'm longing to get a letter from you – a real letter, one in which you're going to tell me such lots and lots of things perhaps you will when you have heard from me I always feel that you write better to me when you have heard from me   And then another thing that strikes me is this – in most of your letters you say "We are getting into so & so tonight." That makes me think that a few hours before you get into a Port, you sit down & write to me, as a duty. Don't you ever feel that you'd like to write a few lines to me & then leave it & write again when you feel like it   Thats how I do [it] darlint, & then when it comes to the last day for posting, I havnt got to sit down & write as a duty.

About books – I havnt read "Mrs Marden" [by Hichens] – I should like to, but I have read "Martin Conisby's Revenge" quite lately & I wasnt very keen on it – it didn't seem up to Jeffrey [Jeffery] Farnol's standard. I don't think I have read "The Chronicles of an Imp" [by Farnol] & yet the title is familiar. However I don't think the book would appeal to me very much from the title

[...]

I'm now reading Eden Philpotts "Secret Woman" darlint I'm not very keen – it takes a lot of reading – its very dry & you know the "Secret Woman" practically at the commencement – if you've got any sense.

Darlint, a little news that you won't like.

Blouses are fashionable again, no more jumpers – I've saved the "little green one" for you, do you want it? I'm longing for Sept. 23rd to come, although you say I shant see you, just to know you are in London will be good.

I wonder what you're going to say to my first letter to you at Colombo.

I'll be awfully anxious to get your answer – be kind to me darlint – our pleasures together are so few – no, I'm going to stop now – because I shall start railing against Life & Fate & everything – & I do want to try not to – I want to B.B. only for you darlint – cos I know you will be pleased with

PEIDI.

54

Not put in evidence, this letter contains one of Edith's most instinctual and lovely sentences: 'I just tried to make you live in my life.'

It was also replete with human interest – for instance the fact that Avis, the overlooked sister, was now acting very much like the one with 'pride of possession' when it came to Freddy Bywaters. Full of what he had done and where he was going, the constant thought of him spilling eagerly out of her mouth... Had *they* been writing to each other? It certainly seems that way. The remark 'we all think we'd like to die at certain moments', with its air of slightly unconvincing worldly wisdom, was presumably meant to suggest that he had been pining for Edith but now was robustly indifferent. Two sisters squabbling over an attractive young man: how ordinary it all was! How was it possible that an almighty cataclysm was on its way – now less than a month away – to overwhelm the tiny gaslit parlour in Shakespeare Crescent and destroy the lives of these sniping, gossiping people?

Then this business of the anonymous letter, sent from a 'wellwisher'.

Edith was clearly suggesting the involvement of Lilian Bywaters, who went 'up west' once a week on Wednesdays (she would do so with Freddy on 4 October, the day that he was arrested). Had Lilian discovered that her son called his lover 'Peidi', and written the note in order to warn Edith off? That is the implication here, which of course ignores the far more likely scenario that Freddy himself was the author of the note, which he had sent to somebody in England to post. If this were the case, then the deliberate use of the initial 'P' was designed to underline his authorship; designed, moreover, to prevent Edith from avoiding knowledge of it.

Yet she did. She dances around it in this letter, which displays what appears to be real shock, but also a desire to exculpate her lover from such crude behaviour. Perhaps she could not bear to believe him capable of it and therefore, in characteristic fashion, simply decided that it was not so. However, the real explanation for this apparent willingness to ignore – and to forgive – may lie elsewhere.

After the murder, Mr Carlton made a statement to the police containing a couple of sentences that went almost unnoticed, but are somewhat mysterious. 'The paper of the anonymous letter shown to me by the Police,' he said, 'appears identical with the paper which is known as "Manifold Paper" which we have in use.'

There is no way of knowing what document he was shown, nor why he was shown it, but the only anonymous letter that played any part in this case is the one that Edith received on 7 September. 'Manifold Paper' was not, of course, only obtainable via Carlton and Prior. Nevertheless, the strong implication has to be that she herself wrote the note – having disguised her handwriting – and, when one thinks about it, this is by far the most psychologically convincing explanation. It is reminiscent of the 'Miss P. Fisher' episode at the General Post Office. Drama, always – or in this case melodrama – but with a purpose. It would have maintained the breach of suspicion between Lilian Bywaters and her son, which Edith pretended to lament. And it would have been a means of provoking her lover, another ruse to recapture him: she knew very well that he would be roused by any such letter.

That said, it remains a possibility that Freddy did write it (as a ship's clerk he may well have had access to this particular kind of paper), that Edith suspected as much, and that she chose to carry on anyway – as did he.

⚜

Mr F. Bywaters P&O, RMS *Morea*, Marseilles
Postmark: London EC, 11 September 1922, 2.30 p.m.

Today is Sept 7th darlint, do you remember it last year – I think it was the day the "Morea" left England – am I right? I had rather a shock this morning – I am enclosing you the cause of it – just as I received it   Do you know anything about it? I don't suppose you do darlint, but I'm just asking   I'm sure if you had reasons for not wanting to see me – you'd tell me and tell me the reasons – you couldn't resort to letters of this description. I dont think it can be from anyone I know – or from any relation of mine, because I am addressed as "P" you will notice – & no one knows you call me anything but "Edie"   Also darlint I cant help noticing that it is posted in the West End on a Wednesday. Write and tell me what you think about it & if you have no use for the letter – destroy it – because I dont want it   I can't talk to you very much darlint – it seems such a long time since you really talked to me and nothing can break down this barrier but a real long talk with you – I am so looking forward to it   Avis was over last night and told me you had seen Harold She also said that they (231) were looking forward to the "Morea" coming in – to hear all about Harold from you & when I said "But I understood he was not coming to England" she said "Oh that was a lot of rot he was talking. I expect he has thought better of it since we all think we'd like to die at certain times but we all get over it and I suppose he has done the same by now." She also told me that the "Morea" is due for China & Japan next trip – is this so? darlint – its even longer than Australia isnt it? – Oh I can't wait all that time its awful here in England without you

*****

There has been some unpleasantness with Mrs Lester – she is not attempting to get out and its nearly 2 ½ years now – so he told her if she wasn't out by Dec (she promised to get out for certain by this September) he would take the matter to Court   We have had our solicitors advice on this matter & he says she wouldn't have a leg to stand on – 2 ½ years is tons of time for anybody to find something else. But I suppose she is waiting for something at the same figure (30 /- a month) & of course she will never get it. However she's horrid to me – of course she can't do anything to irritate him, as he hardly comes into contact with her – but I do – & she's so nasty – she refuses to take anything in at all – not even bread or milk & has told the window cleaner only to do her side of the house.

Its awfully awkward – I have to rush home on Friday nights & do all my own shopping, carry potatoes etc – because if I only ordered them & had them sent she wouldnt open the door when they came. She wouldn't open the door to Bill the other day when he brought a parcel up for me & she won't open it to the Laundry – so I have to take it & fetch it. She's done some very petty things this last fortnight – I didn't believe she would – especially after what I've done for her & Norah [her daughter]. I am trying to get Ethel [the maid] to come up from Cornwall now – I don't know if I shall be successful – I do hope so – I shan't be able to stand this state of things much longer Darlint. I hope I havent bored you with all this – I have just thought perhaps I have – after I had written it all. Forgive me if I have, I didnt intend to – I just tried to make you live in my life. Will you write & tell me if I am to send your watch to you at Plymouth & the books. I have had it put right and often wear it myself at 168 – the strap is so big it comes nearly up to my elbow – also I have had a gold buckle put on it – did you notice it was only R G [rolled gold]. I didn't when I bought it – or I should have had it altered at the time – however it is done now

Dont forget to write from Marseilles & tell me what to do. Darlingest pal I love you more & more – I always shall I'll never alter.

PEIDI

Enclosed:

※

Miss P. Graydon, C/o Messrs Carlton & Prior, 168 Aldersgate Street, EC1
Postmark: London, W1, 6 September 1922, 3.15 p.m.

September 6th

If you wish to remain the friend of F Bywaters, be careful. Do not attempt to see him or communicate with him, when he is in England

Believe this to be a genuine warning from

A WELLWISHER

55

Later Exhibit 54. Written three weeks to the day before the murder. Could anybody on earth have guessed such a thing, or traced the lines of a strategy from this ardent, vital, impatient, sublimely silly jumble of stuff?

It is a love letter, for sure, and as such it seeks to arouse jealousy; this time by conjuring an image of herself as acquiescent – including sexually – to the man whom Freddy regarded as his natural antagonist. She acquiesces to Freddy also, 'it shall be so, I'm quite reconciled' and the rest of it; this was her female pose but also something innate, which derived strength from the game of submission.

The fact that she appeared to be behaving in the same way with both men – or, put simply, the fact that she was obediently sleeping with Percy – may have had its effect upon her reader. At this stage, however, he was still holding out against a return to their old relationship.

⁂

Mr F. Bywaters, P&O, RMS *Morea*, Marseilles
Postmark: London EC, 12 September 1922, 5.30 p.m.

Darlint Pal,

I've got nothing to talk to you about – I can't think about anything at all – I can't even look forward to seeing you. Now you are nearing England – I keep contrasting this home coming with the previous ones. I have been buoyed up with hope, bubbling with excitement   Just existing with an intense strung up feeling of seeing you and feeling you holding me in your two arms so tightly that it hurts but this time everything seems different. I don't hear from you much you don't talk to me by letter and help me and I don't even know if I am going to see you.

Darlint, I'm an awful little beast I know – I don't want to be either – but I feel so hopeless – just drifting – but if you say 'No I won't see you' then it shall be so, I'm quite reconciled to whatever verdict you send forth and shall say to myself 'It is for the best it must be so.'

Darlint you do love me still tho' don't you? and you will go on loving me even if we don't meet. Things here are going smoothly with me – I am giving all – and accepting everything and I think am looked upon as 'The Dutiful Wife whose spirit is at last bent to the will of her husband.'

This isn't sarcasm or cynicism it's exactly how I feel. I had a little letter from you – by what you said it was written on the 28th of July   I've had nothing – further there are heaps and heaps of questions in my letters to you.

I wonder if you will answer them, or are they already dismissed? On Saturday I was so ill* I had to stop away – it's not very often I give in so much as stopping away from business but on Saturday I really had to   I'm quite alright now tho' darlint.

I don't think I told you I bought a fur coat – at least part of it. It was 27 gns. and I had £13 saved up – so I borrowed £15 from the account and am paying it back at £1 per week – the debt is only £10 now.

Also I've had to fall back on wearing lace shoes – no don't make a face darlint, they are rather nice ones – I wanted grey and could get nothing at all in my usual style – only with one or two straps across – and I don't like these – even if they hid my foot I shouldn't – they look loud, so

___

*   Menstrual pains, one assumes.

I bought lace ones, only to wear with cloth clothes tho' darlint – not with silk.

Yesterday you were at Suez – I suppose you got my Port Said letters there and on Friday or Saturday, you will get these – I think the mail facilities favour you more than me darlint.

Darlingest pal do let me hear an awful lot from you next week – I'm just existing now – I shall live then.

Darlingest, only lover of mine – try to cheer me up.

PEIDI.

56

Not put in evidence. It is fascinating to see Mrs Graydon's grasp of the situation between Edith and Freddy – the fact that the young man wanted to take out her married daughter – together with her less-than-shrewd semi-endorsement of it. Did a dislike of her son-in-law underpin her attitude? Speculation, of course, related to the unknowable question of Percy's character. Anyway she would never have shown such a thing – the wreath that the Graydons sent to his funeral was signed 'From your mother and dad' – but both she and her husband must have known that the Thompsons were imperfectly suited; such was life, however, in the days of till death do you part. And Mrs Graydon's consoling thought, no doubt, was that it would all blow over when Freddy settled down (with Avis?) and when Edith calmed down (with a baby?).

Fascinating, also, to read about Edith in domestic goddess mode... and how quickly she bored of it all. She was described by Mr Carlton, at the Old Bailey, as a 'very capable woman' (capable of anything, the onlookers no doubt thought), and she was indeed adept at pretty much everything that she did, from handling accounts to furnishing her house. But she had absolutely no interest in the stay-at-home role that society expected women to reprise, after the glimpse of liberation offered by the First World War. As with the politicised intelligentsia who were her contemporaries – Vera Brittain, Rebecca West – she staunchly refused to accept that particular fate (Brittain, born four days after Edith, called work the twentieth century's 'great gift to women'). And yet. Because of the *milieu* in which she operated – what the *Daily Express* would call the world of 'humdrum clerks and humdrum milliners'; because she was unprotected by the Oxford quadrangle or the path-smoothing social connections; because she was lower-middle class and suburban and took superior trash as seriously as if it were the work of Tolstoy; because she was upwardly mobile and confident rather than downtrodden and objectively pitiable – because of all these things, so inimical to both English snobbery and love of the underdog, her aspirations were despised, her work ethic distrusted and her bright-spirited desire to transcend her horizons regarded as dangerous subversion.

Such, writ large, was the fate of any ordinary woman who tried too hard to realise her capacity for extraordinariness.

⚜

Mr F. Bywaters, P&O, RMS *Morea*, Plymouth
Postmark: London, 20 September 1922, 5 p.m.

Do you know Darlint I'm getting fearfully disappointed today   I had hopes for hearing from you – but there is nothing yet   I went to G.P O. yesterday and they told me there was nothing for me – that was quite disappointing enough, but I thought perhaps you were late at Marseilles & it would be in to-day (Tuesday) When I asked for the letters for me to-day & was told there was none, I asked if the mail by the "Morea" was in & was told it was – but was not yet sorted – so now I'll have to wait until tomorrow – as its no use me getting letters after business hours – I have nowhere to keep them for safety   However I hope time will fly till tomorrow.

This afternoon I sent you a parcel of books to Plymouth – I thought perhaps it would be too late to catch you if I waited to hear from you   And darlint something was in the parcel for you – I couldnt remember if you told me your hair brushes were worn out – or if it was some one else – was it you? & do you like the "Mason Pearson" brush like wire on a rubber cushion. On Saturday I had very solemn warning that you were expected home this week end & you were sure to visit 231 (This from Mother) & when I said I understood you were not coming to England any more – I was told "Oh that was all bluff – just an excuse to make it easier to take you out that night."

I have been amusing myself making jam – chutney & mincemeat with the apples from the garden. Most people who have tasted it think I have been very successful & Norman [unknown] wants to borrow me as his cook. I'm getting rather proud of myself darlint – but I wish I was doing it to share with you – it would be worth more to me than the whole world's praise. This morning I had a letter from Ethel and she says she will come up to me at the end of the month – that's something anyway – I'm beginning to hate this drudgery – it doesnt even help to stifle thoughts now

I think I'll send you a wire to Plymouth to ask you to send Plymouth letter (if I am to have one) to 168   One letter can't matter can it darlint, anyhow I'll risk it. But I'll wire you because perhaps you won't open this before you leave.

Its 5 now darlingest – I'll put this away till tomorrow I'm thinking about such a lot.

PEIDI

Darlint darlint pal – I'm so happy I've heard from you – such a lot it seems like the very first time I have really heard since you have been gone   I dont know what to say to you – I really dont – but you know how I feel don't you? Today is the 20th and I've got tons of work to do – it is statement day and its also nearly 4 – so I must post this now [...] Must it be pals only darlint? If you say "Yes" it shall be

PEIDI (still loves you)

57

Later Exhibit 28, undated, most likely sent on Thursday 21 September. Perhaps the most significant line in this important letter – one that suggested, as strongly as is possible, Edith's innocence – was the reference to Freddy sailing to 'China or Japan'. Where, in that remark, was there any sense that life was about to be changed forever? As ever it seems that those who read her words, solely with the aim of constructing a case against her, were so intent upon finding 'meaning' that they missed what was actually being said. Freddy had almost arrived, Percy had less than two weeks to live, and Edith – as well as anticipating the arrival of a maid – was sulking about the fact that the next separation from her lover was likely to be longer than ever.

Then there was the fact that she had been told this by her sister: the woman in the know. '231' had put 'things in my head', including a story that Freddy had missed the ship at Sydney, according to Avis because he was drunk. It is interesting that Edith refers back to a promise from Freddy that he would never drink 'too much' – especially given the possibility (unproven) that Percy may have done just that – but it is actually very unlikely that he had been drunk, and much more probable that his behaviour was to do with a girl, possibly *the* Australian girl. If, of course, the story were true, and not something fabricated or exaggerated by Avis. But Freddy had form in this regard (see commentary to Letter 15), so one assumes that it probably did happen; a small signifier of his latent wildness.

Not that Avis minded. She, like Edith, was fighting for him, as stubborn in her way as the husband who fought against him, and of late – it seemed – quite confident of winning the prize, not least because she was free to claim it.

Did Freddy ever really want her? Or did he, at least, realise that choosing her made more sense? The Graydons surely hoped so. Lilian Bywaters would certainly have said so; and, for the first time since the argument during his March leave, he would be staying at his mother's house in Norwood (Edith's resentment against 'them' included his sister Florence). Edith recognised the strength of this enmity. It is near-impossible for a child to hold out forever against a mother, and Freddy did not do so. Edith and Lilian had a lot in common, as it happened: both making their way, impressively, in the commercial world; both veterans in dealing with men; both fiercely possessive of their darlingest boy; both admired and beloved by him – hence, perhaps, the quality of their antagonism, which was that of women who basically understood each other.

As for the 'pals' stuff... how erotically phrased it is, how insinuating and irresistible, the image of the 'iron band that won't expand', which surely came into Edith's head and fell on to the page quite naturally: she had the gift, a true writer's gift, of making the reader feel her feelings, of creating a response that is sensory – immediate – and thus alive forever.

Nevertheless Freddy's letter also gave cause for hope. The way in which he had responded to her own words, point by point. The fact that she was still able to make him jealous, as with the man at the Waldorf who had tried to pick her up.

And as, of course, with Percy, and this famous, beautiful, damning paragraph: 'Yes, darlint you are jealous of *him* – but I want you to be – he has the right by law to all that you have the right to by nature and love – yes darlint be jealous, so much that you will do something desperate.'

Is this an outbreath of fervid excitation – a lover's sinuous cadence, which means everything and nothing? Not, of course, to the forces of law, which saw it gleaming darkly on the page, separate from its fellow words. When asked at the trial what she had meant by 'do something desperate', Edith replied: 'To take me away at any cost, to do anything to get me away from England.' Freddy said much the same. But in context, at the time, is that how he interpreted it? Should the writer have realised that gratifying herself with this kind of literary stimulus was dangerous, in its refusal to understand that a reader's response cannot be controlled?

It sounds absurd; or it would do, were it not for the fact that Percy Thompson was murdered.

At the Old Bailey, it is possible that the part of the passage that most offended was not the 'do something desperate' line, but what preceded it. This is Mr Justice Shearman, speaking to the jury in his summing-up:

> You are told [by Sir Henry Curtis-Bennett] that this is a case of a 'great love'. I am only using it as a phrase. Take one of the letters as a test... 'He has the right by law to all that you have the right to by nature and love.' Gentlemen,*
> if that nonsense means anything it means that the love of a husband for his wife is something improper because marriage is acknowledged by the law, and that the love of a woman for her lover, illicit and clandestine, is something great and noble. I am certain that you, like any other right-minded persons, will be filled with disgust at such a notion.

With regard once more to 'do something desperate': after the executions, when the mood of hysteria had turned to a kind of massive subdued shock, officialdom – which did not feel as entirely comfortable as it would have wished about the guilt of Edith Thompson – was doubling-down on the righteousness of its actions. There was unease, for instance, about a last-minute statement from Freddy Bywaters, to the effect that Edith had had no prior knowledge of his actions. With regard to this the Home Office produced another of its internal memoranda, a howling outrage swaddled in bureaucratic language, designed to soothe the very remarkable conscience of authority.

> Assuming, therefore, that he... wished at any cost to his own memory to exonerate Mrs Thompson, feeling that his words uttered at the last moment must be given the fullest possible credence, his statement nevertheless falls far short of proving Mrs Thompson innocent of murder. That Mrs Thompson incited or persuaded Bywaters

---

* Two of the jurors were female.

to remove or help to remove her husband by poison is proved by her letters as clearly as anything can be in a Court of Law.

Her expression 'be so jealous that you will do something desperate' suggests that she not merely intended that the method of effecting her husband's removal was not to be confined to poison but was indicating the means actually adopted by Bywaters.

Both morally and legally his statement does nothing to exonerate Mrs Thompson.

I think it is well to put this aspect of the case upon record...

❧

I think I'm fearfully disappointed about you not getting in on Friday [22nd] darlint   I'd been planning to get off early – rush to Ilford and do the shopping and rush up to meet you – having had my hair washed in the luncheon hour instead of at night – as I should have said and now all that is no use – so I shan't have my hair washed – it must wait until the next Friday – that will mean an extra hour with you – do you mind me having a dirty head for a week darlint – its very very dirty. I've been hanging it out especially for now.

Why are you so late this time – oh I hate this journey, I hate Australia and everything connected with it – it will be 109 days since I've seen you – and you didn't answer my question about China and Japan next time. I suppose it is right – or you would have told me – it will be worse then

I was surprised about you going home this time darlint – so surprised I couldn't believe I had read rightly at first

You ask me if I'm glad or sorry – darlint I dont know how I feel about it – I'm glad for you darlint – because you know I always felt responsible for the break, I dont think I'm glad for myself tho', I think I'm harbouring just a small petty feeling of resentment against them – I've tried so hard not to – and I think I didnt at first, and it's only just this last time

You say you have reasons darlint I don't know them and you don't tell me them – so I can't be influenced by them one way or the other   Tell me them it'll help darlingest You say you suppose you deserve the Sydney letter – didn't you get 2 darlint˙ – I was sorry as soon as I had posted the first. I do hope you got the 2nd.

Darlingest boy – pal – you're horrid to be cross about the Turkish Delight – you are really [...] If you are still cross – soften a wee teeny bit and forgive Peidi and try and accept her excuse for erring   Darlint – you know "to err is human, to forgive divine," and I'm certainly not going to even hazard a guess why you are not bringing any delight or cigarettes this time, in case I err again or am misunderstood. Please tell me   I think I must have been reading 'The Firing Line' [by R. W. Chambers] at the same time as you – I finished it last Sunday   Why didn't you like it as well as the others darlint?

I liked it but I liked the villain as they call him, too, Louis Malcourt.

I've read it before – ages and ages ago only I was stuck for something decent to read and asked Avis to bring along something belonging to me that they had at 231 – she brought that

I've read "Monte Christo" [Dumas] darlint – but neither of the others you mention.

You're going to get me some books this time aren't you? please darlint.

*****

Darlingest boy – I don't quite understand you about 'Pals.' You say 'Can we be Pals only, Peidi, it will make it easier.'

Do you mean for always? because if you do, No, no, a thousand times. We can't be 'pals' only for always darlint – its impossible physically and mentally.

Last time we had a long talk – I said, "Go away this time and forget all about me, forget you ever knew me, it will be easier – and better for you."

Do you remember – and you refused, so now I'm refusing darlint – it must be still 'the hope of all' or 'the finish of all.'

If you still only mean for a certain time and you think it best, darlint it shall be so – I don't see how it will be easier myself – but it shall be as you say and wish, we won't be our natural selves tho' I know – we'll be putting a kerb on ourselves the whole time – like an iron band that won't expand. Please don't let what I have written deter you from any decision darlint – I don't want to do that – truly I'd like to do what you think best.

I don't sleep much better now – the nights seem so long – I sleep for an hour and lie awake for 2 and go to sleep again for another hour – right thro' the night.

A doctor can't do me any good darlint – no good at all – even the most clever in the land – unless that doctor is you and it can't be, so I'm not going to waste any more money on them. I want you for my doctor – my pal – my lover – my everything – just all and the whole world would be changed. I'm very anxious to know about missing the ship at Sydney. I heard about it from Avis last night – she said 'Oh I suppose he was drunk.' Darlint, thats a lie isn't it – you promised me once that it would never be 'too much.' I'm worrying about it – 23 I have made me worry – by putting things into my head.

Send my letters to 168 as before darlint – I'll risk it and I have a difficulty in getting them at the G.P.O. The Marseilles letter was marked all over "Not known" and initialed about 5 times, I think, and they always question me closely as to not having a permanent address. I'll expect a letter on Monday morning at 168.

I'm not very keen on the sound of "I went home to my cousin's every night – quite domesticated." It sounds like a sneer – I wonder if you did sneer when you wrote it.

Now about that Wednesday I mentioned [...] Do you remember now? taking me to a quick lunch at Evans and coming into 168 and then meeting your Mother up West and then ringing me and asking me what I was doing that evening – and I was going to tea at The Waldorf. You went and slept at Norwood that night and didn't come back to me until the Friday. You sound very despondent when you say about "Time passes and with it some of the pain – Fate ordained our lot to be hard." Does some of the pain you feel pass with time? Perhaps it does – things seem so much easier to forget with a man – his environment is always different – but with a woman its always the same.

Darlint my pain gets less and less bearable – it hurts more and more every day, every hour really.

"Other ways only involve the parting of you and I, Peidi, nobody deserves anything more than I do."

I don't understand this part – try and explain to me please – have you lost heart and given up hope? tell me if you have darlint – don't bear it all alone.

[...]

I think I must be fearfully dense – also my memory has left me in the lurch – because I dont understand what you mean by your question "Peidi do you think you could live with a replica* – you once said No"

When did I say it and what do you mean – what does the question refer to? Its a puzzle to me darlint, but I accept the rebuff my memory has given me and hope you will overlook this omission

[...] Now I'm going to be cross – Don't bully me I never said or even suggested that I should cultivate the Regent Palace Hotel† and there was no need whatever for you to have hurled forth that edict and then underlined it. Ask to be forgiven – you bully! (darlint pal)

---

* Edith had described a baby as a 'replica' in Letter 52.
† This remains obscure.

No, I dont think the man who mistook me for "Romance" was decent darlint, but I do think he was quite genuine in mistaking me, I dont think it was a ruse on his part.

Yes, darlint you are jealous of him – but I want you to be – he has the right by law to all that you have the right to by nature and love – yes darlint be jealous, so much that you will do something desperate.

I've not sent a wire to Plymouth to you – I've changed my mind – I see you left Gibraltar on the 19th and perhaps you will get in Saturday morning – then I shall send you a wire to Tilbury to meet me in the afternoon – if its at all possible for you

Before I finish up this letter I've got a confession to make. Darlingest about the watch – I didn't send it to Plymouth – purposely.

I felt that you were not going to come and see me this time and the feeling was awful – horrid, and I felt that if you refused I couldnt make you.

And then I was tempted – I thought, "Yes I can make him – I won't send his watch – I'll tell him if he wants it – he's to come to 168 and fetch it"

Darlint, was it small? if it was, real big love must make people think of small things, because real, big love made

PEIDI.

Later Exhibit 55.

Edith bought Freddy a tobacco pouch, as promised here, on Monday 2 October. 'Both Mrs and Miss Graydon noticed it,' he told his counsel at the trial. 'Mrs Graydon said to me, "You have got a new pouch, Freddy. Was it a present?" and I said "Yes." She said, "From a girl, I expect?" and I said "Yes." She said, "I expect the same girl gave you that as gave you the watch?" I said, "Yes, the same girl gave it me," and she said, "I know who it is, but I am not going to say. Never mind, we won't argue about it. She is one of the best." I said, "There is none better."'

※

Darlint Pal, please try and use – pour moi, and dont buy a pouch, je vais, pour vous – one of these days.

PEIDI –

Later Exhibit 55a. This, the last card that Edith would play before Freddy's return – almost, as it were, on autopilot – was an old and familiar one.

Extract from *Daily Sketch*, 20 September 1922, page 2, column 4. With headnote:

'Chicken Broth Death
'Rat Poison Consumed by Fowl Kills Woman'

The report states:

That death was due to consuming broth made from a chicken which had eaten poison, containing a rat virus, was the medical explanation at the resumed inquest at Shoreditch yesterday on Mrs. Sarah Feldman (34) of Reliance Square, Hoxton.

Later Exhibits 47 and 48 (the two exhibits, which related to the same telegram, were the original and a copy).

Freddy did not turn up to this meeting, arranged for Saturday 23 September at The Broadway in East Ham. Edith had come back from her half-day at work as usual, cooked lunch for her husband and father, then went out at about 3.00 while the men were working in the garden. She did not return until after 8.00. What she did is unknown (perhaps she got her hair done after all; what amazing confidence, alongside all that abasement and submission, to plan to see one's lover again with it unwashed!). What she felt can only be imagined. Freddy's assertions that he would not see her again – which she had probably, despite her anguished pleading, not really believed – had suddenly acquired reality.

According to Mrs Lester, the sitting tenant, who heard Edith's arrival that evening at 41 Kensington Gardens, Percy 'had words with her over being out so long'.

The following day was Avis's twenty-sixth birthday, so would have been spent at Shakespeare Crescent. Freddy was not there, although he was assuredly uppermost in the minds of several of those present.

Office of Origin – London City, 8
Office Stamp – Tilbury, Essex, 22 September, 1922
Handed in at 9.28   Received here at 9.48
To – Reply Paid Bywaters, Steamer Morea, Tilbury Docks
'Can you meet Peidi Broadway 4 p m.'
Envelope addressed – Bywaters, "Morea". Reply Pd.

Later Exhibits 58 and 59 (as above, an original and a copy of the same telegram).

On Monday 25 September, at 4.30 pm, Freddy was outside Carlton and Prior.

Edith had succeeded.

She was unable to leave the office immediately, and sent her friend Lily Vellender to have a cup of coffee with Freddy (they knew each other slightly) in the Fullers tearoom across the road. Then Edith entered the café in her hat and coat, at which point Lily left. As instructed by Percy, she caught the 5.49 from Fenchurch Street; so, however, did Freddy.

Office of Origin – London City, 8

Office Stamp – Tilbury, Essex, 25 September, 1922

Handed in at 10.03   Received here at 10.16

To – Bywaters, Steamer Morea, Tilbury Docks

'Must catch 5 49 Fenchurch   Reply if can manage.'

Later Exhibit 30.

Letter written by Freddy Bywaters, on the evening of 25 September.

☙

Darling Peidi Mia,

Tonight was impulse – natural – I couldnt resist – I had to hold you darling little sweetheart of mine – darlint I was afraid – I thought you were going to refuse to kiss me – darlint little girl – I love you so much and the only way I can control myself is by not seeing you and I'm not going to do that. Darlint Peidi Mia – I must have you – I love you darlint – logic and what others call reason do not enter into our lives, and where two halves are concerned. I had no intention darlint of doing that – it just happened thats all – I'm glad now chere – darlint when you suggested the occupied carriage, I didn't want to go in it – did you think that perhaps I did – so that there would have been no opportunity for me to break the conditions that I had stipulated – darlint I felt quite confident that I would be able to keep my feelings down – I was wrong Peidi   I was reckoning on will power over ordinary forces – but I was fighting what? not ordinary forces – nothing was fighting the whole of me   Peidi you are my magnet – I cannot resist darlint – you draw me to you now and always, I shall never be able to see you and remain impassive   Darlint Peidi Mia Idol mine – I love you – always – always Ma Chere   Last night when I read your questions I didn't know how to answer them – I have now Peidi?

Darlint I dont think I can talk about other things tonight
– I want to hold you so tightly I'm going to tonight in my
sleep. Bon Nuit Ma Petite, cherchez bien pour votre

FREDDY.

61

Not put in evidence, incomplete and undated, but obviously written on Wednesday 27 September.

So in the blink of an eye Freddy and Edith were back as they had been; except that so much more, in the interim, had been thrown upon the fire. He wrote the letter (above) when he was alone, back in his old bedroom at his mother's house, trying to calm his flesh; he must have handed it to Edith when they met on the 26th, again at Fullers, before again taking the Fenchurch Street train together.

They met on the 27th and 28th, when Edith gave Freddy the letter below.

[...] well let us accept it then – and bear the hard part as willingly as we enjoy the natural part. Darlint, I didnt think you wanted to go into the other carriage – but I suggested it because I felt there would be less temptation there – not only for you but for me too – do you think it is less pleasure to me, for you to kiss me & hold me, than it is for you to do so? I think its more pleasure to me than it can possibly be to you – at least it always feels so & darlingest, if you had refrained from doing these things (not perhaps last night – but at some time before you went) I am not above compelling you to – darlint I could, couldn't I, just the same as if the position was reversed – you could compel me to – because we have no will power. I felt that's how it would be darlingest lover of mine – I was strong enough in spirit, until I was tempted in the flesh & the result – a mutual tumble from the pedestal of "Pals only" that we had erected as penance for ourselves. No darlint, it could never be now – I am sure that you see that now don't you? intentions – such as we had – were forced – unnatural – & darlingest we are essentially natural with each other – we always have been, since our first understanding. Why should we choose to be as every other person – when we're not – is every other person such a model that you & I should copy them? Let's be ourselves – always darlingest there can never be any misunderstandings then – it doesnt matter if it's harder – you said it was our Fate against each other – we only have will power when we are in accord, not when we are in conflict – tell me if this is how you feel. As I said last night, with you darlint there can never be any pride to stand in the way – it melts in the flame of a great love – I'm finished with pride   Oh a long time ago – do you remember? when I had to come to you in your little room* – after washing up   I wonder if you understand how I feel about these things – I do try to explain but some words seem so useless   Please please lover of mine, dont use that word† I dont like it – I feel that I'm on a pedestal & that I shall always have to strive to remain there & I don't ever want to strive to do anything anything with or for you – thats not being natural & when you use that word – thats just how I feel – not natural – not myself. Would you have me feel like that just so that you could use a term that pleases you & you only? Tell me

Do you remember me being asked if I had found "The Great Lover" Darlingest lover of mine – I had & I'd found "The Great Pal" too the best pal a girl ever had. One is as much to me as the other, there is no first and second they are equal

I am glad you held me tightly when you went to sleep darlint, I wanted comforting badly – I cried such a lot – no I wasn't unhappy – I look a sight today.

---

*   See Letter 26.
†   The word was 'idol', as is clear from Letter 63.

Darlingest – what would have happened had I refused –
when you asked me to kiss you? I want to know

from PEIDI.

Later Exhibit 9. The order form was wrongly dated by Edith; the message was written on Friday 29 September.

At 4.30 she had given it to Rose Jacobs – 'Rosie' – to hand to Freddy, who was waiting once more at Fullers. One wonders what Rose made of the handsome young man. Ahead of time he was outside Carlton and Prior, straining at the leash, and Edith sent Lily Vellender to take him back to the tea room.

'I saw him,' Herbert Carlton told the police, 'on 29th September in the porchway of my premises about 4.45. A few minutes later prisoner Thompson asked if she might leave and she left. I cannot say whether she joined Bywaters.'

Later, Edith joined Percy at the Graydon house in Shakespeare Crescent; but before that she and Freddy had wandered together through the streets of the City, anonymous and free, as the sky turned indigo, and as the bells of St Botolph-without-Aldersgate tolled six, then seven.

From Carlton and Prior, 168 Aldersgate
Street, London, E.C.I.
September 30, 1922.
'Come in for me in ½ an hour.
PEIDI.'

Later Exhibit 31.

Letter written by Freddy Bywaters on the evening of Sunday 1 October.

The previous day, he and Edith had spent the morning together in the park, presumably Wanstead. 'Prisoner Thompson was away from business on 30th with my permission,' Mr Carlton told the police. 'She gave no reason for being absent.' That was the closest that Edith ever came to jumping ship, a half-day off agreed by her boss.

Mrs Lester's statement was precise, and implied a deception of Percy, saying that Edith 'left the house as usual to go to business with Mr Thompson. She returned however about 10.30, she had some shopping with her. She brought this into the house and left immediately afterwards, returning about 1.30.'

So it was less than three hours with Freddy, before going back to cook lunch for her husband and spend the evening with him at the Birnages'. But the time in the park was significant; it opened the possibility of rich, physical delights, of an earthly paradise rather than a dreamscape conjured by words. The couple had sex for the first time in three months – also, as it happened, for the last time – and, as will be seen from Edith's letter, and inferred from Freddy's, it was quite different from before: a mutuality of passion reverberated through them on to the page.

They did not meet on Sunday. Lilian Bywaters told the police that her son spent the day at home; according to Mrs Lester's statement, Edith and Percy went out in the evening (it is not known where) and returned home at about 10.30.

Freddy's reference to Avis is impenetrable. Was he asking if Edith would be prepared to keep a secret for her sister? Was he showing interest, concern, even – gauchely – trying to arouse a little jealousy? It is impossible to know. What is certain is that if he had ever wavered towards the younger sister, this was no longer the case; his obdurate and sincere attempts to break with Edith were lost upon the seas. For all his knowledge of the world, his experience with women, his letter is touchingly immature – a lovesick boy's letter, which takes its tone and references from those imparted and iterated by Edith.

She had got him back and lit an almighty flame, that much is clear.

※

Peidi Darlint.

Sunday evening. Everybody is out and now I can talk to you. I wonder what you are doing now my own little girl   I hope that Bill [her brother] has not been the cause of any further unpleasantness* darlint   Darlint little girl do you remember saying "the hope for all". "Or the finish of all." Peidi the finish of all seems terrible even to contemplate. What darlint would it be in practice? Peidi Mia I love you more and more every day – it grows darlint and will keep on growing. Darlint in the park – our Park on Saturday, you were my "little devil" – I was happy then Peidi – were you? I wasn't thinking of other things – only you darlint – you was my entire world – I love you so much my Peidi – I mustn't ever think of losing you, darlint if I was a poet I could write volumes – but I [sic] not – I suppose at the most I've only spoken about 2 dozen words today I don't try not to speak – but I have no wish to – I'm not spoken to much so have no replies to make

Darlint about the watch – I never really answered your question – I only said I wasnt cross   I can't understand you thinking that the watch would draw me to you – where you yourself wouldn't – is that what you meant darlint or have I misunderstood you   The way you have

* The reference is unclear.

288

written looks to me as though you think that I think more of the watch than I do of you darlint – Tell me Peidi Mia that I misunderstood your meaning

Darlint Peidi Mia – I do remember you coming to me in the little room and I think I understand what it cost you – a lot more then darlint than it could ever now. When I think about that I think how nearly we came to be parted for ever, if you had not forfeited your pride darlint I dont think there would ever have been yesterday or tomorrow

My darlint darlint little girl I love you more than I will ever be able to show you   Darlint you are the centre – the world goes on round you, but you ever remain my world – the other part some things are essential – others are on the outskirts and sometimes so far removed from my mind that they seem non existent   Darling Peidi Mia – I answered the question about the word "Idle"* on Saturday – I never mentioned it

Yes darlint – I remember you being asked if you had found "The great lover"   It was when you sang "A Tumble Down Nook"

What have I found darlint? The darlingest little sweetheart girl in the whole world and "The Only Pal" Now darlint pal – I'm anxious about Avis I hope you have found out all there is to know of the other night – I want you to tell me   Supposing she did stay with some fellow and she tells you and asks you not to tell anybody – are you going to tell me Peidi?

---

* Freddy had called Edith an 'idol' – which she did not like, as she explains with beautiful candour in Letter 61.

Darlint I'm enclosing a slip for you for the books in case
I am unable to get them myself – also will you get the
"Tempting of Paul Chester" Alice and Claude Askew.
There is 13/- to pay on the others – but darlint I hope to
be able to get them myself, also and principally I want to
drink Beaune with you.

Good night now darlingest – dearest little sweetheart
and big pal

FREDDY

64

Later Exhibit 60.

This letter, perhaps more than any, shows Edith's writerly gift. It was also the one, again more than any, that condemned her to death.

'Do something tomorrow night'; 'Don't forget what we talked in the Tea Room'. The sentences leap out, even now.

Written in fits and starts, in between the demands of work, the letter is undated. However it clearly begins as a response to Letter 63 – 'yes I was happy', she writes, in answer to his question above: 'I was happy then Peidi – were you?' Therefore Edith did not start to write it until Freddy gave her *his* letter, written on 'Sunday evening'.

As is laid out in the commentary to 65, below, the couple met twice on Monday 2 October, for lunch and tea, so logic suggests that she wrote it between those meetings and handed it to Freddy when they parted in the early evening.

There is, however, a mystery in the question: 'Darlingest lover, what happened last night?' The evidence of Lilian Bywaters and Mrs Lester – and, more so, of Freddy's own letter – makes it clear that the couple did not meet on Sunday.

Equally clear is what Edith is describing; it is possible to feel, even now, through words written one hundred years ago, her last sensations of pleasure. 'You said you knew it would be like this one day...' Perhaps what happened is this? The couple had sex on Saturday in the park and Edith, a woman of astonishingly responsive sensuality and strange self-obsessed innocence, for the first time in her life realized what this could be like for her; for the rest of the day and throughout Sunday she held the memory of it and hovered around the unknown sensation of climax – then, on Sunday night, achieved it. And mentioned this, in her tantalisingly delicate way, at lunch with Freddy on Monday, then referred back to it in the letter that she wrote in the afternoon.

For him, meanwhile, straightforwardly sexual and ardent, this cannot have been easy: the promise that it held and that was soon to be snatched out of reach again – for the *Morea* sailed on Thursday, and in between times Edith, the glorious lover, was back to playing the wifely role, weaving fantasies of the future and doing absolutely nothing ...

Then: 'I tried so hard to find a way out of tonight darlingest boy but he was suspicious and still is' – she had to spend the evening with, of all people, her brother-in-law Richard. That paragraph might be said to hold Edith's defence, against those who contended that she was plotting murder in this letter. What she describes here is a continuation of the situation as it has always been: waiting, lying, planning to go abroad, not daring to provoke matters for fear of losing her job and having to live off Percy (which did not square with what Mr Carlton, who would anyway have wanted to keep her on, would say to the coroner: 'She was capable of getting a job anywhere').

The line 'I could be beaten all over' is of grave interest, given the ongoing questions about Percy's own capacity for violence – the casual way in which it is mentioned compels belief, although with Edith one simply never knows. For she is also, of course, defending herself to Freddy. Everything that she writes in this paragraph has been written before, over and over, although here the pressure of events – the long separation, the tremulous bliss of reunion – give her words an unprecedented poetic force.

They had, in fact, reached the endgame. She was married and apparently always would be. If he too wanted to marry, then it would not be to her. She had reclaimed him at an immense cost to her pride, and with a remarkable expense of effort, but all she had really done was prove that she could do it. He had trailed back to her, her tame wolf, and her response was to go out with her husband: on Saturday, Sunday, Monday, Tuesday.

What did he think, therefore? That she had pulled every trick in the book to get him back in order to say: life won't always be like this, darlint, while at the same time making it perfectly clear that it would? It is possible to interpret her words – her very defeatism – as a challenge, which her prosecutors would call deliberate. Nothing will ever change, unless *you* change it. It is possible, indeed, that this is how Freddy read what she wrote.

The end of the paragraph deals with Edith's attempts to 'forget' her circumstances, to clear her mind of the yearning for things to change. 'Pal, help me to forget again'. Given this, the infamous phrase – 'do something tomorrow night… something to make you forget' – takes on a far less sinister aspect. It links, in fact, to what she had just written about herself. And, placed in such a context, it makes sense of the following exchange at the Old Bailey (where Edith's words would have been greeted with palpable waves of scepticism):

'What', asked the solicitor general, 'had Bywaters to forget?'

'That I was going somewhere with my husband.'

'What was he to do to make him forget that?'

'I wanted him to take my sister Avis out.'

'You say "I will be hurt, I know." What did that mean?'

'I should have been hurt by Bywaters being with a lady other than myself.'

This also explains the line: 'the bargain now, seems so one-sided' – it would be less so, went Edith's reasoning, if the fourth party in the Thompson–Bywaters triangle were to be reintroduced. It was characteristic in its masochism, and indeed one might say in its kindly cruelty towards Avis, whom of course Freddy had mentioned – slightly ambiguously – in his letter of Sunday evening.

And the remarkable fact of the matter is that Freddy *did* ask Avis out on the night of 3 October, when he visited the Graydon house before walking to Ilford. She told the court: 'As I was letting him out of the door he said to me, "I will be down to take you to the pictures tomorrow evening." That arrangement was made by him just as I was letting him out the front door.'

Then – again in reply to Freddy's letter – Edith returned to the prolonged saga of his watch, which she had held on to in the hope that he would come to get it, even though at that time he was adamantly refusing to see her – an episode now consigned to the past, but which (as lovers do) they delighted in picking over.

Then a brief mention of the bronze monkey that Edith kept on her desk – 'He's still well' – which perhaps had been mentioned at lunch.

Then: 'Don't forget what we talked in the Tea Room, I'll still risk and try if you will – we only have 3 ¾ years left darlingest.

'Try & help'

To her accusers, this seemed to offer up Edith's guilt on a plate. It conjured – in truth it still does – a final breathless meeting at Fullers, in which the couple plotted the following night's murder over the tea-cups.

'Look at the end of that letter,' the solicitor general said to her. 'What had you discussed in the tearoom?'

To which she replied: 'My freedom.'

The oddest thing about it is that this 'Tea Room' talk almost certainly does not refer to the meeting in Fullers on 2 October. The entirety of Edith's letter relates to Monday – she describes, for instance, 'thinking of tonight and tomorrow when I can't see you'. Therefore if she handed it to Freddy when they met at tea, she cannot have been writing about what they discussed that day. The only other possibility is that she wrote this final sentence *after* they met. She might have left the letter at the office and added a coda the following morning, before giving it to Freddy on Tuesday 3rd. Which sounds convoluted, and not very likely.

So if her reference was to a conversation of *the previous week*, in which they met at the tea room three times, it does rather take the heat out of it. There is no knowing what they talked about on, say, Friday 29 September. Obviously they dreamed about their future – the usual talk of 'risk', which may well have meant separation from Percy, moving abroad; 'we only have 3 ¾ years left darlingest', which alluded to the suicide pact and the desire for life to change. There was no evidence whatever to say that this meant change brought about by murder.

Yet this is how the passage was analysed in the closing speech for the prosecution: 'I ask – what did they talk about in the tea room? I put it that there was a long course of suggestion resulting in a desire to escape from the position, and a fresh suggestion was made in the tea room...' With regard to the murder, and Freddy's waylaying of Percy on his way home from the theatre: 'There is the undoubted evidence in the letters upon which you can find that there was a preconcerted meeting between Mrs Thompson and Bywaters at the place'. This quite extraordinary statement, which defines the word 'evidence' in the most terrifying possible way – as meaning whatever the forces of law choose it to mean – can only have referred to the 'tea room' conversation. How was it that Edith's defence did not emphasise that a) nobody knows what was talked about on that occasion; and b) there was no proof of when it took place? But the defence seemed in a dream, as if dazed by the impossibility of arguing against a case of shreds and patches.

In his ineffable Home Office memorandum of 28 December, written to bolster the case for the executions proceeding as planned, Sir Ernley Blackwell stated smoothly: 'Undoubtedly Bywaters knew their plans [where the Thompsons would be on the night of 3 October] and the Jury were certainly entitled to infer that at tea time, when they were together in the teashop, they arranged for the attack.'

It will be noted that 'tea rooms' had now, mysteriously, acquired a proven connection to crime-plotting (even though on the 3rd, the day of the murder, the couple spent no time at all in Fullers – as Sir Ernley must have known), and that the correlation with Edith's letter of the 2nd was now so loose as to be almost irrelevant. Effectively, Sir Ernley's statement meant this: that it was legitimate to hang a person on what the jury inferred from a conversation of which nobody really knew anything, including when it happened.

There remains, however, the truly unanswerable question, the one that was no business of the law: what did *Freddy* understand by Edith's words?

❧

Darlingest lover of mine, thank you, thank you, oh thank you a thousand times for Friday – it was lovely – its always lovely to go out with you

And then Saturday – yes I did feel happy – I didn't think a teeny bit about anything in this world, except being with you – and all Saturday evening I was thinking about you – I was just with you in a big arm chair in front of a great big fire feeling all the time how much I had won – cos I have darlint, won such a lot – it feels such a great big thing to me sometimes – that I can't breathe

When you are away and I see girls with men walking along together – perhaps they are acknowledged sweethearts – they look so ordinary then I feel proud – so proud to think and feel that you are my lover and even tho' not acknowledged I can still hold you – just with a tiny 'hope.'

Darlint, we've said we'll always be Pals haven't we, shall we say we'll always be lovers – even tho' secret ones, or is it (this great big love) a thing we can't control – dare we say that – I think I will dare   Yes I will   I'll always love you – if you are dead – if you have left me even if you don't still love me, I always shall you

Your love to me is now, it is something different, it is my life and if things should go badly with us, I shall always have this past year to look back upon and feel that 'Then I lived'   I never did before and I never shall again

Darlingest lover, what happened last night? I don't know myself I only know how I felt – no not really how I felt but how I could feel – if time and circumstances were different.

It seems like a great welling up of love – of feeling – of inertia, just as if I am wax in your hands – to do with as you will and I feel that if you do as you wish I shall be happy, its physical purely and I can't really describe it – but you will understand darlint wont you? You said you knew it would be like this one day – if it hadn't would you have been disappointed. Darlingest when you are rough, I go dead – try not to be please.

The book is lovely – it's going to be sad darlint tho', why can't life go on happy always?

I like Clarie* – she is so natural so unworldly

Why ar'nt you an artist and I as she is – I feel when I am reading frightfully jealous of her – its a picture darlint, just how I did once picture that little flat in Chelsea – why can't he go on loving her always – why are men different – I am right when I say that love to a man is a thing apart from his life but to a woman it is her whole existence

I tried so hard to find a way out of tonight darlingest but he was suspicious and still is – I suppose we must make a study of this deceit for some time longer. I hate it   I hate every lie I have to tell to see you – because lies seem such small mean things to attain such an object as ours. We ought to be able to use great big things for great big love like ours. I'd love to be able to say 'I'm going to see my lover tonight.' If I did he would prevent me – there would be scenes and he would come to 168 and interfere and I couldn't bear that – I could be beaten all over at home and still be defiant – but at 168 it's different   It's my living – you wouldn't let me live on him would you and I shouldn't want to – darlint its funds that are our stumbling block – until we have those we can do nothing. Darlingest find me a job abroad   I'll go tomorrow and not say I was going to a soul and not have one little regret   I said I wouldn't think – that I'd try to forget circumstances   Pal, help me to forget again – I have succeeded up to now – but its thinking of tonight and tomorrow when I can't see you and feel you holding me

Darlint – do something tomorrow night will you? something to make you forget   I'll be hurt I know, but

I want you to hurt me – I do really – the bargain now, seems so one sided – so unfair – but how can I alter it?

*****

About the watch – I didn't think you thought more of that – how can I explain what I did feel? I felt that we had parted – you weren't going to see me – I had given you something to remind you of me and I had purposely retained it   If I said "come for it" you would – but only the once and it would be as a pal, because you would want me so badly at times that the watch would help you not to feel so badly – and if you hadn't got it – the feeling would be so great – it would conquer you against your will.

Darlint do I flatter myself when I think you think more of the watch than of anything else   That wasn't a present – that was something you asked me to give you – when we decided to be *pals* a sort of sealing of the compact   I couldn't afford it then, but immediately I could I did Do you remember when and where we were when you asked me for it? If you do tell me, if you don't, forget I asked.

How I thought you would feel about the watch, I would feel about something I have

It isn't mine, but it belongs to us and unless we were differently situated than we are now, I would follow you everywhere – until you gave it to me back

He's still well* – he's going to gaze all day long at you in your temporary home† – after Wednesday.

Don't forget what we talked in the Tea Room, I'll still risk and try if you will – we only have 3 ¾ years left darlingest.

Try & help

PEIDI.

---

* At the trial, Mr Justice Shearman would suggest – in all seriousness – that this phrase referred not to the bronze monkey but to Percy Thompson; the implication being that 'he' would not be 'well' for much longer.
† The 'temporary home' was the RMS *Morea*, a painting of which was being delivered and which Edith intended to hang in her office 'after Wednesday', that is to say the day after the murder.

65

Later Exhibit 10. Written on Monday 2 October.

'On the 2nd Oct at 8.30 a.m. I answered a telephone call,' Lilian Bywaters told the police. 'It was a woman's voice and I called my son and he answered it. My son left the house shortly before 11 a.m.'

Surprising, perhaps, that Edith was willing to ring Freddy at his mother's house, but such now was her confidence that she did not fear Lilian's influence; and Lilian, clearly, had learned what seemed to be the wisdom of silence.

The couple arranged to meet for lunch that day. But instead it was Percy, spying as was his wont – unappealing yet pitiable – who turned up at Carlton and Prior at around 12.30.

A boy who worked at the firm told the police: 'Miss Graydon called me into her office which is on the ground floor, she was alone, she was in the act of wrapping up an order form with some writing on it... After she had wrapped it up she placed it in a white envelope, sealed it and said "Take this... to Aldersgate Street Station and give it to the gentleman who is wearing a blue overcoat and a trilby hat."'

That was the message below. Edith then wrote another note, which was not put in evidence:

> Mr Carlton has gone out to lunch now & I must wait until he comes back – Miss P. is not back yet – do you mind waiting there – I am sorry to ask you to wait such a lot but its awkward today – I had a terrible half hour.

The boy took this message to Freddy some five or ten minutes after the first note. 'The second letter,' he said, 'I delivered ten yards from Osman's shop.'

Osman's stood on the other side of the alley that ran alongside Carlton and Prior; it was a shop that sold knives.

Eventually the couple had lunch – their favoured venue was in Cheapside – and later had tea at Fullers. Then Edith left to spend the evening with her brother-in-law Richard Thompson, and Freddy to the infinitely warmer and more welcoming arena of 231 Shakespeare Crescent, where he stayed until around 10.30 p.m.

From Carlton and Prior
'Wait till one he's come.
PEIDI.'

66

This letter, not put in evidence, is undated.

❋

Darlingest Boy,

Thank you – ever, ever so much for all those things I
received – are they all for me tho? there seems such a lot
& what am I to do about them? Wear them now? or wait,
I know when you sent them you wanted me & expected
that I would wear them, but now – well I suppose its not
to be.

I've nothing to talk about darlint, not a tiny little thing
– Life – the Life I & we lead is gradually drying me up
– soon I'll be like the "Sahara" – just a desert, like the
"Shulamite" you must read that book, its interesting –
absorbing, arent books a consolation and a solace? We
ourselves die & live in the books we read while we are
reading them & then when we have finished, the books
die and we live – or exist – just drag on thro years & years,
until when? who knows – I'm beginning to think no one
does – no not even you & I, we are not the shapers of our
destinies

I'll always love you darlint,

PEIDI.

PART II: MURDER AND AFTER

On the morning of 3 October, stated Lilian Bywaters, 'the phone went and my son answered it. He did not tell me what the message was. He left the house somewhere before 12 o'clock but did not say where he was going.'

He had gone to the City, as usual, where he took Edith to lunch and later met her at Fullers, although they did not stay more than a couple of minutes.

They parted at Aldersgate station at around 5.30.

Edith travelled to Piccadilly station, for an evening at the Criterion Theatre with Percy, her aunt Lily and uncle John. Freddy went to the Graydons' house, where he would again spend the evening. The knife was in his inside coat pocket. Later he would say that he always carried a knife.

'A knife of that size and character?' asked the solicitor general.

'Yes, handy at sea.'

'Handy at sea, but was it handy at home?'

'Yes.'

To the coroner, Mr Graydon stated that Freddy had arrived at Shakespeare Crescent at about 7 p.m., and that, during the course of the evening, Avis 'said that she had received a telephone message from Percy informing her that he and his wife were going to the Criterion Theatre that night. I am sure Bywaters heard her saying it. He remained with us till 10.55 p.m., then left simply saying "Good night" and we naturally thought him to be going home... he had one glass of ale and may have had two, but no more. I could see nothing unusual in his manner.'

Freddy himself would say that he had learned from Edith, earlier that day, that she would be going to the theatre that night (in fact her letter of 2 October mentions that she would not be seeing him on the 3rd).

Either way, therefore, he knew where to find Percy. If he knew it from Edith, he had time to plan what he might do. If he heard it from Avis that evening, and if she presented the theatre visit in clever language designed to make trouble – oh Edie and Percy, they're good as gold together really! – there is a possibility that a remark of this kind, with its sharp deviation from the relationship as presented by Edith, set him on his course of action.

It is possible, too, that Avis suspected as much, all her life.

That said, he already had the knife; although there is ample reason to doubt that he walked to Ilford with the intention to kill (see commentary to Letter 10).

What, then, did he intend? The story had reached its impasse and he wanted, one might say, to bring matters to a head. He was very young – one must never forget that, the heat in the blood, the vital unwillingness to let it cool – and he was impelled to do something, although probably he himself did not know what. Have it out with the husband, yes. Have it out, at any rate. There is in fact a mysterious sense in which his antagonist was not Percy Thompson, but Edith; who – through her presence, but mainly through her words – had brought him to a state of scarcely tolerable frustration over a situation that, in his sane self, he did not even want.

He was arrested the following evening, at the Graydon house. Edith had tried her hardest not to mention his name to the police, whose first best guess was that Percy was a victim of stranger murder. It was Richard Thompson who suggested to detectives that Freddy might be a person of interest, whereupon the case acquired an entirely new dimension; although without the letters they could have suspected Edith all they liked, and she would have eluded their grasp.

On the morning of 4 October, clearly acting on Edith's instructions, Avis went to Carlton and Prior. There she asked Rose Jacobs to take 'Miss Graydon's box' from the desk in Edith's office and keep it safe. Inside the box (first mentioned at the very start of this story, in Letter 1) were the two love letters that became Exhibits 30 and 31, plus Freddy's photograph, as well as the 'Dear Edie' letter that became Exhibit 14 and was kept as a blind (see note to Letter 6).

One of the strongest practical arguments against Edith's foreknowledge of her husband's murder is that those two letters had not yet been destroyed, which (as far as she knew) would have severed all evidential links with Freddy. It is actually impossible to believe that she would have conceived a plot, yet failed to get rid of those letters. The other argument is that Edith, had she been involved in such a plot, would have surely pushed the murder forward a day and arranged it for 4 October – knowing that, within a matters of hours, Freddy would be sailing off and out of harm's way. But these points in her favour were never raised.

She would never have been so stupid as to have left the letters in her desk had she known about the murder; yet it was immensely stupid to leave them in the care of Rose Jacobs, whom she had patronised and befriended while failing to recognise that the girl – like so many of her sex – seethed with spite towards her.

The first real breakthrough in the case came on the evening of the 4th, when the police visited Lilian Bywaters. A detective inspector on the case reported that he searched Freddy's bedroom, at Lilian's own request: as she herself put it, 'I took him to my son's bedroom where I saw him take some letters.' In a writing case inside a suitcase, not locked, the detective found Exhibits 28, 47, 54, 55, 58 and 60: the letters received while Freddy was in England. In a coat pocket were what became Exhibits 9 and 10: the notes scribbled on Friday 29 September and Monday 1 October. It would seem that Lilian, who had immediately grasped the situation, had taken the view that if her son was going down for murder, he was taking Edith with him.

Around the same time, the police obtained evidence from that young Judas, Rose Jacobs, who gave the following statement:

> On Wednesday or Thursday 4th or 5th October, when
> I heard of the Ilford murder, I went to Mrs Thompson's
> desk and took possession of a small tin box – locked, a
> book, and inside the book was a photo of Bywaters and

also in the desk was the letter which I had addressed to Miss Fisher [the one used as fake identification at the post office]. Mr Carlton asked me about it. I told him what I knew and he gave me the letter which I later burnt, together with the photograph. I kept the box.

Rose took the locked box back to her home, as Avis had requested (it seems that Mr Carlton did not know about this). Then she handed it over to a detective sergeant.

At about 11.30 a.m. on Wednesday 4 October, Edith had been taken with her mother in a taxi to Ilford police station. She was not arrested or put in a cell, but she would never go home again. She made a statement, which did not identify Freddy as her husband's assailant.

On the 5th, having been tricked by a staged encounter (for which the detectives responsible would be criticised at the Old Bailey), she was suddenly confronted by the figure of Freddy Bywaters in a corridor at the station and screamed: 'Why did he do it? I didn't want him to do it! Oh God, oh God, what can I do!'

Her outburst was analysed thus by Mr Justice Shearman in his summing-up: 'Again it is noticeable that she is throwing the blame on him, "Why did he do it?" and she is excusing herself.'

Edith then made another statement, admitting that on the night of 3 October she had recognised Freddy as the man who attacked Percy.

On the 6th, Edith and Freddy attended a hearing at Stratford Magistrates' Court; afterwards she was taken to Holloway prison and he to Brixton.

On the 12th, a detective inspector from the Port of London police made a search of Freddy's cabin on the *Morea* at Tilbury. There he found the locked box that contained the rest of Edith's correspondence.

1

Letter sent to Edith from Freddy. It is one of the few to exist in its original form: a thin folded sheet of closely spaced lines, covered in tidy slanted script.

It is not known when the couple started writing to each other again, nor how often they did so. At this stage both were on remand but, as yet, only Freddy was due to stand trial. On 23 October, the inquest had brought in a verdict of wilful murder against him. Despite the discovery of the letters, Edith had been charged with nothing.

The following day, extracts from the letters were made public for the first time when the presiding magistrate at Stratford ruled them admissible. It was reported that Edith collapsed and had to be removed from the courtroom when a detective sergeant read her words aloud.

Nevertheless she continued to write to Freddy; that desire had not evaporated.

On 21 November, however, a man named J. H. Wall, from the Prison Commission department within the Home Office, wrote to the Governor of Holloway, Dr Morton:

> Please note that letters written by the woman Thompson to the man Bywaters will not be posted. She will not, however, be told of this. If she writes any, they will be sent up to this Office, where they will be retained.
>
> If she has written to him, or if she has received letters from him, why were they not submitted to the Commissioners. None appear to have been sent up.

The reply from the Governor read:

> Noted. Only 2 letters have been sent out by the woman Thompson, and 3 have been received from Bywaters, none of which appear to have any bearing upon the trial. Two of the letters received from Bywaters were destroyed

by Thompson, but I attach the third letter [below] for the Commissioners' perusal.

Minuted in the Home Office files was the reply from Wall:

The letter should not have been passed & two prisoners connected in the same case & such a grave case should not have been allowed to correspond without first obtaining the Commissioners' instructions.

On 23 November, as Edith entered the dock for the final day of the hearing at Stratford Magistrates' Court, she shouted out to Freddy in her old, spirited voice, asking if he had received two letters that she had sent that week. It was her last act of defiance against the legal machinery that was about to swallow her whole. She had gone to the court that day expecting to be released; her family was there, optimistic in its belief that she would be leaving with them. Mrs Graydon was heard to cry out, 'My child, my child' as instead, at the end of proceedings, both Edith Thompson and Frederick Bywaters were formally charged with murder and conspiracy to murder. Edith Thompson was further charged with administering poison with intent to murder Percy Thompson; with soliciting and proposing to Frederick Bywaters to murder Percy Thompson; and with soliciting and inciting Bywaters to conspire with her and agree to murder Percy Thompson.

※

No 8696 Nov: 18th 1922 [Saturday]

Name F. Bywaters

Brixton

G.M.M.C. [Good Morning Ma Chère]

Today I want to finish the conversation of yesterday. It was rotten - wasn't it - when I was feeling in a mood to talk for a long time I had to desist owing to lack of material. Now P.m. [Peidi mia] comment ca vas [sic]-

Why haven't you written to me so that I recd. letter first post this morning? Answer - A change for me to be in this position? - I'm going to take full advantage of the opportunity. The enclosed cutting* - Is the part I have underlined quite correct? If it is - I shall have to use spectacles. Now suppose we have a conversation about the book. My opinion now - yours when you answer. In the first place don't think I liked it as much as I did 'Atonement'. The best parts I see you noticed. I think Coict made quite an unnecessary sacrifice - though - she was prompted by the highest motives. If she had told Grier she would never had those times of torment - which - you can understand - but I cannot. (It was explained very well by A. & C. Askew - in 'The Shulamite'). Did you like Grier? Or Bently?†

Funny. - I dreamt last night that you wrote to me & told me that you had been able to finish 'His Daughter' [by Gouverneur Morris]. I would talk about 'Sam's Kid' [by F. E. Mills Young] more, only I have no particular wish to explain my feelings to an audience - you alone yes - it is different.

You understand fully - don't you Pal? You asked me what I do all day - I suppose practically the same as you. Sit on a chair - think or read, eat at specified times & then sleep; One day is over. I look forward to the day

---

* This did not survive.
† This book, and *Atonement*, are unidentifiable.

at Court – it breaks the monotony. Do I sound a bit morbid & down – I don't feel over exhilarated: – One of those 'One little hours' would be good now. But this I suppose is only a passing phase – not the longing for 'One little hour' – the other part. I'm going to finish now p.m. Carissima mia. Goodbye

FREDDY

The trial of Thompson and Bywaters began on Wednesday 6 December, and ended on the 11th. The jury spent a little more than two hours deliberating, then returned verdicts of 'Guilty'.

Freddy can have expected nothing else. Edith had hope, of course; although it is hard to know how, when she was up against the desire to condemn that pervaded almost every area of the Old Bailey, including the judge's seat. This, from his summing-up, shows the way in which prejudice and preconception had invaded the very processes of logic.

> It is said by the prosecution that from beginning to end of these letters she is seriously considering and inciting the man to assist her to poison her husband, and if she did that, and if you find that within a week or two after he came back the poisoning is considered no longer possible, he has no longer studied or has not studied bichloride of mercury, but has read *Bella Donna* without seeing how *Bella Donna* can be of any use to him, they would naturally turn to some other means of effecting their object, and it is said to you they naturally would, when you find them meeting day after day, parting at half-past five, meeting the husband at six, and she telling him where they were going, and he immediately, as soon as he gets an opportunity, if you believe he waited for them coming back, and knew they were there – gentlemen,

you may say here are circumstances following the long-studied incitement for him to help her to poison.

Basically she never stood a chance. This, sometimes, is what 'justice' decides to do.

When Edith's family went to see her in the cells, before she was removed to Holloway, she held Mr Graydon's coat and said: 'Take me home, Dad.'

2

Letter from Edith, thought to be to her school friend Bessie Akam. The 'Thursday' to which she refers is the date of the appeal, 21 December.

❧

Holloway Prison, Monday 18 December, 1922

Dear —

I have just received your letter and I hasten to answer it.

Yes, it was awful last Monday. I can't explain what it felt like. I suppose no one knows unless their position is the same. It would be so much easier to bear if I knew or even felt I deserved that verdict, but I'm hoping for such a lot on Thursday. Everyone seems so hopeful for me. I suppose it is catching.

The time here, on the whole, seems not as long as on remand – so many things are different. I can't tell you because it is against the rules, but it is a fact, and I sleep better here than I did there; really I have very good night's rest.

There is plenty of time and opportunity to think all day long, so that by the time the night comes my brain is quite worn out and rests quite naturally.

This is something I am really pleased about, because I never – no, I think, not once – had a really good night's sleep. I have asked and obtained permission for you to visit me. Now, as you are going away on Friday, I wonder if you will have time, but if you don't come I shall quite understand, and hope that you will have a real good rest over the holidays.

I remember it was mother's birthday yesterday, and wrote to her. I'm glad you went down to see them. I expect they want cheering a little.

You know, dear, it's really about them I worry far more than about myself. It must be painful for them – the publicity alone must be more than they can cope with. You see I am shut away here and know nothing of all that. However, perhaps things will come right even yet.

Ask — to write: only tell him to mind his p's and q's. Now there is nothing else I want to say except to thank you – I can't tell you how much – for all you have done for me and for mother during this time.

It has helped tremendously to know that everybody, friends and relatives, have all stood by me during this time and have believed in me and still do.

I can't say any more, but I'm sure you will understand how I feel, and remember that all I want you to do now is to wish me luck for Thursday.

EDITH

3

Part of a letter from Freddy to an unknown recipient, possibly his sister Florence. Date also unknown – although the reference to 'last Friday week' is surely to Friday 8 December, the day on which Edith began her testimony at the Old Bailey, to which this letter is a powerful reaction.

Whereas Freddy had done everything in his power to shield her – to the point of, perversely, damaging her cause, since he looked so noble and was so obviously lying – she, in contrast, had not protected him at all. She had shielded him after the murder, by not giving his name to the police, but that was self-protection also and anyway had got her nowhere; in fact it had given ineradicable substance to the accusation that she was a liar (lying to the forces of law is always regarded as peculiarly wicked. Almost comical, in this case, where even the judge was not averse to a bit of fact-elision).

At the trial, meanwhile, she had not been brave or self-possessed. Having demanded the right to testify, surely a sign of innocence, when the twisty lawyerly 'yes or no' questions were put to her she had no weapons against them whatsoever (see commentary to Letter 14). And in her floundering inability to explain what she had barely understood herself, she had implicated Freddy without a care for him.

This, for instance, was an exchange with the solicitor general regarding Letter 43. He read out the passage 'why arnt you sending me something... if I don't mind the risk why should you?', then said:

'You were asking Bywaters to send something which he had said, according to you, he was going to bring?'

'That is so.'

'What was it?'

'I have no idea.'

'Have you no idea?'

'Except what he told me.'

'What did he tell you?'

'He would bring me something.'

'Did he not say what the something was?'

'No, he did not mention anything.'

'What did he lead you to think it was?'

'That it was something for me to give my husband.'

'With a view to poisoning your husband?'

'That was not the idea, that was not what I expected.'

'Something to give your husband that would hurt him?'

'To make him ill.'

'He suggested giving your husband something to hurt him?'

'He had given me something.'

'Given you something to give your husband?'

'That is so.'

'Did the suggestion then come from Bywaters?'

'It did.'

'Did you welcome it when it came?'

'I read it.'

'What?'

'I read it and studied it.'

'Did you welcome the suggestion that something should be given to your husband to make him ill?'

'I did not.'

'Did you object to it?'

'I was astonished about it.'

'Did you object to it?'

'I did, at the time.'

'And although you objected to it you urged Bywaters to send it more quickly than he intended?'

'I objected at the time. Afterwards I acquiesced.'

Later, this would provoke the following from Mr Justice Shearman's summing-up, which in the strange circumstances was not unreasonable: 'You have noticed, I daresay, in the course of the case that where the woman made statements they are mostly something excusing her and implicating the man, but in some of them, when the man is making statements, they are always exculpating the woman. It is said that is chivalry and that is why he is doing it.'

Hence, perhaps, a little-known incident, referred to in a confidential Home Office file dated 23 December 1922 and headed:

'Interview with Mr Whiteley'. This was Cecil Whiteley, Freddy's defence counsel and a lawyer of high repute.

The handwritten minutes read:

> Bywaters' counsel Mr Whiteley would have liked to see Sir E. Blackwell. He was anxious to say something & not in writing.
>
> Finally he told me.
>
> Bywaters says that between 17–20th March, under pressure from Mrs Thompson, he gave her a large quantity of a white powder, calling it cocaine. She gave it to Thompson. This is the elephant dose [see Letter 27]. It was quinine.
>
> B. says he never procured poison for her (But he did stick a knife three* times through her husband's neck).
>
> This helps B. very little & damns Mrs T.
>
> Mr W. also said B. is a good chap & that his father was killed in the war.

This, then, was Freddy's revenge for Edith's betrayal in the dock. One suspects that he was encouraged in it by Lilian Bywaters, but it was also the behaviour of a man capable of deliberate action. He had offered this information to his counsel and told him to do something with it. He was twenty years old, he did not want to die. One is reminded of Ruth Ellis, full of fortitude after her condemnation in 1955, but – just before her execution – calling in a new solicitor, giving a new statement, naming the person who, she claimed, had given her the gun with which she shot her lover David Blakely.

Completely understandable, in other words. Nevertheless it is unclear how Freddy really thought that it would help him. The more evidence there was against Edith, the more likely *he* was to hang; his only chance of reprieve would have been if the authorities reprieved

---

* In fact it was twice. Not that it makes much difference; it is just interesting to note that these prim, precise men were so often careless with their facts.

her, which they were most keen not to do. So as much as anything it was revenge.

As to what he actually said to Cecil Whiteley... He had danced and dodged about the 'quinine' business in the witness box (see commentary to Letter 22), giving nonsensical answers about humouring Edith in her desire to commit suicide. Now, almost certainly, he was telling the truth. This could only be proved by his own letters to Edith, and they still could not prove what he actually gave to her. It may in fact have been cocaine, obtained for him by the mysterious Dan. Whatever it was, Edith may have merely pretended to use it.

But this recently discovered piece of information does probe certain myths that have grown up around the Thompson–Bywaters case: that he was an essentially decent hothead; that she, except when writing about the need to self-abort, was essentially a fantasist. Both these characterisations are accurate. Neither goes far enough. They are too simplistic, given this immensely complex story, in which facts are few and interpretations multifarious.

And – with regard to the possibility that Edith was a husband poisoner, which a century ago almost everybody believed: people did do such things. Madeleine Smith and Adelaide Bartlett, attractive women of the Victorian era, had not seemed likely to poison a lover or a husband, and they both got away with doing so, but it is almost beyond doubt that they did exactly that. So why not Edith Thompson?

Reading the letters from the spring of 1922 one does discern a heightened quality, a compulsive quickening, as if the dreams of murder had acquired an *element* of the factual – a first tentative step across the chasm that separates fantasy from reality – which the information from Freddy, as above, undoubtedly confirms. Whether Edith made the leap, and dropped something – just once, perhaps, just the smallest pinch – into her husband's food or drink, is unknowable; all that is known is that it did not kill him. She was not guilty. At the same time, and this perhaps is what Freddy was grappling with in his cell at Pentonville, she was guilty of something.

Quite soon, however, he abandoned his sense of betrayal by Edith's testimony and fought to save her with all that was good in him – which was a great deal (the Governor of Pentonville would later write: 'I looked at this lad, and I thought, Is it necessary to take his life?'). After the shock and trauma of the trial, Freddy was honest enough to accept that Edith had spoken as she did out of terror, that she had spoken something of the truth, and that she had been sitting there giving evidence because of what he himself had done. That his, in the end, was the greater guilt.

꙳

Can you understand the feeling I have?

Gradually, bit by bit, the trust and faith that I have put in somebody seemed to be dragged out and thrown in my face, and it hurts. When I have said that, I have said all. Put yourself in the position I occupy and just think. I tried to think after last Friday week, but really I could not muster one clear thought. Everything seemed topsy-turvy, but things seem clearer now. I suppose it is one of the hardest things in this world for a person to recognise and admit that he or she has misplaced their trust.

Letter sent by Edith to her parents after the dismissal of the appeals on 21 December (Mr Graydon had attended the hearing).

The Governor of Holloway, Dr Morton, who would soon be stuffing Edith with remarkable quantities of drugs in an attempt to numb the actuality of what was happening to her, sent the letter to the Prison Commissioners for approval. He wrote:

> In view of your instructions as to letters of prisoners under sentence of death I beg to submit the attached for your perusal. Although this woman has written a number of letters since she was condemned to death I may say they have all been couched in a more or less frivolous style.
>
> This is the first letter she has written in which she shows that she has begun to realise what her sentence means.
>
> Also I beg to draw your attention to para. commencing 'However I suppose' and ending 'I know that certain events were landmarks.'

The reply was: 'The letter may be posted.'

Dearest Mother and Dad –

Today seems the end of everything. I can't think – I just seem up against a black, thick wall, through which neither my eyes nor my thoughts can penetrate.

It's not within my powers of realisation that this sentence must stand for something which I have not done, something I did not know of, either previously or at the time. I know you both know this. I know you both have known and believed it all along.

However, I suppose it is only another landmark in my life – there have been so many when I look back, but somehow they are not landmarks until I look back upon the journey, and then I know that certain events were landmarks.

I've tried to unravel this tangle of my existence, this existence that we all call life. It is only at these times that we do think about it.

It has been an existence, that's all, just a 'passing through'; meeting trials, and shocks and surprises with a smiling face and an aching heart, and eventually being submerged and facing Death, that thing that there is no escaping – no hope of defeating.

You both must be feeling as bad and perhaps worse than I do today, and I do so hope that this will not make things harder to bear, but I really felt that I should like to talk to you both for just a little while, after I was told the result.

Even now I cannot realise all it means; but, dearest mother and dad, you both must bear up – just think that I am trying to do the same, and I am sure that thought will help you.

EDITH.

5

Letter from Edith to her aunt, Edith Walkinshaw.

☙

Holloway Prison,
Saturday 23 December, 1922

Dear Auntie – It was good of you to send me in the book; it will help to pass a good many weary hours away, when my mind is more settled.

At present I can't think – I can't even feel. When I was told the result of the appeal yesterday, it seemed the end of everything.

In Life, Death seems too awful to contemplate, especially when Death is the punishment for something I have not done, did not know of, either at the time or previously.

I have been looking back over my life, & wondering what it has brought me – I once said "Only ashes and dust and bitterness", and today it seems even less than this – if there can be less.

This last ordeal seems to be the ultimate end of that gradual drifting through Life, passing each event, each disappointment, so many of which I have encountered and met with a smiling face and an aching heart.

Auntie dear, I have learnt the lesson that it is not wise to meet and try to overcome all your trials alone – when the end comes, as it has to me, nobody understands.

If only I had been able to forfeit my pride, that pride that resents pity, and talk to someone, I can see now how different things might have been, but it's too late now to rake over ashes in the hope of finding some live coal.

When I first came into this world, and you stood to me as godmother, I am sure you never anticipated such an end as this for me. Do you know, people have told me from time to time that to be born on Christmas Day was unlucky, and my answer has always been, "Superstition is only good for ignorant people", but now I am beginning to believe that they are right; it is unlucky.

However, what is to be will be. Somewhere I read "The fate of every man hath he bound about his neck", and this, I suppose, I must accept as mine.

I'm glad I've talked to you for a little while. I feel better – it seems to lift me out of this abyss of depression into which I have fallen, and I know you will understand, not only what I have said, but all my thoughts that are not collected enough to put on paper.

Thank Leonard [her aunt Edith's son, aged 15] for me for his letter. It made me laugh, and it's good to laugh just for five minutes. I'll write to him another day. I can't now – but I know he will understand.

EDITH

6

Letter from Edith, thought to be to Bessie Akam.

❧

Holloway Prison,
Tuesday 26 December, 1922

Dear —

I wanted to write to you yesterday and yet I couldn't. I could do nothing but sit and think. Who was it said, 'Some days we sits and thinks, and some we simply sit'? Well, yesterday was a 'sitting and thinking day'.

I got your letter on Saturday. Yes, the result of the appeal was a great shock – I had such hopes of it – not only hopes for mercy, but hopes for justice; but I realise how very difficult it is to fight prejudice.

If you have facts to fight, and you fail, you seem more reconciled, but when it's only prejudice – oh, it's awful.

You talk about not having to pay the extreme penalty. Do you know that I don't dread that at all. I feel that would be easier than banishment – wrongful banishment for life. I feel no apprehension of what might lie ahead after this life.

Yesterday I was twenty-nine; it's not really very old, I suppose, and yet it seems so to me.

Yesterday I was thinking about everything that has ever happened, it seems to help in all sorts of ways when I do this. I realise what a mysterious thing life is. We all imagine we can mould our own lives – we seldom can, they are moulded for us – just by the laws and rules and conventions of this world, and if we break any of these, we only have to look forward to a formidable and unattractive wilderness.

I've often thought how good it would be to talk, to pour out everything, it might have pained as well, but it would be pain that comes with sudden relief of intolerable hurt.

However, I'm going to forget all that now. I'm going to hope – because everybody tells me so. I'm going to live in those enormous moments when the whole of life seems bound up in the absolute necessity to win.

Thank you so much for writing to me, and helping to keep me cheerful.

EDITH

7

Letter from Avis Graydon to Prime Minister Bonar Law, dated 30 December 1922.

The points that she raised were answered in Home Office minutes, thus:

> The passage marked 1) is quite inconsistent with Mrs T's explanation of a passage in her letter of 2 Oct. 'Do something tomorrow night'. She said this meant 'Take my sister Avis out'!
>
> As regards 2) She did not tell her mother of her adulterous connection with B or of the letters she was writing to him for a year planning to get rid of her husband by poison or any other available means.
>
> PT is described as a popular young man without an enemy in the world. There is no reason to believe that he treated his wife badly or that he was unhappy with her until Byw. came on the scene: and the pictures* of the pair taken this year show that she was pretending be on terms of great affection with him – although she was writing at that time of poisons with wh. to get rid of him!

The assertion that Percy was 'popular' lacked any evidential basis: nobody described him as such. There was, however, some evidence that he 'treated his wife badly'. But any points in the letter that questioned the prevailing narrative – good points, in the main – were ignored as if they had never been made; notably the reference to Bernard Spilsbury.

The line regarding Edith's sanity is strange and desperate. Avis, as has been seen, was shocked beyond expression by her sister's letters.

Her own life, which ended in Ilford in 1977, was spent in an ongoing aftermath of these events: in her 1973 interview she said that

---

* This referred to the photograph taken at Boscombe – see commentary to Letter 51.

she still expected Edith to come walking through the door. She never married. Her conversion to Catholicism (see note to Letter 3) was connected to the fact that a kindly priest had given her sister some comfort in the death cell, although he was forbidden to visit her at the end: the authorities, whose capacity for bureaucratic sadism seemed to know no limits, insisted that unless Edith were to convert (when?) she must be attended by an Anglican.

❧

I beg you kindly to read this letter in the hope that some of the points will enable you to see my sister's character other than presented to the public, by the pros.

[1] I can assure you Sir that my sister had no idea that her husband was going to be murdered, as it had been arranged a fortnight before that, I should accompany them to the Theatre, & spend the night with her in Kensington Gdns, & she had no idea until she met her husband in the evening that I was not going to be of the party. Her husband telephoned me late in the afternoon & I told him that I had already made arrangements to go out for mother.

How can they pass sentence of Death on her?

Mr S[pilsbury] gave evidence that there was no trace of poison in the deceased's body, how then can it be said, she poisoned him.

Why was all the evidence of defence put on one side, & only the black side – the foolish letters of an overwrought, unhappy woman – placed before the Jury.

It is untrue that my sister was happy until B came into her life.

Mrs Lester can prove, & also others with whom she lived before, that she was unhappy; only her great respect & love for her parents prevented her bringing her troubles home. [2] If she had done anything wrong at anytime, she would have told mother at any cost, also my brother in law, would have spoken to my dad.

I should like to say, that PT being of a peculiar character had no friends of his own, & naturally very soon disagreed with my sister's friends.

The man is dead, but why should he die blameless. His case was just the same as my sister's which you can see by the letters, not produced.

Mrs T was a hard working woman of a generous, loving nature & no doubt after B seeing her unhappiness, she turned to him for sympathy. Her great mistake being – afraid to confide in her family who loved her above everything. Why was it so emphatically said 'She incited B'? it is obvious her letters were answers to questions, where are B's letters to prove his statement that Mrs T is innocent? Why has no benefit [sic] of the doubt been given in this case to the accused.

Can it be my sister is insane! Is this question having the prison doctor's attention.

If you had seen my sister at any time, there could not be any doubt in your mind that the verdict is wrong.

I beg you to shew mercy on her, for her parents sake, you are a father therefore understand their feelings. We are helpless & know she is not Guilty.

May the Great Judge of all guide you in coming to your

final decision, to which the family are just clinging, as the last hope

Committing the above to your kind attention. I remain in anticipation...

8

Letter from Lily Laxton to 'the Gentlemen of the Cabinet', forwarded
to the Prime Minister. Dated 31 December 1922.

Again the letter was addressed in Home Office minutes, thus:

> As regards plea 1) within Mrs T is shewn by her own
> letters to be quite capable of talking of these arrangements
> for the future as a 'blind' so that she wd be able to refer
> to them as proving that the attack upon her husband was
> a surprise to her.
>
> Cf her ref to the prescription incident [see Letter 12].
>
> As regards plea 2) the story of self defence was an
> afterthought* and is quite incredible. If it had been true
> he must have said so at once: but even if true it wd still
> have been necessary to explain away the carrying of
> that dagger. He clearly took it there for the purpose of
> killing T.
>
> We must not discuss her views on cap punishment.
> Crimes of this sort must necessarily bring sorrow &
> disgrace upon parents and families.

> As the Home Secretary has left the decision [...] to you, I
> feel I must make a final appeal on their behalf.
>
> My husband & I were the aunt & uncle with whom
> Mr and Mrs T spent the evening at the theatre, & I
> assure you Gentlemen, [1] that from Mrs T's manner,
> conversation & also arrangements we all made to go to
> dances, dinners, & other theatres, during the season, it

---

* This is strictly true, and the detail about fearing that Percy had a gun was absurd, but
Freddy always stated that he had had a fight with Percy.

was absolutely impossible for Mrs T to have entered into any arrangement with B to commit the crime.

Moreover, knowing the late mr T very well, [2] I say the lad's story is true & undoubtedly he acted as he thought in self-defence, Mr T being just the kind of man who would bluff having a weapon.

But Gentlemen, my real plea is on behalf of the parents. By hanging the unhappy couple it is not them who suffer but the family left behind. I know it is a difficult decision for you to arrive at, & possibly it will make a precedent for the abolition of Cap Pnishment, but Gentlemen, being a new Gov it is possible for you to do this. If burning at the stake was not a deterrent to crime, I am sure the more merciful way of hanging is not. These things or crimes are only committed in a moment of passion & not premeditated. The punishment of yrs of confinement is bourne [sic] by the offenders, but the punishment of hanging, is bourne by the parents & relations. May I therefore ask once again for 'Mercy' [...]

9

Letter from Freddy to Edith, sent from Pentonville and not delivered. It is unknown whether Edith attempted to write to her former lover during their time under sentence of death. She did have contact with his sister Florence, whose antagonism had dissolved in the most remarkable and impressive way.

❦

Tuesday 2 January, 1923

Edie – I want to ask you not give up hope. I know & you know & some others know also, that you should not be in the position that you find yourself. I'm still hoping that the powers that be, will exercise some common sense & displace their suppositions with facts. I know this must be a terrible strain on you, but Peidi mia, don't lose heart – B.B. I am keeping quite well & I've heard [presumably from Florence] that you are a lot better. I'm glad.

I have seen Florrie today & she told me that she had written to you explaining the misunderstanding. I should dearly like to pull the snub nose of a certain person – Do you know to whom I refer?* I've read two books by Baroness Von Sutton [Baroness von Hutten] 'Pam' & 'What became of Pam' – one of Hichens 'An Imaginative Man' & one of Rolf Wyllards [Dolf Wyllarde's] 'There was a Crooked Man'. Since I've been here. If you are able, will you write? I want to say a lot, but cannot, you understand. I can only hope & trust that some time in the future we will be able to talk to one another.

* This is unclear.

Goodbye, Peidi mia – B.B. –

Always,

Freddy

10

Letter from Edith, thought to be to Bessie Akam.

❦

Wednesday 3 January 1923

Dear —

I know I ought to have written to you yesterday – but I didn't feel I wanted to – that's my only excuse.

Thank you [for] sending along the book. I haven't [received] it yet, but I soon shall have. When I think I have been longing to get it for three months now and you have had it all the time. I feel so cross that I didn't mention it before. However, I am going to prepare myself to enjoy it to the full, after waiting so long.

Does it seem three whole months since I first came here to you? Some days it seems like three weeks and others like three days. Time is always our enemy, don't you think? It either goes too fast or too slowly always.

I've read lots of books since I've been here; usually I get through one every day – but they, none of them, have been very striking, nothing in them to impress one, or to make you remember them. Of course, I read 'If Winter Comes'. Auntie — sent it in to me. That I enjoyed; it is quite differently written from the usual type of novel, and that fact alone made it interesting, but the plot (which doesn't really appear until quite the end of the book) was even more interesting to me under these circumstances.*

Have you read it? You should. Then I read 'A Witness for the Defence' by A. E. W. Mason. I wonder if you have 'The Four Feathers' by him? I should like to have that. Oh! And I read 'His Daughter', a Yankee book by Governor [Gouverneur] Morris, but there was nothing much in that; at least, nothing much I can discuss in writing.

I could talk to you about it, but I couldn't write. Now I am starting Dickens again. I think I have read all his at least three or four times, but you can always pick up one and feel interested in it at any time

I remember at school we used to have what was called a 'Reading Circle'. A Dickens book was chosen by our teacher, we read it at home, not at school, and then we each chose a character from the book and wrote a little essay on him or her, as the case might be. These essays we would all take to Wanstead Park on a Saturday afternoon: we would each read our own out loud, and then it was discussed in general.

We usually took our tea to the park and made a little picnic party of it. I remember an essay I was highly commended on by the teacher. It was on 'Quilp'.

Today it is lovely; the sun is shining and everywhere looks bright and cheerful. I begin to feel quite cheerful myself – isn't the sun wonderful, it always raises your spirits. But I don't like it as cold as this. I'll be ever so glad when the

* This recently published novel by A. S. M. Hutchinson dealt with an unhappy marriage and divorce leading to scandal.

summer comes: the heat I love, but I never did like the cold – not out of doors, at any rate. I don't think I should mind inches of snow outside if I was inside in a huge armchair before a great, big fire, with a nice book – yes, and some nuts, I think.

I've still got faith – I'm still hoping. They say "you can always get what you want if you want it enough, but you can't control the price you have to pay", and I think that's so every time.

I got — letter. Thank him for me; it was very sedate and proper, tell him. I really didn't think he could be like that – I think that is part of him I don't know yet.*

Shall I see you again soon – Edith.

_____
* The writer is unknown, perhaps Bessie's husband Reg?

11

Letter from Freddy Bywaters to the Home Secretary, Sir William Bridgeman.

This highly intelligent, intensely perceptive document was, as before, parsed in Home Office minutes, thus:

> It has been conclusively shown that the construction which he sought to put upon the letters is an impossible one. Apart from what is in the letters themselves they must be construed in the light of what actually occurred – the deliberate murder of T.
>
> As regards the passage marked 1.:- On 20th Sept. Mrs T. wrote a letter to meet him at Plymouth on 23 Sep (10 days before the murder) "Darlint you are jealous of him but I want you to be... desperate". On 2 Oct she wrote:- "Don't forget what we talked in the tea room, I will still risk... if you will."
>
> As regards 2. it is certain that B wd have been convicted if he had made no statement & had not given evidence, assuming that Mrs T. had said what she did & that the knife had been found & the ownership traced to him.
>
> 3. The admission that he had the knife with him at lunch on 3 Oct is of some importance. Did he shew it to Mrs T. & what comment did she make upon it?
>
> ... As regards the facts relevant to the murder charge I do not think that either he or Mrs Thompson has told the truth with (in any?) single particular. They have lied consistently as to the position between Mrs Thompson & her husband vis a vis of her intrigue with Bywaters: as to the meaning of the letters; and as to the circumstances in which Thompson was attacked & murdered.

There is nothing to say about this, really, except to observe that the leaps of logic and disregard for actual evidence displayed at the trial were now so embedded into the narrative that it had taken on the status of established truth. What it was, instead, was a particular reading of a multi-layered text. As has been seen, several are available; and the most convincing is probably the one offered here, by the man to whom the letters were written.

Whether he read them so objectively at the time, of course, is another question.

※

Wednesday 3 January, 1923

I am writing to ask you to use your power to avert a great catastrophe and also to rectify a grave injustice. Edith Thompson & I have been found guilty & today stand condemned upon a charge of which we are innocent. In the first instance I wish to speak to you of Edith Thompson. The case for the prosecution was based entirely upon a series of extracts from letters written by her to me. There were, mentioned in these letters, names of some poisons & broken glass. It was suggested that Mrs Thompson had been administering poison & broken glass to her husband. The body was exhumed & no trace of any alien substance was found, but still, Mrs Thompson was committed for trial on the charge of having administered poison to her husband. I am asking you believe me, sir, because what I say is the truth, that Mrs Thompson never had any intention or the slightest inclination to poison her husband or to kill him in any way. The only way to treat those letters is the way in which I read them. She is a hysterical & highly strung woman & when writing letters to me she did not study sentences & phrases before transferring them to paper, but, as different thoughts, no matter what, momentarily flashed through her mind, so they were committed to paper. Sometimes, even I could not understand her. Now

337

sir, if I had, for one moment, thought or imagined, that there was anything contained in Mrs Thompson's letters to me, that could at any time, harm her, would I not have destroyed them? I was astounded when I heard the sinister translation the prosecution had put to certain phrases, which were written quite innocently. Those letters were the outpourings of a hysterical woman's mind, to relieve the tension & strain caused by the agony she was suffering. If you like sir, merely melodrama.

1. Furthermore I wish to say that she never suggested to me that I should kill her husband. She is not only unjustly condemned, but it is wicked & vile to suggest that she incited me to murder. God knows that I speak the truth when I say that there was no plan or agreement between Mrs Thompson & I to murder her husband. I can do no more sir, than ask you to believe me – the truth – & then it is for you to proclaim to the whole world that Edith Thompson is "Not Guilty" & so remove the stain that is on her name. It was said by an officer of the law, when the result of the exhumation was known, "The case against Mrs Thompson has failed". Why then sir, was she committed for trial? I ask you, I implore you sir, in the name of humanity & justice, to order the release of Edith Jessie Thompson.

I have not much space sir, so will try & be as concise as possible in laying before you my case. I wish to bring to your notice 2. that the evidence against me is only that which has been supplied by myself. I was asked at Ilford if there had been a fight & I said yes. I was not asked for details & I received No caution. When I saw my solicitor on Oct. 9th I told him exactly what had happened the same as I did to the Judge & Jury at the Old Bailey. When I was at the inquest at Ilford, I was advised by a law officer to get the charge against me reduced. I mentioned this to my solicitor who said it would be best to say nothing until the trial at the Old Bailey. You now know sir, why my explanation was not made known before. Mr Justice Shearman suggested to the Jury, that my knife was in my pocket for one reason only – namely that I had agreed with Mrs Thompson to murder her husband on Oct 3rd. I saw Mrs Thompson at midday on Oct. 3rd & it was then for the first time I learned that she was going to the Criterion Theatre that evening. 3. My knife was in my pocket then & it had been there since 23rd Sept. I was in the habit of carrying either a knife or a revolver. At the inquest, Dr Drought* in his evidence stated that the first blow had been delivered from the front. That is quite true, you have my statement made in the witness box at the Old Bailey. If I could speak to you I could explain any point you might wish, more fully, but my space here is limited.

I ask you to accept my word, sir, or perhaps you can show me some way in which I can prove to you that I am speaking the truth.

I hope & trust that this will receive your careful & favourable consideration sir, & that you will order another hearing of the case.

I am, Sir, yours respectfully, F.E.F. Bywaters.

---

* Percy Drought, police surgeon.

12

Letter from Edith to Florence Bywaters. Amazingly it retains a glimmer of Edith's former voice; that 'I don't quite feel satisfied' is very characteristic.

This is, in fact, a love letter, sent to Freddy through the medium of his sister.

☙

Wednesday 3 January, 1923

Thank you for your letter, but even now I have it I don't quite feel satisfied.

You mention about the monkey,* that your mother would naturally like to have it and, of course, I quite understand how she feels, and, believe me, I would quite willingly part with it to her if Freddy so wished, but you don't tell me what he does wish – you only say 'Probably mother misunderstood'.

Don't let there be any misunderstanding. Just tell me what he really does wish. Also, while we are on the subject, will you ask him what I am to do with the watch?

In myself I am better, and am trying to keep cheerful, but it is so terribly hard. I often wonder if it is worth while and then, after my people have been, I feel I must keep up just for them.

Tell Freddy I am trying to be what he always told me,† and

---

* The bronze monkey given to her by Freddy.
† The reference is to Freddy's old exhortation to B.B. – be brave.

hope he is, too. Tell him it is always now, as it always has been, and it always will. I can't write a message; I want to say it; he'll understand. You'll write again, wont you?

Sincerely,

Edith T.

13

Letter from Florence to Edith, sent on 6 January 1923. The previous day it had been announced that there would be no reprieves.

The note on the Home Office file read: 'This letter will not be passed.'

11 Westow St.
Upper Norwood
Jan. 6th 1923

Dear Mrs Thompson,

I received your letter this morning and read it out to Mick* when I saw him. Oh God what can I say to you now? Words are such poor things. Mother is nearly mad today. I wonder if she will pull through?

But I dare say you are anxious to hear what Mick had to say. First of all re: the monkey. He says for you to keep that – but that he would like Frankie (my little brother) to have the watch.† So you could perhaps have it sent on. He told me to tell you he understands the message and it is reciprocated. Also he sent his love and says to try and bear up. He has written to you but the letter was sent to the Home Office – so I doubt whether you will get it now. Of course Mick poor devil – didn't know [about the reprieves] when I saw him. Even then he didn't seem much concerned over himself – his one thought was for you. Oh what a

---

* Within the family Freddy was sometimes known as 'Mick'.
† The same watch that Edith had bought for Freddy and kept after having it mended.

great heart he must have. But then you must of course know that as well as I.

I'll be ever so glad if you would drop me a few lines – so that I could let him have any message – will you? I can't say any more now – my heart is too full. With our kind thoughts and wishes.

Sincerely yours,

FLORRIE BYWATERS

14

Telegram sent, in duplicate, from Ethel Graydon to Queen Mary at Sandringham and King George V at Buckingham Palace. Dated 6 January 1923.

> May I humbly beseech Your Majesty as last resort to
> exercise your Royal prerogative of mercy towards my
> daughter Mrs Thompson now under sentence of death
> I am broken hearted at the terrible injustice of her
> sentence caused entirely by prejudice Mrs Graydon

15

Letter from Edith to her father, William Graydon. Dated 4 January 1923, five days before her execution on Tuesday 9th.

It was the last letter that Edith wrote, and part-censored by the prison authorities.

※

Dearest Dad

Somehow today I feel I'd like to write to you. It seems such a long time since I saw you – and yet it isn't. It's only the same distance from Saturday as it was last week. I wonder why some days seem so long ago and others quite near?

Of course nothing different happens here, every day is the same. The best part of each day (and of course the quickest) is the half an hour's visit I have. It never seems to be longer than ten minutes.

Do you remember the book I told you I wanted? They tell me it is out of print, and I couldn't help thinking that even in little things my luck is entirely absent.

[...] I've been reading Dickens's 'Our Mutual Friend', but the print is so frightfully small and indistinct that I can't see anything if the light has to be on, and it is after dark always that I feel I would like to read the most.

Yesterday mother showed me the sketch of the Morea [Freddy's ship]. It looks nice in its frame, don't you think? I was quite pleased about it.

I'm getting quite used to things here now. It's really astonishing what you can do without when it's 'Hobson's choice'.

You'll be coming to see me on Saturday, won't you? On that Saturday of last year, I wonder if you remember what we did?

I do, quite well. We were all at Highbury, and the huge dinner Harold ate I can see now if I close my eyes. And then there were the rattles and trumpets and whistles in the Tube and Avis getting out without her ticket and we throwing it out of the carriage on to the platform when it was too late. Oh, dear! What a lot can happen in a year!

I hope Saturday comes quickly, it's been such a terrible long week. Au revoir until then.

EDITH.

AFTERWORD

On 9 January Edith and Freddy were executed, simultaneously, at 9 a.m.

It was said that before he died, with fortitude, he confessed to being sincerely sorry for what he had done. Three days earlier he had told his mother that he killed Percy Thompson in a fit of rage. 'I just went blind.' Then he said: 'She is innocent, absolutely innocent. I can't believe they will hang her.' For his sake, Lilian Bywaters tried to save the woman whom she believed had destroyed her son, and passed on his words.

The rope was being softened and stretched at Holloway as Edith's solicitor chartered a small aeroplane and travelled to the country house of the Home Secretary; who took the view that there was nothing new in what Freddy had said, and the law must take its course.

The stories about Edith's execution are many, and atrociously distressing. The accounts that compel assent – including from a young female doctor who was in attendance, who spoke about the event in 1956 – are less horrific than the rumours; essentially, Edith was so full of drugs that she was, one prays, not wholly aware of what was happening. The persistent tale that she was pregnant cannot be true. Dr Morton would have known it, and it would, quite frankly, have been a great relief to the authorities had they been able to reprieve her – and indeed Freddy – for a reason that was out of their hands. They knew that there was a contentiousness about this case, which is why they were so obdurate about it; they knew that removing a shell of a woman from the scene would not be an end to the matter, although societal pressure had made them determined to do it; pregnancy would have got them off the hook without any loss of face.

Eight* more women would be executed in Britain after Edith, with Ruth Ellis the last in 1955, and the last executions of all took place in August 1964. There would be many false starts with regard to abolition. Yet this case, not so much a miscarriage of justice as a misapplication of it – an intrusion of the law into places where it should not go – was the beginning of the end. The authorities, for all their adamantine rectitude, were like Virginia Woolf, unable to sleep at her house in Bloomsbury, recording in her diary for January 1923 that she heard a woman cry, 'as if in anguish, in the street, and I thought of Mrs Thompson waiting to be executed.'

Edith was under the nation's skin. Somewhere, she still is. Her letters have vanished; her words remain, along with any interpretation that the reader chooses to find in them.

Laura Thompson, 2022

---

* Susan Newell in 1923; Louie Calvert in 1926; Ethel Major in 1934; Dorothea Waddingham in 1936; Margaret Allen in 1949; Louisa Merrifield in 1953; Styllou Christofi in 1954; and Ruth Ellis.

ACKNOWLEDGEMENTS

I should like to thank my dear friend John Mitchinson, to whom I pitched the idea of publishing Edith's letters. He responded to her story instantly, with a characteristic generosity that infused the brilliant people at Unbound; among whom I give especial, heartfelt thanks to Alex Eccles, Aliya Gulamani, Mark Ecob and Rina Gill.

The information in this book – some of which was revealed for the first time in my *Rex v Edith Thompson* (Head of Zeus, 2018) – comes from Home Office files, notably the huge two-part file (HO 144/2685) held under the hundred-year rule and opened slightly prematurely. I read this in a sealed room at the National Archives in Kew. I also read, for the first time, the typed reproduction of Edith's extant letters.

The National Archives hold the physical document written by Freddy Bywaters in Brixton prison, as well as reproductions of his other surviving letters, and the various pleas sent to the authorities by Edith's family after the trial.

The 1973 interview with Avis Graydon comes from a BBC recording (T10391RC1) held at the British Library.

In further reading, along with *A Pin to See the Peepshow* by F. Tennyson Jesse (Heinemann, 1934), I recommend *Criminal Justice* by René Weis (Hamish Hamilton, 1988), a moving and impassioned book, the depth of whose research has helped to inform my knowledge of this case.

A NOTE ON THE AUTHOR

Laura Thompson, who is unrelated to Edith, has been fascinated for many years by the Thompson–Bywaters case. She re-examined it in *Rex v Edith Thompson*, which was shortlisted for the CWA Gold Dagger for Non-Fiction in 2018. Her other books include *The Last Landlady*, a memoir of her publican grandmother, published by Unbound in 2018; the Edgar-nominated biography *Agatha Christie*; and the *New York Times* bestseller *The Six*, about the lives of the Mitford sisters.

Unbound is the world's first crowdfunding publisher, established in 2011.

We believe that wonderful things can happen when you clear a path for people who share a passion. That's why we've built a platform that brings together readers and authors to crowdfund books they believe in – and give fresh ideas that don't fit the traditional mould the chance they deserve.

This book is in your hands because readers made it possible. Everyone who pledged their support is listed below. Join them by visiting unbound.com and supporting a book today.